THE IRON BRIDGE

SYMBOL OF THE INDUSTRIAL REVOLUTION

Of all the works of man, there is not any one which unites so well with natural scenery, and so heightens its beauty, as a bridge, if any taste, or rather if no bad taste, be displayed in its structure. This is exemplified in the rude as well as in the magnificent; by the stepping stones or crossing plank of a village brook, as well as by the immortal works of Trajan.
Robert Southey

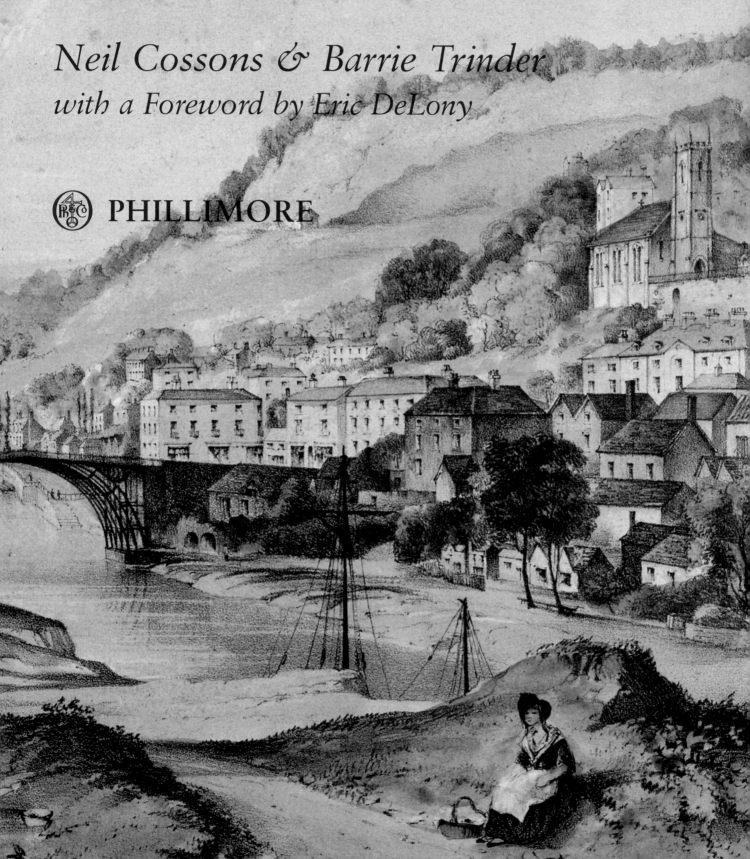

THE IRON BRIDGE
SYMBOL OF THE INDUSTRIAL REVOLUTION

Neil Cossons & Barrie Trinder
with a Foreword by Eric DeLony

PHILLIMORE

First published in 1979 by Moonraker Press

This second edition published 2002 by
PHILLIMORE & CO. LTD
Shopwyke Manor Barn, Chichester, West Sussex

ISBN 1 86077 230 7

Printed and bound in Great Britain by
THE BATH PRESS
Bath, Avon

Contents

List of Illustrations

Illustration Acknowledgements

Neil Cossons, 91, 131, 133; Eric DeLony, 89, 140, 141; HAER collection, Library of Congress, Joseph Elliott, photographer, 139; Illustrated London News Picture Library, 13; Ironbridge Gorge Museum Trust, frontispiece, 2, 6, 8, 11, 14-16, 21-6, 27, 29-31, 33-40, 42, 47, 49, 55, 56, 81-4, 128, 130; Andrew Jenkinson, 7; James Lawson, 9; le musée Marmottan, Paris, 48; NKK Corporation, 134; John Powell, 86; Harold Richardson Collection, 136; Royal Commission on the Ancient and Historical Monuments of Scotland, 62; Royal Commission on the Ancient and Historical Monuments of Wales, 53; Science Museum, London, 59; Shrewsbury Borough Museums, 1; Skandia Corporation, Stockholm, 18; Staffordshire Record Office, 50; Sunderland Art Gallery, 60, 61; Hugh Torrens, 107; Barrie Trinder, 3-5, 10, 12, 17, 19, 20, 28, 32, 41, 43-6, 51, 52, 54, 57, 58, 63-80, 85, 87, 88, 90, 92-106, 108-27, 129, 132; US National Archives, 137; US Patent & Trademark Office, 135, 138.

Foreword

BY ERIC DELONY

What is it about old bridges that make them so appealing? Is it the catenary soar of the Humber or the Golden Gate, their diaphanous cables and suspenders etched like harp strings against the afternoon sky? Is it the Erector-set exactness of a metal truss or cantilever – chords and struts held by rivets and pins, defying gravity as they leap broad rivers? Or is it that bridges rendered in more traditional materials and shapes – wood, stone or cast-iron arches – remind us of less hectic and troubled times?

This book is about the latter, cast-iron arches, of which England enjoys the world's largest and most distinctive collection. Constructed during the pinnacle of the Industrial Revolution when England was at the height of its manufacturing and engineering prowess, these bridges illustrate an astounding flourish of technical and artistic creativity that was emulated by other countries, but rarely duplicated. The nearly 130 surviving examples represent a 50-year period, 1780-1830, when the material for bridge construction changed from wood and stone to cast iron, the miracle material of the 19th century. England paced the world during this period of manufacturing and technological advancement. Surviving bridges are the tangible evidence of this important phase of Britain's technological development.

During the bicentennial of the world's first iron bridge in 1979, a retrospective review of its origins and history was prepared by Neil Cossons and Barrie Trinder. Twenty-three years later, the two authors have prepared an update, encapsulating the knowledge of and scholarship on iron bridges that has amassed since that memorable occasion. Cossons was then Director of the Ironbridge Gorge Museum, and Trinder was its honorary historian and noted scholar on the surrounding Shropshire Coalfield. The bicentennial celebration of the world's first iron bridge took the form of a conference and monograph published by Cossons and Trinder.

Earlier that decade, I was an intern at the Iron Bridge Gorge Museum during the summer of 1971 when stabilisation of the Iron Bridge began. The nearly 200-year-old structure was being crushed as the banks of the River Severn slid inward. I was fortunate to have won a year-long Fulbright Fellowship to study the Industrial Revolution and how the British were studying, preserving and interpreting its artifacts and relics. During that eventful year, I saw more of England's industrial heritage than most Englishmen see in a lifetime. The first nine months were spent in Bath, Somerset, with Angus Buchanan at his Centre for the Study of the History of Technology where the National Record of Industrial Monuments (N.R.I.M.), the official arm of the British government for industrial archaeology, was headquartered. In addition to my own personal field trips, I travelled with Keith Falconer (who had recently replaced Rex Wailes as chief survey officer for N.R.I.M.) to the Midlands, Devon and Cornwall inventorying engineering and industrial relics. It was at Buchanan's Centre that I caught an infectious enthusiasm for steam engines thanks to George Watkins, a walking encyclopedia of steam engine technology who also was stationed there.

Equally profound were three months in the Ironbridge Gorge where I worked with Neil, Barrie and Stuart Smith on some of the first projects of the Ironbridge Gorge Museum. Stuart and I rescued an 18th-century iron canal boat, that a local farmer was using as a watering trough; I oversaw the work of Borstal boys chipping bricks by the thousands; students from the museum programme at Leicester University and I recorded the warehouse at the Coalbrookdale Ironworks; and I got to meet Prince Philip. The Fulbright afforded me the opportunity to share some of the fascination, scholarship, and hard work that many of us were beginning to experience during the early 1970s when the new field of Industrial Archaeology was being invented. We were among a growing group who were pioneering a whole new way to look at engineering relics and the industrial landscape. One of the prominent hubs of this activity was the Ironbridge Gorge which claimed birthplace status as one of the key locations where the industrial revolution originated.

Upon returning to the United States, I applied some of the lessons and techniques learned in England to the recently established Historic American Engineering Record of which I have been chief for the last fifteen years. H.A.E.R. is a programme of the National Park Service, created in 1969, to document engineering and industrial heritage in the United States. For the last 33 years, we have been racing to capture the evidence of America's industrial and engineering heritage with drawings, photographs and histories before it is lost. The records become part of the national collection at the Library of Congress. Though over three decades have passed since that memorable summer, all of us continue to work towards the celebration, documentation, preservation, and interpretation of engineering heritage and the industrial landscape. I think it is safe to say that the Iron Bridge is not only an outstanding symbol of the industrial age, but also served to bring a number of people together, imbuing many of us with a passionate regard for engineering and industrial heritage.

Preface and Acknowledgements

The first edition of this book was written in 1977-8 and was one of four substantial academic works published in association with the Ironbridge Gorge Museum Trust in 1979, the bicentennial year of the Iron Bridge.[1] It has long been out of print, and its publisher, Moonraker Press, has ceased to exist following the death of its owner, Anthony Adams, who first suggested that a study of the Iron Bridge would be appropriate in a series of books on landmarks in transport. We were honoured when a Japanese edition was published by Kensetsu in 1989 and pleased that the book continues to be of interest, and that Phillimore consider it worthy of a second edition. Such has been the pace of research during the last two decades that this is in effect a new book.

Several reviewers of the first edition complained, legitimately, that it lacked references, but this was a feature of the series, and a fully-referenced edition of the essential arguments appeared in a contemporary article in a learned journal.[2] Nevertheless we have corrected that fault in this edition.

In 1979 we were able to build on the work of past generations of scholars, on the writings of Samuel Smiles, and on the extraordinary antiquarian labours of the centenarian John Randall (1809-1909), china painter, geologist of national repute, and our link to some precious historical sources that are now lost. We were able to take forward the work of the late Dr Arthur Raistrick (1896-1991) who was the first to use in print the minutes of the proprietors of the Iron Bridge.[3] The principal new sources for the history of the bridge available in the 1970s were the personal account books of Abraham Darby III, deposited in the then Shropshire Record Office by his descendant, the late Rachel, Lady Labouchère. We were also able to draw on James Lawson's research on Thomas Farnolls Pritchard, which had been stimulated by the discovery of the architect's drawing book in the library of the American Institute of Architects in Washington DC in the 1960s. We benefited from conversations with the late A.H. (Sam) Blackwall, a civil engineer who had a vivid sense of the history of his profession, and are delighted that his book, *Historic Bridges of Shropshire*, was published posthumously in 1985. Sam Blackwall, if anyone, deserves to be credited as the restorer of the Iron Bridge.

It is pertinent to review some of the advances in scholarship of the past quarter century that have influenced this second edition. Julia Ionides has brought into the public domain the contents of Pritchard's drawing book,[4] although her book does not add to our detailed knowledge of the Iron Bridge project. The study of the Darby family has progressed through the publication of Lady Labouchère's biography of Abiah Darby, who, curiously, recorded few comments in her diary about the Iron Bridge, and through Emyr Thomas's book which enlarges our understanding of the family's legal and financial affairs.[5] Some newly-published accounts of Coalbrookdale written by 18th-century travellers have added to our understanding of the Iron Bridge, and several attempts to explain how it was constructed were published before the discovery of the sketch by Elias Martin, preserved in Stockholm, revolutionised thinking on the subject. We acknowledge the achievement of the BBC Timewatch programme, broadcast in January 2002, in demonstrating the feasibility of the method of assembly that Martin illustrates, and our delight in the use of the museum at Blists Hill as an archaeological laboratory. Much was learned about the Iron Bridge from the programmes of restoration carried out between 1972 and 1980, and in 1999-2000. We are grateful to Shelley White and Paul Belford of the Ironbridge Archaeology Unit for discussions on the latter programme, and anticipate with interest the publication of a full report on the archaeological investigation of the bridge by the Unit and by staff of English Heritage.

While our knowledge of the Iron Bridge has expanded steadily since 1979, the evidence of succeeding generations of iron bridges has grown out of all proportion, but we take some satisfaction that our broad interpretation of the history of iron bridges between 1781 and 1830 has been followed by other historians. We acknowledge with gratitude the work of the late J.G. James whose publications, listed in the bibliography, and whose card index, housed in the library of the Institution of Civil Engineers, have been an invaluable source of data. We would also like to acknowledge the work of Peter Cross-Rudkin who has been largely responsible for the appropriate section of the Institution's Historic Engineering Works database on which we have drawn for information on a variety of bridges, some of which in 1979 were unknown to us, or to anyone else interested in iron bridges. This is not the place to investigate in detail every bridge of the early 19th century that might have been cast in iron. This is a continuing process, and the stream of evidence shows no sign of drying up. Most of the previously unknown structures are of relatively minor significance, although their very number shows the need for continual re-interpretation of the data. We can nevertheless be confident that not even the most diligent researcher will track down a previously unknown structure of the merit of Mythe or Craigellachie.

Several people have been helpful in allowing access to bridges or architectural features on their properties, or to documentary records in their care, and we would like to record our thanks to Mr and Mrs George Williams of Ludlow, to Jennifer Crombie of Culford School and to John Crompton of the National Museum of Scotland. We are also grateful for help from Richard Hayman and Wendy Horton, archaeological consultants, the staff of Shropshire Records & Research, the Social History Group of the Friends of the Ironbridge Gorge Museum, and Susan Bennett, formerly archivist to the Royal Society of Arts. Peter Wakelin of Cadw, Peter White, Stephen Hughes and Brian Malaws of the Royal Commission on the Ancient and Historical Monuments of Wales and Miles Oglethorpe of the Royal Commission on the Ancient and Historical Monuments of Scotland, Andrew Scott of the National Railway Museum, Paul Smith of l'Inventaire, Bernard Marrey, Dr Ivor Brown, David Crossley and Neville Flavell have provided information while this book was being written.

Many others over recent decades have in various ways enlarged our understanding of the Iron Bridge and of iron bridges in general. Stuart Smith has passed on references to iron bridges over many years. It has been a delight since his stay in Ironbridge in 1972 to discuss the history of bridges with Eric DeLony, now chief of the Historic American Engineering Record. Hugh Torrens of the University of Keele has brought to our notice several important sources of information about the Iron Bridge, and more particularly the documentary material relating to the Trentham Bridge. We owe particular debts to two librarians, Mike Chrimes, of the Institution of Civil Engineers, and John Powell, librarian of the Ironbridge Gorge Museum.

Finally it is pertinent to reflect that it is 23 years since the publication of the first edition of *The Iron Bridge: Symbol of the Industrial Revolution*. We do not expect to be responsible for the book that will succeed this second edition, certainly not if it does not appear until 2025. We nevertheless anticipate keenly the new understanding that will come to light from continuing documentary and archaeological research, and trust that this volume will provide a sound launching pad for the curiosity of future generations of scholars.

Neil Cossons
Barrie Trinder

Shropshire, May 2002

Conventions and Abbreviations

Dates of birth and death are indicated in the text on the first occasion on which an individual is mentioned. National Grid references to bridges are provided only when the structures concerned are not listed in any of the tables at the end of the volume.

Most of the bridges discussed in this book were designed using Imperial measurements, which are therefore quoted in the text. Metric equivalents are given for measurements relating to bridges, although not for approximate distances between places. We see no necessity in this particular study to give metric equivalents for Imperial tons and hundredweights, nor for shillings and pence.

The following abbreviations are used in the references:

I.G.M. – Ironbridge Gorge Museum
S.R.R. – Shropshire Records & Research

Perspectives

A Symbol

The iron arch that links the parishes of Madeley and Benthall across the River Severn in Shropshire remains in 2002, as it was in 1802, or in 1979 when the first edition of this book was published, a recognised symbol of the 'Industrial Revolution', but if the Iron Bridge is a symbol, precisely what does it symbolise?

The debate amongst historians about the significance of the economic and social changes in Britain between 1700 and 1850 took several new directions during the last two decades of the 20th century. Econometricians expressed doubts about the magnitude of macroeconomic change over the period. Economic historians emphasised the commercial nature of British society in the early 18th century, and the lack of change in the means of production of consumer goods by 1850. Social historians were concerned to relate economic developments to the persistence of custom, and to analyse the role of women in relation to their families and to employment. Other scholars have demonstrated that the rapid development of the coalfields in the western portion of Great Britain was part of an Atlantic trade pattern.

Such arguments are refinements that add to our understanding, but they should not diminish our appreciation of the scale of the changes that did occur. The Industrial Revolution should not be perceived in celebratory terms as a succession of innovations, nor was it a continuous process of 'immiseration'. It is nevertheless a term that encapsulates dramatic changes in economic and social life. In many parts of Britain the landscape was transformed between 1700 and 1850. The growing availability of coal created new sources of mechanical power, transformed metallurgical and chemical processes and reduced energy costs for enterprises of all kinds. The expansion of textile manufactures prompted new manufacturing communities, introduced the concept of factory production, and had many positive consequences for public health. Inland navigation, and later railways provided systems for distributing goods that linked every town of consequence. The changes of the second half of the 19th century, the extension of the factory system to the production of food, furniture, footwear and clothing, the rapid growth of suburbs, the use of steel in civil and mechanical engineering, the application of electric power, were all dependent on developments that had taken place during the 'Industrial Revolution'. Above all the scale of the changes in Britain in the late 18th and early 19th centuries can be measured by the reactions of contemporary commentators, particularly those from abroad. From their very different perspectives, Karl Marx and Alexis de Tocqueville were agreed that British society had fundamentally changed, and that it had done so in ways that would be imitated in other countries.

The Iron Bridge represents in particular two of the significant changes in Britain in this period. First it was a well-publicised demonstration of the importance of the iron industry, and one that was to have many direct consequences. Iron was exported in many forms, as axes, nails or cooking pots, or as bars from which overseas customers could forge their own artefacts. From the mid-1790s some textile mills were built around iron pillars and beams and many of the machines they contained had iron frames. The machines were driven by iron waterwheels, or by steam-engines with cast-iron cylinders, beams and pump barrels, and fed with steam from wrought-iron boilers. Canals were controlled by locks with wrought-iron fittings, and their bridges were protected by cast-iron fenders. Access to the newly-enclosed fields of the agricultural Midlands was through gates hung with wrought-iron fittings, and in fields and barns increasing use was made of iron machinery. Iron ships multiplied in the first half of the 19th century, and by 1851 most towns in Britain were connected to a network of 6,000 route miles of iron railway. The Industrial Revolution has with some justice been called the 'iron revolution'.

The Iron Bridge should also be interpreted in the context of civil engineering. Between 1700 and 1850 the British enlarged their understanding of a range of ancient civil engineering techniques, including road-building, the improvement of natural waterways, the digging of artificial canals, and the construction of masonry arch bridges. At the same time they developed new techniques, the ability to build embankments, cuttings, tunnels, and iron railways, together with new forms of bridges and aqueducts, including arches of cast iron, of which the bridge at Coalbrookdale was the most celebrated. New methods came to be based on scientific calculations, which were published and became the foundations for the education of future generations, whilst those who took responsibility for building bridges, roads, waterways and railways gained professional status through the establishment of the Institution of Civil Engineers in 1820. Innovation was encouraged by learned bodies, most notably by the Society of Arts which, in 1787, recognised the significance of the Iron Bridge by presenting its gold medal to Abraham Darby III.

The Iron Bridge demonstrated the potential of iron as a construction material. It showed that iron *could* be used rather than how to use it, but its influence was none the less potent for that. It was a step in the dark to a greater extent than can readily be appreciated after two centuries of subsequent technological change. Thomas Tredgold (1788-1829), who understood the properties of iron as thoroughly as anyone of his generation, reflected in 1824 that 'One of the boldest attempts with a new material was the application of cast iron to bridges'.[1]

Regional Context

The Iron Bridge can be interpreted as the product of a particular period of British history. It was also the achievement of a particular region. The Coalbrookdale

Coalfield in Shropshire extends about eight miles north and two miles south of the Severn Gorge. The manufacture and application of iron had already by the 1770s been further developed in the area than in any other part of Great Britain. In 1709 Abraham Darby I (1678-1717) had succeeded in making iron of reasonable quality, using coke rather than charcoal, at the ironworks in Coalbrookdale. In subsequent decades his process was further developed until by the 1750s coke-blast iron was competitive in most respects with that made with charcoal. Steam power was first employed at an ironworks in 1743, when a Newcomen engine was used to re-circulate water between the pools of the Coalbrookdale ironworks. Iron cylinders for Newcomen engines were being cast at Coalbrookdale by the early 1720s, and by the end of that decade iron wheels for wagons running on the local wooden railways were being cast there. In the late 1760s Richard Reynolds (1735-1816) introduced iron rails in the district.[2]

By the late 18th century iron was becoming part of the fabric of the district, giving it a distinctive character that it retains. Many of the cottages in and around Coalbrookdale have windows with iron lintels, frames and sills, doors with iron doorsteps, chimneys with iron pots, fireplaces with iron grates or ovens. Iron grave-slabs are found in the local churchyards, and the pews in one parish church are entered through iron doors; shop fronts are decorated with iron cornices; roads are measured by cast-iron mileposts; iron plate-rails serve as fence posts, fireplace lintels or supports for well-covers. Wrought-iron rattle chain has been pressed into service as a fencing material. Haystack boilers and wrought-iron tub boats have been used as water tanks.[3] It is hardly surprising therefore that the most important innovations in the use of iron in the last quarter of the 18th century, its application to bridges, boats, rails and multi-storied buildings, should have been made in Shropshire. In no other district were the techniques of handling the material so well understood. The Iron Bridge can be interpreted as the logical outcome of the evolution of technology in the Coalbrookdale Coalfield over the previous 70 years.

The coalmines in the Severn Gorge became prosperous in the reign of Elizabeth I, and by the mid-17th century were amongst the most technologically advanced in Europe. Potteries, tar distilleries, tobacco-pipe manufactories, lead smelters, saltworks and brickworks grew up, availing themselves of cheap supplies of fuel. Before Abraham Darby II (1711-63) blew in the first blast furnace at Horsehay in 1755, there were only four blast furnaces in the vicinity, but by 1759 there were 13, and in the next half-century Shropshire was the leading iron-producing county in Great Britain. Many of the leading figures of the Industrial Revolution had connections with the district. Its principal spectacles, the Coalbrookdale ironworks, the Tar Tunnel, the Coalport chinaworks, the Hay inclined plane on the Shropshire Canal, were visited by countless tourists both from Britain and overseas.

The economic lifeline of the district was the River Severn, along which barges cheaply transported the produce of local coal mines, and distributed raw materials and semi-finished products to the widely dispersed charcoal ironworks in the West Midlands and the Borderland. Iron goods from the Coalbrookdale area were taken by river to Stourport and thence by canal to Birmingham, Manchester and

1 Afternoon View of Coalbrookdale (William Williams, 1777).

Liverpool, while groceries and other imported goods were brought upstream to Shropshire from the port of Bristol. The river was also used for short-distance carriage, of limestone for example, over the two miles from Buildwas to the Calcutts. Considerable quantities of raw materials and semi-finished products were carried across it, including iron ore from Ladywood to Coalbrookdale and pig iron from Horsehay to Willey. Yet there was no bridge across the Severn in the Gorge itself.[4]

If the Severn was an essential element in the economy of the Coalbrookdale Coalfield; it was also, locally, a barrier to commercial and social life.[5] The riverside parishes were all part of the ancient borough of Wenlock, and burgesses who lived in Madeley on the north bank needed to cross the river to gain access to the borough courts. People also needed to cross to attend markets or Quaker meetings, to settle accounts with barge-owners or to purchase the products of the Jackfield potteries. The nearest bridges to the Gorge in the early 1770s were the medieval structure at Buildwas, two miles upstream from the site of the Iron Bridge, and the ancient crossing at Bridgnorth, nine miles downstream. Several ferries carried passengers over the river in the Gorge, but they could not accommodate vehicles, and were dangerous in times of flood.

Bridging the Severn in the Gorge posed problems that could not readily be solved with existing technologies. The banks were precipitous and unstable, and no system of construction that involved the hindering of navigation could have

2 Buildwas bridge under reconstruction, *c.*1791, showing the wooden centring on which the voussoirs would be erected (Samuel Ireland).

been contemplated. Road access was difficult. There were no points at which roads on both sides of the river converged. The only turnpike road to approach the river was that from Madeley towards Buildwas Bridge, which descended the side of the Gorge by the steep track now called Lincoln Hill, but on the opposite bank from the foot of the slope were the cliffs of Benthall Edge.

The Engineering Context

The traditional method of bridging a river was by a masonry arch, or series of arches, a technology that derived from the ancient civilisations. It was only in the 18th century that engineers in Britain were beginning to match the achievements of the Romans in building stone bridges. Piers or abutments for a bridge would be constructed, and a wooden centring erected between them on which the voussoirs (wedge-shaped pieces of stone forming the arch) would be erected towards the crown of the arch, where the keystone would be placed. When that had been done, the centring would be taken away, and if it had been well-constructed the arch would remain intact.

Masonry arches were well-suited to the most commonly used bridge-sites in England. Most bridges in use in the 18th century were the descendants of those erected in medieval times on the sites of ancient fords, on gravel bars, at locations where rivers could easily be approached. On such sites it was relatively easy to build multi-span masonry bridges, for firm foundations could be obtained for the piers. A wide flood plain enabled height to be gained by embanking the road on either side of the bridge. Examples of bridges of this sort built at about the same time as the Iron Bridge are John Gwynn's (d.1786) bridge over the Severn at Atcham of 1769-76 (SJ 540093), which remains in its original form, John Smeaton's (1724-1792) Coldstream bridge over the Tweed of 1767 (NT 848401), and Thomas Telford's Mont-

3 William Edwards's bridge at Pontypridd of 1755. The pierced abutments lightened the load on the arch.

ford Bridge over the Severn of 1794 (SJ 432153). The tradition of building masonry arches still flourished in the 18th century, and was being improved by experiment. In 1755, after several trials, William Edwards (1719-1789) succeeded in lightening the load on a masonry arch by piercing the abutments in his bridge at Pontypridd (ST 074904).[6] The widest masonry arch in Britain was not built until 1827-34, and Thomas Telford and John Rennie (1761-1821) made many refinements to the tradition in the early years of the 19th century.[7] Nevertheless, the traditional masonry arched bridge was not a solution to the problem of crossing the Severn in the Gorge, and apart from the medieval bridge at Buildwas, which was upstream from the Gorge itself, no masonry arch has ever spanned the Severn in this area.

There was one stone bridge in the region that crossed a steep-sided river in the vicinity of an ironworks. A bridge over the River Teme near the Bringewood ironworks (SO 453750) in the Downton Gorge, a few miles upstream from Ludlow, had been constructed in 1772. The Teme is not so wide as the Severn, nor did it carry heavy barge traffic. The bridge served only local needs. Thomas Farnolls Pritchard, who later designed the Iron Bridge, did work on the Downton estate and would certainly have known of the bridge, even if he did not design it.[8] The Downton bridge must certainly be regarded as part of the context of the iron bridge in the Severn Gorge.

The other tradition of bridge-building involved the use of wood, either in the form of arches, as at Walton, Kew and Battersea on the Thames, or at Preen's Eddy on the Severn, or as beams and trestles as at Selby on the Yorkshire Ouse. The technology of timber construction was never as capably practised in 18th-century Britain as it was in some continental countries, or in Quebec and the north-eastern parts of the United States. In Switzerland there was a continuing tradition extending from such medieval covered bridges as the Spreuerbrücke and the Kapellbrücke in Lucerne to the 19th century. The initial cost of a timber bridge was less than that of a masonry arch, and the construction process was quicker,

4 The bridge of 1772 over the River Teme at Downton near Ludlow, close to the Bringewood ironworks, that was probably designed by Thomas Farnolls Pritchard.

5 Thomas Telford's wooden bridge of 1799-1800 at Cressage, Shropshire. It had a life of just over a century and was replaced in 1914.

but maintenance was expensive. In 1800 the appearance and safety of the wooden bridges over the Thames in London were the causes of scandal, and it was predicted that such structures would shortly disappear from the English land-scape.[9] Nevertheless, new wooden bridges continued to be built. Thomas Farnolls Pritchard contemplated the erection of a timber arch over the Severn at Stourport in 1773, and in 1799-1800 Thomas Telford built a wooden trestle bridge at Cressage (SJ 593045), only six miles from Coalbrookdale.[10] The only wooden bridge erected in the Severn Gorge, at Preen's Eddy, had a life of only 15 years.

Iron precursors

No one in literary and scientific circles in the late 18th century doubted that the Iron Bridge at Coalbrookdale was the first of its kind, although this claim can be qualified. An iron bridge was projected at Lyons in 1755. It was never built, but French engineers of the late 18th century were certainly aware of the structural possibilities of iron.[11] Robert Mylne (1734-1811) prepared drawings in 1774 for two iron bridges at Inveraray.[12] In 1946 engineers working for the London & North Eastern Railway removed from the Milby Cut (SE 4067) near Boroughbridge in Yorkshire a simple cast-iron beam bridge, now in the reserve collection of the National Railway Museum, York. The waterway was dug in 1769, but there is no evidence that the bridge was built then.[13]

An iron bridge was built elsewhere in Yorkshire in 1769. A newspaper reported that an arch of 72 ft. (22.2m) span and 6 ft. (1.8m) wide, made by a Leeds whitesmith and ironmonger, Maurice Tobin (c.1703-73), had been erected over an ornamental waterway in Sir George Armytage's (1734-83) park at Kirklees Hall (SE 170222) in the West Riding. The bridge was probably of wrought iron, since it was described as an 'ornamental iron bridge with roses', and Tobin was accustomed to supply to his gentry customers such items as fenders and hinges, and, on one occasion, a wrought-iron staircase. The bridge cost less than £200. It remained uncelebrated until mentioned in a standard work on 18th-century ironwork in 1911, and nothing is known of its subsequent fate.[14]

The Iron Bridge at Coalbrookdale was both celebrated and influential. Its design, while obviously based on precise calculations and measurements, was not derived from structural theory. Nevertheless, it was a spectacular demonstration of what could be achieved. As a leading structural historian has commented, 'neither the form given to the arch nor the framing around and over it reflect any of the current thinking of architects, engineers and mathematicians ... It had little influence on later designs, but, becoming quickly famous, it was an important stimulus to the use of iron'.[15] Thomas Telford wrote in 1824 of 'the merit of promoting a great arch of cast iron, introducing a material almost incompressible, which is readily moulded into any shape, and which is peculiarly applicable in the British Isles where the mines of iron are inexhaustible and the means of manufacturing cast iron unrivalled'.[16] No one benefited more than Telford from the achievements of those who built the Iron Bridge.

The first half of the 19th century was the heroic age of British civil engineering. From that time we inherit the practice of speaking of engineering achievements as those of individual designers – Telford's Menai Bridge, Rennie's Lune Aqueduct, Brunel's *Great Britain*, George Stephenson's *Rocket*, Robert Stephenson's Britannia Bridge. It does not belittle the achievements of those engineers to suggest that it is unhelpful in trying to understand how the Iron Bridge at Coalbrookdale came to be built to look for one person who was solely responsible for it. We should not seek to explain it in the terms of a later era, and it may be salutary to reflect that we do not regard the great civil engineering achievements of the 20th century, the road crossings of the Severn, Thames, Humber and Forth, or the Honshu-Shikoku bridges in Japan, as the works of individuals. If we wish to understand how the bridge came to be built we need to ask pertinent questions and to use evidence rather than fantasy in seeking answers.

II

The Project

Progenitors

The proposal to build an iron bridge linking Madeley with the south shore of the Severn originated in a letter written in 1773 by Thomas Farnolls Pritchard (1723-77), a Shrewsbury architect, to John Wilkinson, the ironmaster.[1] Wilkinson (1727-1808) sprang from an ironworking family. He was the son of the Lancashire pot-founder Isaac Wilkinson (c.1704-84), and brother of William Wilkinson (c.1744-1808) who applied British ironworking techniques at Indret and Le Creusot in France. Their sister had married the scientist Joseph Priestley (1733-1804). In 1757 Wilkinson was one of 12 partners who formed the New Willey Company in Shropshire, and by 1774 he had gained complete control of the concern. In that year he took out a patent for boring cannon, and was consulting with Matthew Boulton (1728-1809) and James Watt (1736-1819) about the boring of cylinders for steam engines, consultation which in 1776 resulted in the application of the second Watt engine to blow the New Willey blast furnace. By the mid-1770s Wilkinson had established an ironworks at Bradley near Wolverhampton, and was preparing to erect another at Snedshill near Oakengates in Shropshire.[2] He loved innovations. In the late 1780s he built the first iron river and canal craft, and the younger Joseph Priestley wrote of his Bradley works:

> independent of the scope there is for exertion in every branch of the business, there is a pleasure and advantage in being concerned in a works of such large extent, and where so many improvements are daily making that no consideration can overbalance.[3]

It was therefore within Wilkinson's character to be connected with the first iron bridge. He was, except for one short period, a shareholder in the project while the bridge was being built. There is no evidence that he was directly involved in the process of construction, but it seems that it was he who took the first steps to making Pritchard's proposition a reality. Thomas Telford, who was acquainted with many of those involved with the project, wrote that he did not know who first proposed building the bridge, but that ' the late Mr John Wilkinson had some share of the merit, certain it is that he was very active in promoting the first iron bridge'.[4]

Thomas Farnolls Pritchard was, by 1773, a successful West Midlands architect.[5] He was born in 1723, the son of John Pritchard, a Shrewsbury joiner, and he in

6 John Wilkinson, depicted on one of his own trade tokens.

turn became a joiner in his native town. His maternal grandfather, Thomas Farnolls, an innkeeper and farmer, died in the year of his birth. On the death of his maternal grandmother in 1748 Pritchard inherited a modest income derived from property, which he shared with his two brothers, and a personal legacy of a silver tankard.[6] By 1760 Pritchard was practising as an architect, the patron of several skilled craftsmen. Amongst the buildings he designed or re-ordered were Swan Hill Court House and the Foundling Hospital (now part of Shrewsbury School) in Shrewsbury, Hosyer's Almshouses, the Guildhall and No. 27 Broad Street in Ludlow, Hatton Grange near Shifnal, and Croft Castle in Herefordshire. In 1767 he leased a turret at Eyton-on-Severn, a remnant of the great Jacobean mansion of the Newport family, where he spent the concluding years of his life, concerning himself with the design of bridges and buildings rather than with practical craftsmanship. In 1765 he had surveyed the old Stone (or English) bridge in Shrewsbury. His plan for its replacement was rejected in favour of a design by John Gwynn (d.1786), but he was responsible for the temporary timber bridge on which traffic crossed the Severn after the demolition of the old bridge until the completion of Gwynn's structure in 1774. Pritchard advised the Shropshire Quarter Sessions on the projects to build new bridges over the Severn and Tern at Atcham in the 1770s, although his designs were not used. In 1773 he was appointed surveyor for a bridge over the Severn at Stourport in Worcestershire, where the river was joined by the newly-opened Staffordshire & Worcestershire Canal. His initial plan in December 1773 was for 'a commodious wooden bridge … with stone

7 A view of Stourport in 1776 showing Pritchard's bridge, completed the previous year.

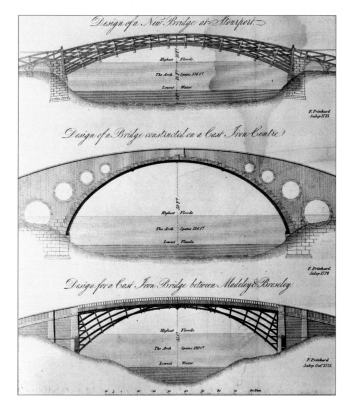

8 Pritchard's bridge designs, progressing from a timber structure, to a masonry arch constructed on iron centring to his first plan for an Iron Bridge in the Severn Gorge, from J. White, *On Cementitious Architecture* (1832).

abutments', that was based on the bridge across the River Thames at Walton in Surrey, but he appears to have decided to build a brick bridge on an iron centre, lightened in the spandrels by circular perforations, like those used by William Edwards in his bridge at Pontypridd. An advertisement in June 1774 requesting trustees particularly to attend a meeting at which 'a matter of some consequence' was to be discussed, suggest that the design may have been changed at that time. Stourport bridge was completed in 1775, and consisted of three arches, two of 42 ft. (13m) and one of 48 ft. (14.8m) span, with 49 land arches on the approaches across the riverside meadows. It is illustrated in a print of the canal port published in 1776, that shows rusticated stonework on the undersides of the arches. This could be artist's licence, and it remains a possibility that the bridge was built on iron centring, although the completed structure does not resemble Pritchard's drawing. The first Stourport Bridge had a life of only 20 years. No detailed description remains.[7]

John White argued in 1832 that 'Pritchard made a gradual progress in the application of iron to the erection of bridges', and that after completing Stourport he came to favour the erection of a wholly iron bridge, observing that the architect had been encouraged by 'the spirited ironmasters of Coalbrookdale', including Abraham Darby, John Wilkinson and Mr Onions. Pritchard certainly knew the ironmasters as suppliers and clients. His 'Drawing Book', held in the library of the American Institute of Architects, shows that in 1765 he ordered a cast-iron grate from Coalbrookdale during his restoration of Shipton Hall in the Corvedale. He designed the memorial for Ann, first wife of John Wilkinson, which remains in the parish church at Wrexham, and in 1769 he provided a chimney-piece for *The Lawns*, Wilkinson's house at Broseley. He designed fireplaces at Benthall Hall for the Harries family and for Blythe Turner at Broseley Hall, where he built a summer-house in

9 The memorial in Wrexham parish church, designed by Thomas Farnolls Pritchard, to Ann, first wife of John Wilkinson.

the Gothick style. He probably did work for Abraham Darby III at the Hay Farm, Madeley, for Darby's accounts record payments in 1776 to Joseph Bromfield, a plasterer, and John Nelson, a carver, who regularly carried out commissions for Pritchard.[8]

The Launching of the Project

Wilkinson's support for Pritchard's scheme came to fruition during the winter of 1773-4. In February 1774 local newspapers reported that the people of Broseley and Madeley Wood were proposing to petition Parliament for leave to bridge the Severn near Coalbrookdale. It was already intended to build an *iron* bridge, a single arch of cast iron, with a span of 120 ft. (37m). A year passed before a meeting was held at which a subscription was raised to cover the legal expenses involved in presenting a petition at Westminster. The proposed dimensions of the bridge remained unchanged, and it was claimed that an iron bridge would be more durable and less expensive than one built of conventional materials. In the summer of 1775 the promoters published notices of their intention to petition Parliament, heading them 'Iron Bridge over the Severn'.[9]

10 The summer house at Broseley Hall, designed by Thomas Farnolls Pritchard, that appears in the book of his drawings by the American Institute of Architects in Washington D.C.

The first formal meeting of the subscribers took place at the home of Abraham Cannadine (d. 1785), a Broseley cooper and probably an innkeeper, on 15 September 1775. Cannadine's house regularly accommodated public meetings, and he appears to have had no other connections with the bridge project, except that he occasionally supplied tubs or barrels to Abraham Darby. A subscription of between three and four thousand pounds was promised, and a design by Pritchard was accepted for a bridge 'of very curious construction'. Abraham Darby III agreed to build the bridge and the approach roads, and accepted the post of treasurer to the project.[10] He and Pritchard subsequently prepared an estimate of costs to which they appended a list of potential subscribers.[11]

Apart from Darby and Pritchard, most of the supporters of the Iron Bridge project lived in Broseley. Charles Guest was a grocer and proprietor of a soap works, a member of the family from which sprang the dynasty who controlled the Dowlais ironworks in South Wales. Leonard Jennings worked two windmills, and sometimes supplied bran to Abraham Darby's farms. John Thursfield of Benthall Hall was a surgeon, but his family were best known as potters. He shared an interest in coalworks at Barnetts Leasow, Broseley, with another shareholder in the bridge, John Morris (d. 1797), who lived in Cockshut Lane, Broseley. John Nicholson was landlord of the *Swan Inn*, Coalbrookdale, a hostelry established about 1760, where the bridge proprietors often met. Other individuals held shares for short periods during the time of promotion and construction, but their roles appear to have been insignificant. The secretary to the proprietors was Thomas Addenbrooke (d. 1787), a respected solicitor who lived at Buildwas, although his address was often published as 'Coalbrookdale'.[12]

The subscribers met on 17 October 1775, when they examined Pritchard's plans and estimate, commissioned Abraham Darby III to build the bridge, and compiled a list of commissioners to be named in the bill for presentation to Parliament. As was usual with bills of this kind, the list included all the gentry and clergy from a wide area around who could be regarded as sympathetic, including the Earl Gower, Sir Henry Bridgeman, Sir Watkin Williams Wynn, George Forester, William Pulteney (1729-1805) and John Fletcher, vicar of Madeley. Such people did no more than express support, and it was the subscribers who were responsible for carrying the project into effect. The principal signatures on the petition that was presented to Parliament, distinguished from the rest, are those of Abraham Darby III, John Wilkinson, Leonard Jennings, Edward Blakeway, a substantial investor in the iron and ceramics industries of the Severn Gorge, John Wyke, a Broseley surgeon, and William Goodwin (1748-97), a timber merchant who lived at Severn House, Coalbrookdale. Other signatories included many clerks from the Coalbrookdale ironworks, Roses, Gilpins and Hortons, and nine Severn bargemen. Richard Reynolds, the husband of Abraham Darby's step-sister, and his partner in the Coalbrookdale works, appears not to have given public support to the project.[13]

Pritchard's first design for the bridge, a cast-iron arch with a span of 120 ft. (37m), was published by his nephew, John White, in 1830. White saw the design as the result of an evolutionary process that began with Pritchard's drawings for a wooden bridge at Stourport, dating from 1773, and continued with his plan for a masonry arch on a cast-iron centre. The cast-iron bridge for Coalbrookdale was to have four ribs, each of them 9 in. × 6 in. (0.23 × 0.15m) in section.[14] Pritchard and Darby estimated that the bridge could be built for £3,200, of which £2,100 was to be spent on 300 tons of cast iron and wrought iron, and over £500 on dressed stone. They calculated that pumping, scaffolding and trans-port would cost £200, surveying

11 The estimate of costs for the construction of the Iron Bridge, prepared by T.F. Pritchard and Abraham Darby III in September 1775.

and making drawings £120, making and providing materials for new roads £250.[15] These figures proved over-optimistic, and, like many pioneering projects, the construction of the Iron Bridge took place in an atmosphere of financial crisis.

The Parliamentary Process

Early in February 1776 Thomas Addenbrooke travelled to London by the *Diligence* stage-coach and stayed there for nearly a month, arranging for the petition calling for an Act to build the bridge to be presented to Parliament, and observing the passage of the subsequent bill through the Commons and Lords. He employed as his barrister John Harries of the Middle Temple, probably a kinsman of the Rev. Edward Harries. Addenbrooke was paid for 24 days' work at half-a-guinea a day, while John Harries received a fee of £100.[16]

Charles Baldwyn (1729-89), one of the two members for the County of Salop, presented the petition for the bridge to the House of Commons on 5 February 1776. The petitioners contended that:

> a very considerable traffic is carried on at Coalbrookdale, Madeley Wood, Benthall, Broseley &c. In iron, lime, potters' clay and coals, and persons carrying on the same frequently are put to great inconveniences, delays and obstructions by reason of the insufficiency of the present ferry over the River Severn, particularly in winter.

They claimed a bridge would improve trade and affirmed that 'it would ... be of public utility if the said bridge were to be constructed with cast-iron'.[17] The petition received more notice than most applications for leave to bring in local or private legislation. Lord North (1732-92), the Prime Minster, and Fletcher Norton (1716-89), the Speaker, expressed interest in the project, and called for drawings to be displayed in the House. Pritchard's plans were brought forward, and, according to reports, 'gave great satisfaction'. The petition was referred to a committee of the House, whose members included Charles Baldwyn.[18]

A little over a week later the committee reported back to the House. Thomas Addenbrooke was examined on the advantages that would follow from the building of a bridge. He expressed his opinion that it would be of particular benefit to the china manufactory at Caughley, and drew attention to the difficulty of taking carriages over the Severn, since none of the ferries in the Gorge was able to carry vehicles. Leave was then given for the introduction of a bill to be prepared by Charles Baldwyn, Sir Henry Bridgeman and Mr Noel Hill (1744-89), the other member for the County of Salop.[19]

Thomas Addenbrooke and John Harries had doubtless already prepared the draft of the bill that was presented by Charles Baldwyn and given its first reading on 19 February 1776. Its second reading followed eight days later. After minor amendments at the committee stage, a third reading was given on 8 March. The bill was introduced in the House of Lords the same day, and passed quickly through that House, receiving the Royal Assent on 25 March 1776. The preamble of the Act repeated the arguments of the petition, but the commitment to build a bridge of iron was qualified, the trustees receiving authority to make a structure of 'cast-iron, stone, brick or timber'.[20]

A Winter of Dissent

For the next 18 months the trustees could not decide how to proceed. From the beginning of 1774 the intention had been to build a 120 ft. (37m) bridge of iron, a proposal that had been formalised when Pritchard's design was approved in October 1775. At the same meeting, the trustees authorised Abraham Darby to take responsibility for building the bridge, but on 15 May 1776 the trustees rescinded this commitment, and decided to advertise in the Midlands press for people with plans for a single-arch structure of 120 ft. 'in stone, brick or timber'. People willing to build such bridges were invited to a meeting on 28 June 1776, but it appears that no satisfactory proposal was made, for the trustees then agreed to go ahead with Pritchard's design, and to seek contractors for the masonry abutments. On 24 July Pritchard was instructed to prepare a model of the intended bridge.[21]

A schism developed among the subscribers during the summer of 1776. On one side were Abraham Darby III and others committed to building a bridge in iron. On the other were the more conservative trustees who preferred a less unorthodox structure. On 1 October Leonard Jennings and John Wilkinson made over their shares to Abraham Darby III on condition that the bridge would be erected by Christmas 1778. It seems unlikely that Wilkinson would have been apprehensive about an iron structure, and the reason for this transaction may have been to strengthen Darby's position by increasing his personal shareholding. Within twelve months Wilkinson and Jennings had regained their holdings. The factions amongst the remaining trustees divided up at a meeting on 18 October 1776, at which it was re-affirmed that the trust would erect a cast-iron bridge, and that Darby would complete it by Christmas 1778. Seven trustees – Rev. Edward Harries, Richard Harries of Shrewsbury, Charles Guest, John Hartshorne, Sergeant Roden, John Morris and John Thursfield – opposed the use of iron unless the whole project, including the access roads, could be completed for 3,000 guineas. Abraham Darby agreed to indemnify these seven from further demands over and above the £50 per share that they had originally agreed to subscribe. If more money was needed, it was to be raised by Darby and his fellow supporters of the use of iron, Pritchard, Edward Blakeway and John Nicholson. Darby guaranteed on the credit of the bridge tolls to pay the proprietors five per cent interest on their shares should completion be delayed beyond Christmas 1778. Although the seven who opposed the use of iron formed a majority of the trustees, they held a minority of the shares, only ten, compared with the 42 held by Darby and his allies.[22]

In spite of this apparent agreement, no progress was made on the construction of the bridge during the winter of 1776-7. Doubts remained about the decisions made on 18 October 1776, and about the legality of the system under which shares had been assigned. On 31 March 1777 the trustees agreed to seek the opinion of a learned counsel, Thomas Mitton of Cleobury, on the interpretation of the Act of Parliament, and on the assignment of shares. Mitton's opinion, received at a meeting on 14 July 1777, was that no undertaking could be given to any trustee that he would receive interest on his shares in any other manner than by normal dividends arising from tolls and other forms of income specified in the Act. He recommended, and the trustees agreed, that the whole agreement of 18 October 1776 should be rescinded, and that a new form of assignment of shares should be drawn up. There were henceforth to be 64 shares. The seven shareholders who had opposed the use of iron agreed to raise further capital by making donations of £2 10s. 0d. per share, while Abraham Darby, his supporters, and any new trustees, were to pay £5 per share. Darby still accepted that the bridge and its access roads could be completed by Christmas 1778, and agreed that, if it would not be finished by then, he would pay five per cent interest on such sums as had been paid to him. On 20 October 1777 the 64 shares under the new system were assigned: Abraham Darby III took 15 and his brother Samuel four. John Wilkinson had 12, Leonard Jennings and the Rev. Edward Harries 10 each, Thomas Farnolls Pritchard, Edward Blakeway, Charles Guest and John Morris two each, and no other subscriber had more than one. The legal and financial foundation of the project was settled, at the cost of Mitton's two-guinea fee, and the projectors were able to face the practical problems of making the bridge a reality.[23]

The design had been altered by July 1777. The proposal was now for a bridge of 90-ft (27.7m) span instead of 120 ft. It is likely that the span was subsequently increased to 100 ft. 6 in. (30.95m) to accommodate the towing-path, and that the plan agreed by July 1777 was essentially for the bridge as it was actually built.[24]

Pritchard's Model

Pritchard was instructed to prepare a model of the proposed bridge on 24 July 1776, and in September 1779, almost two years after his death, but soon after the ironwork had been erected, the proprietors made a payment of nearly £40 to his brother 'for making drawings, model &c'.[25] This was not the mahogany model now displayed in the Science Museum, London, which was made after the bridge was completed.[26] It is possible that Pritchard's model was that held by the National Museum of Scotland.[27] When an American Quaker Jabez Maud Fisher stayed with Abraham Darby III on 20 August 1776 he was shown 'a very elegant and compleat Model of the plan on a scale of ¼ inch to a foot' (1:24), which is precisely the scale of the model held in Edinburgh.[28] The abutments on the model are notional and not as built, suggesting that when the model was made the design of the ironwork was settled, but that decisions remained to be taken about the approaches. The model may therefore have been made before the bridge was completed. The abutments are identical on each side, with pairs of triple-stepped buttresses with flared capping stones flanking land arches in which the key stones are prominent, the latter a detail that can be observed in several of Pritchard's buildings, on the rear elevation of No. 27 Broad Street, Ludlow, for example. Pritchard's model may have been sold soon after the bridge was completed, although the sale is not itemised in Abraham Darby III's accounts. In 1782 Sir

12 The gazebo in
the garden of No.27
Broad Street,
Ludlow, that was
probably designed by
Pritchard. The ogee
and circle
ornamentation
match the decorative
elements on the Iron
Bridge.

Edward Smythe (d.1811) of Acton Burnell paid
£2 12s. 0d. to a Shrewsbury firm of heraldic
painters for painting a model of the bridge.[29]
The sum represents the labour of two skilled
men for about a fortnight, which would be
consistent with the amount of work required to
paint the Edinburgh model. The Civil
Engineering Department of King's College,
London passed the model in the spring of 1927
to what was then the Science Museum, Edinburgh, where it was formally registered in
January 1928.[30] The model was apparently given
to King's College by Queen Victoria as part of
the collection of philosophical instruments and
astronomical apparatus formed at Kew by King
George III. It appears prominently in an
engraving showing Prince Albert opening the
museum displaying the collection at the College
in June 1843.[31] Whether the king obtained the

model from Sir Edward Smythe cannot currently be established, and it is possible
that it has another provenance.

13 The model of the
Iron Bridge now held
by the National
Museum of Scotland,
part of the collection
made by King
George III, being
presented by Prince
Albert to King's
College, London in
1843. The model can
be seen above the
doorway. *Illustrated
London News*, 1 July
1843.

Pritchard in Retrospect

Thomas Farnolls Pritchard died on 21 December 1777 in his tower house at Eyton-
on-Severn. Groundwork for the construction of the Iron Bridge had only just
commenced and, before examining how the bridge was built, it is appropriate to
examine the contribution that Pritchard had made. His obituary records that he had

14 Thomas Farnolls Pritchard, 1723-77 (artist unknown).

been ill for more than a year, which explains why he attended no meetings of the bridge trustees after October 1776.[32] Nevertheless, he remained a subscriber up to the time of his death, and was assigned shares under the new allocation of October 1777. He must, almost certainly, have been consulted about the alteration of the span of the proposed bridge during the summer of that year. The evidence, quoted above, of White, Tredgold and Telford, based on manuscript sources which do not survive, seems conclusively to establish that it was Pritchard who first proposed to build an iron bridge at Coalbrookdale, and there is no doubt that the plan for a 120 ft. (37m) arch in cast iron that first aroused interest in the project was his. That Pritchard had a significant share in the design of the bridge as it was actually built is suggested by the payment to his brother for the model and drawings. Stylistic evidence also links Pritchard with the bridge. The decorative circles in the spandrels recall the pierced abutments of the Stourport bridge, and the combination of the circle with an ogee appears in the summer house at 27 Broad Street, Ludlow, where Pritchard carried out alterations to the main building. The architect revealed his affection for the ogee in his design for the garden temple at Broseley Hall that stands only a mile from the Iron Bridge.[33]

The building of the Iron Bridge brought together two traditions. One was the innovating zeal of the ironmasters of the Coalbrookdale Coalfield who by the 1770s had already applied cast iron to a variety of new functions; the other was the tradition of craftsmanship in stone, brick and timber from which the two professions of architect and civil engineer were beginning to emerge in the English provinces in the mid-18th century. Thomas Farnolls Pritchard belonged to the second tradition, but through his contacts with the ironmasters and his own zeal for innovation, he came to bestride the two. Many other people contributed to the Iron Bridge project, but whoever inscribed on Pritchard's portrait 'Thomas Farnolls Pritchard, Archt., Inventor of Cast Iron Bridges, 1774' was not far from the truth.[34]

III

Realisation

The Third Abraham Darby

Whatever the extent of Thomas Pritchard's contribution to the Iron Bridge, from December 1777 the creative genius of the project was the third Abraham Darby (1750-89), offspring of the second Abraham Darby (1711-63), the ironmaster who had initiated the expansion of the iron industry in Shropshire in the 1750s, and of his second wife, the pious and strong-minded Abiah (1716-93), a member of the Maude family of Sunderland. Darby was born in 1750 and educated at the school of James Fell, a Worcester Quaker. He was 13 when his father died in 1763, and he was subsequently apprenticed to Richard Reynolds (1735-1816), who managed the works from 1763. In 1768, five years after his father's death, Darby took responsibility for the Coalbrookdale foundry.[1]

Much of the history of the Shropshire ironworks in the years that followed was shaped by the relationship between Darby and Richard Reynolds, 15 years his senior, the husband of his half-sister Hannah (1735-62), offspring of his father's first marriage to Margaret Smith. Reynolds, a Bristolian and son of an iron merchant, had moved to Coalbrookdale in 1756 to represent the interests of Thomas Goldney (1696-1768), partner of Abraham Darby in most of his mining and ironworking concerns. The following year he married Hannah Darby, acquired a half-share in the iron and coalworks that had been established by his father-in-law and Thomas Goldney at Ketley about four miles north of Coalbrookdale, and settled at Ketley Bank House. His first wife died in 1762, and in 1763, after the death of Abraham Darby II (1711-63), he went to live at Coalbrookdale, marrying for the second time in December of that year, but returned to Ketley Bank House after Abraham Darby III took over management of the foundry. Reynolds was a shrewd businessman who became very rich through his participation in a range of enterprises, many of them, in Bristol and elsewhere, unconnected with his Shropshire interests.[2] His son, William (1758-1803), eight years the junior of Abraham Darby III, was the most creative of the Shropshire ironmasters. He studied with Dr Joseph Black (1728-99), physician and physicist of the University of Edinburgh, and was an enthusiastic collector of scientific data and samples. According to the ironmaster Richard Crawshay (1739-1810), William Reynolds had 'more Metalurgie and Chemical Skil than any other of my friends'.[3] In his late teens, he discussed the installation of steam engines with James Watt, whom he regarded as 'one of the greatest philosophers in Europe', and by 1781 he was exchanging friendly letters with him.[4]

For most of his business life Abraham Darby III owed money to Richard Reynolds. Hay Farm, the home to which he moved in 1780, was mortgaged to Reynolds in April 1774 for £4,000. Nevertheless, he continued to acquire new properties in the mid-1770s, notably control of the lordship of the manor of Madeley, and the Madeley Wood ironworks. In 1777 Darby and his brother Samuel (1755-96) mortgaged to Reynolds their shares in the Ketley and Horsehay ironworks for £8,000. Darby also borrowed money on a large scale from his brother-in-law, Joseph Rathbone (1746-90) of Liverpool.[5] Richard Reynolds may have considered that the project to build an iron bridge was at odds with the financial prudence that he cherished and, except for a period of less than a month in the autumn of 1778 when he held ten shares,[6] he had no involvement in it until after the structure was completed.

The life of Abraham Darby III is reasonably well-documented, and it is possible to place his involvement with the Iron Bridge in the broader context of his family and business life. In 1776 Darby became a Quaker elder in February, and married Rebecca Smith (1752-1834) of Doncaster in May.[7] Apart from his interests in the Coalbrookdale ironworks, and from 1776 in the furnaces at Madeley Wood, he began from 1774 to control the lime works at Lincoln Hill on the eastern side of Coalbrookdale.[8] He invested in overseas trade, having shares in the ship *Darby*, trading from Liverpool to Danzig (Gdansk) in 1771, for which he received compensation from an insurance company after the loss of the vessel two years later, and in the brigs *Endeavour* and *Industry*, trading from Bristol, in 1779.[9]

Darby lived in some comfort, buying some luxury items, such as a red leather hatbox from traders in Bristol, but obtaining some necessities locally. In 1776 he bought nightcaps and stockings from an itinerant Scots pedlar. He subscribed to newspapers and in 1771 purchased a camera obscura and an 'electrical machine', both of which remained amongst his possessions throughout his life. He appears to have been well-read, having amongst his books Samuel Johnson's dictionary, scientific volumes by Joseph Priestley, the works of John Milton, a life of Oliver Cromwell and a study of minerals. His possessions also included mathematical instruments, a microscope and a pair of Senex's globes. While he was in London he participated in the activities of the Society of Arts of which he became a fellow in 1777, following the election of his brother Samuel the previous year. He enjoyed fishing and shooting, and kept two spaniels whose leather collars bore his name.[10]

Darby's family life and his business affairs were disturbed during the period when the Iron Bridge was under construction by the mental instability of his brother Samuel. The Coalbrookdale partners had a foundry in Southwark, and in 1775 Darby bought a property adjacent to George Yard, from which Samuel, having finished his apprenticeship in Liverpool, was to manage the partnership's affairs in the capital.[11] Although only just of age, Samuel married in 1776. He became severely ill during 1779 and recovered in Shropshire, but after his return to London it became evident that the foundry in Southwark was making losses, and it was sold in November of the same year. His illness was linked with nervous problems that prevented him from taking a responsible part in the family's business concerns during the remaining 17 years of his life.[12]

15 View of Coalbrookdale before the building of the bridge (William Williams, *c.*1777).

The most recent chronicler of the Darbys has revealed that Abraham Darby III was remembered by subsequent generations of his family as having 'failed in business'.[13] It appears that his ambition to establish his family's ironmaking business on secure foundations was combined with a measure of financial recklessness. During the period when he was responsible for building the Iron Bridge he was newly married and preparing to move to a new home at Hay Farm. His brother was ailing, and he was increasingly indebted to Richard Reynolds, his partner and kinsman, amongst others. Furthermore he only attained the age of 30 in the year before the bridge opened.

Sources

There is no single straightforward account of the construction of the Iron Bridge which enables the stages to be narrated with the precision with which the erection of the Menai Suspension Bridge or the Britannia Bridge can be described, but there are six principal sources which taken together enable a coherent if incomplete narrative to be compiled.

The first is the information given on two of the earliest views of the bridge published at about the time it was opened to traffic, a woodcut published by John Edmunds (d.1807) of Madeley, and a plan and elevation published by J. Phillips of London in 1782. The latter is the basis for the much-quoted description of the building of the bridge that appears in Richard Gough's (1735-1809) edition of William Camden's (1551-1623) *Britannia*, published in 1789. Where these accounts can be checked with other sources the information they give is confirmed, and it is reasonable to regard them as accurate, if incomplete.[14]

Shropshire's county newspaper, the *Shrewsbury Chronicle*, began publication only in 1772, and its news coverage was limited in the decades that followed. It includes several items about the construction of the bridge that are invaluable in establishing the chronology of events, but none describes the methods of erection.

The proprietors' minute book includes scarcely any detailed information from the period of construction, and the most authoritative documentary sources are the financial records of Abraham Darby III, in which the accounts showing how money was expended on constructing the bridge are mingled with details of his other business activities and with trivial items of personal expenditure. Two sets of documents survive; a ledger,[15] and two cashbooks in which some items are described in more detail than in the ledger.[16] Darby's accounts record the purchase of construction equipment, payments to sub-contractors, and the wages of the workers directly employed on the construction of the bridge. Payments were made fortnightly, according to the custom in the local mines, and the level of expenditure can be plotted throughout the period of construction. The average wage at the Horsehay ironworks in this period for such tasks as breaking limestone was about eleven shillings a week, which can be used as an approximate measure of the numbers employed on the bridge at any one time. Darby's accounts do not reveal the costs of the iron and stone, and contain only some ambiguous references to the acquisition of the land on which it was built.

The writings of travellers are also a source of pertinent evidence. Arthur Young (1741-1820) and the American Quaker John M. Fisher visited Coalbrookdale in 1776 when plans for the bridge were being discussed, and John Wesley (1703-91) actually observed preparations for its erection in 1779.[17] Others, during the 1780s, talked with people involved in the project, and recorded local perceptions of the events of 1773-81 and of the personalities involved.[18] To their journals may be added the writings of Thomas Telford who from the early 1790s was acquainted with many people close to the construction project. His account in the *Edinburgh Encyclopedia* is clearly well-informed and can be regarded as an original source.[19]

Pictorial evidence is a further source. Many images of the Iron Bridge were published in the years after its completion, but until recently only one detailed view of the banks of the Severn before the bridge was complete was known, William Williams's (c.1740-98) pencil sketch, which, from its title, was obviously made in 1776 or 1777.[20] In 1997 a Finnish scholar drew attention to a watercolour by Elias Martin (1739-1818), apparently one of a series showing the bridge under construction. The watercolour hangs in the museum of the Skandia Company in Stockholm, and challenges past interpretations of the process of construction.[21]

Finally there is the archaeological evidence provided by the bridge itself. The outer ribs bear the inscription 'This bridge was cast at Coalbrookdale and erected in the year MDCCLXXIX'. English Heritage has since the 1970s been responsible for photogrammetric recording of the structure. Some archaeological observations were made when the scaffold was in place for the final stages of the restoration of the bridge in 1980, and a more thorough programme was carried out during re-painting in 1999-2000.[22]

Building the Bridge

The construction of the Iron Bridge can best be understood not through a chronological narrative, for which the sources provide insufficient evidence, but by attempting to answer a series of questions in which what is known can be balanced with current gaps in our knowledge.

The Act of Parliament decreed the location of the bridge.[23] It was to cross the Severn from a point in Benthall parish near the house of Samuel Barnett, a barge owner, to the opposite shore close to the house of Thomas Crumpton, also a barge owner. The site was adjacent to a ferry, with access on the southern bank to a road leading up the valley of the Benthall Brook towards Broseley, where it made a junction with the Wenlock turnpike road. On the north bank it was within reach of The Wharfage, the quay built alongside the river in the first half of the 18th century. Samuel Barnett's house was demolished and rebuilt, for which he was compensated by the proprietors. A payment in June 1780 of £50 to Edward Harries, lord of the manor of Benthall, 'for Roden's house, as valued', may also have been compensation for the demolition of property on the south bank.[24] The bridge proprietors bought a piece of ground on the north bank from the barge owner Richard Beard. Its purchase was unrecorded in Darby's accounts, but is mentioned in the minutes of the proprietors of the *Tontine Hotel*. The plot accommodated the abutment of the bridge, the *Tontine*, and, probably, most of the land later developed as the market square.[25] A few months after the bridge opened, the proprietors had to ensure the removal of George Armstrong's hog sty, probably on the south bank. In the following year they secured the demolition of Owner Pool's brewhouse and Owner Crumpton's warehouse on the north bank, and in 1785 insisted on the removal from the road of Pool's pig and pig sty.[26]

One of the first concerns of the proprietors was the maintenance of the existing ferry. The privilege of working the ferry belonged to the lords of the manors of Madeley and Benthall, Abraham Darby III and Edward Harries, both bridge proprietors, who appear to have passed their rights to the trustees without payment. The boat was let year by year to Daniel Day, who was probably the previous operator of the ferry. He was committed to carrying without toll timber for use in constructing the bridge, and was paid for the use of his boat during the construction process in 1779 and 1780. Day also had the right to collect tolls from those using the road leading south from the ferry, up the valley of the Benthall Brook.[27] It is evident that he was respected by the trustees, who, when he was an old man in 1800, gave him clothes as a gratuity.[28]

Construction of the bridge began in November 1777, but the amounts spent during the following months suggest that no more than two or three men were employed. It is evident that much work was done on the Benthall road, but the main task of the summer of 1778 would have been the digging of the foundations for the abutments, and the building of the platforms on which the ironwork was to rest. The source of the stone used in the bridge is not known. It is a grey, coal measure sandstone, found commonly in the district. Expenditure increased during March, reached a peak of over £45 a fortnight in early May, and further peaks exceeding £30 a fortnight in early July, mid-October and mid-November. Except for a brief spell in late July and early August, the traditional time for friendly society feasts, it appears that well over 20 men were employed for most of the summer. A payment of nine guineas for ale at the end of October perhaps marked the end of a phase of construction. A ledge in the wall of the platform on the north bank, below the clay of the river bed, and about 2 ft. (0.6m) wide at the downstream end, tapering to nothing at the upstream end, was discovered during repair work in the winter of 1973-4. It suggests that either the wall had been started at an incorrect alignment, or that alterations to the planned line or even to the span of the bridge were made early in 1778.[29]

While the platforms were being prepared, iron-founders were casting the ribs of the bridge. The Phillips text relates that 378 tons 15 cwt. of iron were used in the structure, and there seems no reason to doubt this contemporary figure.[30] The same text relates that the castings were made in open moulds, which is confirmed by the concave surfaces and the air holes still visible in the bridge. Detailed observation has shown that the bridge consists of more than 800 castings, of only 12 different types.[31] Such a weight of iron would have strained the resources of the Coalbrookdale works, quite apart from the practical difficulties of casting the large ribs, each about 70 ft. (21.6m) long and weighing 5 tons 5 cwt. The weekly output of a Shropshire blast furnace at this time was no more than about 20 tons, producing less than two tons at each tapping, so it is evident that, quite apart from considerations of quality, the ribs would have been cast from an air furnace, the type of reverberatory furnace then used for re-melting iron in a foundry.

Where the ribs were cast remains uncertain. No records survive for the 1770s for the Coalbrookdale ironworks, nor for any other foundry in the area. The Edmunds text records that the bridge was cast at Coalbrookdale in the year 1778, which there is no reason to doubt, but 'Coalbrookdale' could mean the Severn Gorge

16 The forehearth of the Old Furnace, Coalbrookdale. The upper beams provide evidence of the re-building of the ironworks in 1777. It is likely that the ribs of the Iron Bridge were cast at an adjacent air furnace from pig iron smelted in the Old Furnace.

17 The inscriptions on the Iron Bridge.

at that date. The Upper Furnace at Coalbrookdale had been continually in blast for seven years prior to the substantial re-building recorded by the date '1777' cast on the beams, and confirmed by archaeological evidence, that was part of a comprehensive programme of improvement affecting all parts of the ironworks.[32] About 20 years later travellers recorded two conflicting pieces of evidence. When Charles Hatchett (1766-1847) visited the ironworks in 1796 he was told that 'the celebrated Iron Bridge over the Severn was cast in this Foundry', but in 1801 the Rev. Richard Warner (1763-1857) learned that iron for the bridge was 'cast into the proper pieces in open sand upon the spot',[33] which gives credence to the opinion of several practical ironworkers that the easiest way to make the castings for the bridge would have been to erect an air furnace on the banks of the river.[34] Nevertheless, there is no suggestion in any of the original sources that this is how the castings were produced. Abraham Darby III acquired the Madeley Wood (or Bedlam) ironworks just before the bridge was built, but the foundry at Madeley Wood was always small – it closed in 1803 – and it seems unlikely that castings of nearly six tons were made there.[35] The most likely source of the castings remains the Upper Furnace complex at Coalbrookdale, if only because from the mid-1790s lengthy ribs for other bridges were certainly cast there, and because the patterns for the bridge were stored in an adjacent warehouse until 1902-3.[36]

The ironwork was erected during the summer of 1779. On Friday 26 March about noon John Wesley preached at Broseley and afterwards, walking to Coalbrookdale, he 'took a view of the Bridge which is shortly to be thrown over the Severn', commenting, 'I doubt whether the Colossus at Rhodes weighed much more', implying that he saw castings laid out on the bank awaiting erection.[37] The county newspaper reported that the first pair of ribs was erected and secured on Thursday and Friday 1 and 2 July 1779,[38] which is in keeping with the pattern of fortnightly expenditure on construction which dipped below £30, and then only marginally, only twice between the end of March and late November. Darby's accounts provide evidence that timber and ropes were purchased on a large scale during 1779. Over £150 was spent on timber, chiefly softwoods from Danzig, and more than £60 on ropes, as well as a smaller payment for 'scaffold poles and cords'. An owner, Thomas Sutton, was paid nearly £15 for the use of his trow, while the boat belonging to the ferryman Daniel Day was also employed.[39] The chronology is therefore well-established, and it is clear that a large quantity of timber was used, that a 'scaffold' was built, that a Severn trow was employed, and that much use was made of ropes.

18 A sketch of the Iron Bridge under construction (Elias Martin).

Older accounts of the construction of the bridge have suggested that the timbers were used to erect towers.[40] Our understanding of the subject has been changed by the discovery of the picture by Elias Martin, which shows an elegant wooden framework, rather like a set of goalposts with the cross-bar supported by diagonal struts, which was used to raise the half-ribs from the deck of a vessel on the Severn. It appears that the base plates were fixed on to the masonry platforms on either side of the river, and the uprights inserted into the base plates. One of the main half-ribs was then inserted into the base plate, and then the other, the two halves being fixed with vertical and horizontal pins in a crown piece, a complex component that could only have been cast with great skill. A re-enactment construction of the bridge, using components half as large as the originals, was staged during a BBC Television 'Timewatch' programme in January 2002, and established that this was a feasible mode of construction. Martin's watercolour shows three sets of ribs completely erected, and was probably made in mid-July 1779. Once the main ribs were erected a stable platform would have been completed. A payment for 'scaffold poles and cords' was made early in September.[41] The 'scaffold' may have been a series of decks, erected on the main ribs, from which other components, the middle and back ribs, the cross stays and braces, the deck bearers and the ornamental circles and ogees, could have been inserted. Most pieces were joined by dovetails, wedges or shouldered joints according to wood-working practice. An accurate drawing of the crown piece was made during the re-painting programme of 1999-2000, when numerals marked on the ribs were recorded, but appeared to relate to the order of casting rather than the order of erection.[42]

The principal parts of the bridge were, according to the Phillips text, erected within about three months, without serious accidents to the workmen, and without delaying traffic on the river. While there is an element of rhetoric about this statement – the passage of a heavily-laden barge would scarcely have been

19 The half-scale reconstruction of the Iron Bridge across the Shropshire Canal at Blists Hill, undertaken for the BBC *Timewatch* programme broadcast in January 2002, illustrating the method of construction shown in the Elias Martin sketch.

20 The crown pieces which held together the half-ribs of the Iron Bridge, illustrated in the half-scale reconstruction at Blists Hill, 2001.

welcome on 1 or 2 July 1779 – it can be taken as substantially correct. The completion of the work may have been marked by an ale-drinking for which nearly £6 was expended in mid-August.[43] It is thus reasonable to suppose that the period of three months during which the ironwork was erected ran from mid-May until mid-August, that much of the ironwork, as John Wesley had observed, was already on site by late March, that the first stages, the installation of the base plates and uprights on the masonry platforms took a little over a month, that the main ribs were erected quickly, beginning on 1 July, and that most of the rest of the structure was completed six or seven weeks later. Abraham Darby's accounts show that Job Goff or Gough (d.1782), who kept a tavern in Broseley, removed the scaffold late in November.[44]

The numbers working on the bridge diminished during the winter that followed, and during January 1780 there were probably fewer than a dozen men employed. The labour force during 1780 never reached the levels of previous years, but between the beginning of May and the end of August Darby never paid out less than £20 a fortnight, indicating a workforce of around two dozen. Work continued on the Benthall Road, and on a new road on the north bank joining the turnpike road at the top of Lincoln Hill (the present Church Hill), on which construction had begun in September 1779.[45] Teams of horses were hired to convey sand and lime, and some use was made of boats on the river, perhaps to ferry materials from one side to the other. The other main task of 1780 was the construction of the abutments behind the ironwork erected the previous summer. During restoration work in 1972 it became evident that the abutments had been built cheaply and apparently hurriedly, an indication, perhaps, that by this time costs of the bridge considerably exceeded the estimates. The masonry appeared to be solid, but in many areas it formed only a thin facing over a rubble filling.[46]

Some Personnel

Several sub-contractors or consultants were employed during 1780. James Deag, who had previously carried out masonry work for Abraham Darby, and may have built the abutments, received over £130 between April and October. Denis Edson was paid more than £50 for work carried out between early May and late November. Edson was an engineer practising from Chester, where he had worked on the Chester Canal. In June 1780 he contracted to carry out improvements on the turnpike road from Cainscross near Stroud through Nailsworth to Bath. He subsequently worked on the Stourbridge, Gloucester & Berkeley and Grand Surrey canals. It seems likely that he supervised the final stages of the construction of the roads running to the Iron Bridge.[47]

George Parker, who took over from Charles Hornblower at the beginning of October 1778, supervised the erection of the ironwork. Parker was in charge of Abraham Darby's limeworks on Lincoln Hill at this period, and in 1778 had supervised brick-making and other work in the Madeley collieries, as well as overseeing work on parish roads for which Darby was responsible as parish surveyor. Thomas Gregory succeeded him at the beginning of 1780. According to Samuel Smiles (1812-1904), writing in 1863 and quoting evidence provided by William Gregory Norris, then manager of the Coalbrookdale works, Gregory was foreman of pattern-makers at Coalbrookdale, and was responsible under Darby's superintendence for the design of the bridge as it was erected. He clearly had wood-working skills appropriate to a pattern maker since he subsequently built the model of the Iron Bridge now displayed in the Science Museum, and was recorded in the parish register as a carpenter when he died in 1799. It was he who conducted the brothers La Rochefoucauld around the Coalbrookdale ironworks in 1785.[48]

In their accounts of the Iron Bridge, Telford, Tredgold and White all included Daniel Onions amongst those who were responsible for its construction, the latter naming him amongst the ironmasters who had encouraged Pritchard to persevere with his plans. This was probably the Daniel Onions, partner in Banks & Onions, owners of the Benthall ironworks, who lived at a riverside inn at Gitchfield, in Broseley parish. He appears to have been the father of John Onions, a more famous ironmaster, and was certainly involved with the Preen's Eddy Bridge. He is not mentioned in Darby's accounts, and he was not a shareholder in the Iron Bridge, but it does seem that at some stage he fulfilled a significant role.[49]

Completion and Costs

The Iron Bridge was opened on New Year's Day 1781.[50] Less than £10 was expended on labour in the last fortnight of 1780, but a few men were kept on until the end of January 1781. The last payments by shareholders in the Iron Bridge were made in February 1781.[51] Promotion by the proprietors ensured that it became one of the celebrated monuments noticed by every tourist who kept a diary or journal.[52]

Many questions remain to be answered about the costs of the bridge. Darby originally agreed to construct it for £3,250, and £3,150 was promised by the initial subscribers, payment of which was completed after the opening of the bridge. It is evident that the true costs of the bridge substantially exceeded that figure, and that they were met by Darby himself. The accounts show that the costs of erection, that is, of labour employed directly, of Pritchard's and Edson's professional services, of sub-contractors, of hiring boats and teams of horses, of compensation paid to occupiers of demolished houses, and of such expendable materials as ropes and scaffolding, amounted to £2,373 4s. 4d. The estimate put the total cost of such items as no more than £550. The cost of the land on which the bridge stood is unknown, although some of the plot on the north bank possibly belonged to Darby as lord of the manor, and that on the south bank to Edward Harries. While the Benthall Road pre-dated the bridge project and belonged to Harries, the new road on the north bank (the present Church Hill) must have incurred land purchase costs, even if it avoided existing buildings. The costs of the castings, reckoned to be £2,100 in the original estimate – it would have been rather more since more iron was used than had been anticipated – and of dressed stone, which was forecast to be £500, are unknown.

Several visitors to the Severn Gorge recorded that Abraham Darby was financially embarrassed by the Iron Bridge project. Samuel Butler, a Warwickshire gentleman who inspected the bridge on 14 March 1782, learned that the undertaking had cost 5,000 guineas (i.e. £5,250).[53] Lord Torrington in 1784 was informed that the bridge had cost £6,000 and that Darby had suffered 'for his noble undertaking'.[54] The young French aristocrats, the brothers La Rochefoucauld, gained the impression in 1785 that Darby was on the point of bankruptcy.[55] It is ironic that Richard Reynolds, whose connection with the project had been marginal when it had been a venture involving much risk, purchased 15 of Abraham Darby's shares in December 1781 and July 1782. In due course they passed to his daughter Hannah Mary (1761-1839), widow of William Rathbone (1757-1809), and remained with the Rathbone family until the bridge was passed to Salop County Council in 1950.[56] By the time the bridge was opened Darby's own finances were exceedingly troubled. He and Samuel Darby together owed £60,000 to their brother-in-law, Joseph Rathbone, a level of indebtedness far beyond that which could have been incurred by the building of the bridge.[57] The Coalbrookdale Company and its allied concerns were re-structured during 1782 and, while Abraham Darby III evidently lived in some comfort at Hay Farm, he still owed large sums to his kinsmen. His possessions were sold immediately after his death in 1789.[58]

The ultimate financial irony concerning the Iron Bridge is that within less than a decade it became a prosperous concern. The tolls were let for £350 in the autumn of 1783, £393 in 1786, £561 in 1793, £636 in 1814 and £690 in 1829, and by the mid-1790s a dividend of four guineas (8 per cent) was being paid on each £55 share.[59] The value of Pritchard's vision and Darby's persistence had been realised in financial terms.

Conclusions

Many of those who contributed to the building of the Iron Bridge are unknown by name. Pattern-makers created wooden patterns for huge castings with such accuracy that the ribs could be threaded through uprights and fitted to dovetail joints; moulders prepared moulds of shapes and sizes to which they were wholly unaccustomed. Never before had molten iron flowed into shapes like those of the ten half-ribs of the bridge, and only steam-engine cylinders amongst the usual products of the foundry were comparable in weight. Thomas Sutton and his crew manoeuvred their trow between the masonry platforms. Skilled men erected the wooden frame on which the ribs were raised. Doubtless every man on the payroll strained on ropes to lift the ribs into position, while one individual perched precariously on the end of the first half-rib, fitting the second into the crown piece. Others, less glamorously, created a measure of order from the chaos of obstructions on the Bridge Road, and hacked through the rocks on the side of the Gorge to link the bridge with the Madeley turnpike. The Iron Bridge was the brainchild of Thomas Farnolls Pritchard. The scheme to build it was launched through the encouragement of John Wilkinson and the legal and political skills of Thomas Addenbrooke. The bridge became a reality as a result of Abraham Darby's personal commitment to the project. It was also, as the writer of the Edmunds text remarked, 'an indisputable proof of the abilities of our mechanics and workmen'.[60]

IV

The Completed Bridge

Old and New Roads

The opening of the Iron Bridge changed patterns of communication and settlement in the Severn Gorge. The bridge became the meeting point of roads, and a centre for commerce and business. A town, taking its name from the bridge, developed at its northern end. The bridge has been closed to vehicles for nearly seven decades, but remains in 2002 the focus of transport systems in the area. The roads approaching the Iron Bridge were either made into public thoroughfares by the proprietors or were specially built during or after the period of construction to cater for people using the bridge.

The site of the bridge, as shown above, was determined by the topography of the Gorge.[1] It was built in the first instance to serve local needs. The preamble of the Act of Parliament and the petition that preceded it fail to mention any benefits likely to accrue to long-distance travellers from the proposed structure. By contrast the contemporary Preens Eddy Bridge, two miles downstream, was expected to benefit people journeying between Wales and the Midlands.[2] Road access to the Gorge was so difficult that some castings from the Coalbrookdale ironworks consigned to Stafford were sent by river to Bridgnorth before being transferred to waggons or carts.[3]

The bridge proprietors improved Edward Harries's private road up the valley of the Benthall Brook to make a connection with the Wenlock turnpike network, providing access to the centre of Broseley, a route through Broseley to Bridgnorth and one through Posenhall to Much Wenlock. A gate was installed at the junction with the turnpike. Pool dams, the stunted remains of kilns, piles of iron slag and brick- and tile-wasters can still be seen along the quiet residential backwater that is now Bridge Road, for the area has had a busy past, and for half a century after the Iron Bridge was opened there were conflicts between those who worked there and travellers passing through. The bridge

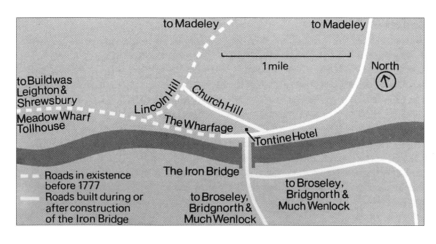

21 The roads constructed during and after the building of the Iron Bridge.

proprietors agreed with Edward Harries that the produce of the Benthall estate should pass toll-free, but they found it necessary a few months after the bridge opened to affirm that all traffic originated elsewhere should pay the full rates. Later that year the leading pottery concern, Bell & Thursfield, compounded their payments, and in 1790 the British Tar Company, which had ovens at the Benthall Ironworks, followed the same course. In October 1781 the proprietors complained to the owners of the ironworks that slag and ashes were blocking the road, and two months later they demanded that a fence be built around the boring mill pool. The fence was replaced with a wall in 1819-20. In 1783 the trustees widened the road by demolishing pottery buildings, and in 1791 removed some slip-pans to a greater distance from the carriageway.[4] Proposals to by-pass Bridge Road by a new route running parallel to the Severn past Ladywood, before climbing the side of the Gorge to join the Wenlock turnpike road near to the *Forester Arms* at Broseley, were made in 1826-7, and the bridge proprietors contributed £600 towards the cost. The new road was first used by a stage-coach on 18 November 1828, and the bridge proprietors formally took over responsibility for it in 1832.[5]

On the north bank the bridge was approached by a quay lined by warehouses, controlled by the Coalbrookdale Company, and even then called The Wharfage, that had been laid out during the first half of the 18th century. At the foot of Lincoln Hill it joined the Madeley turnpike road to Buildwas Bridge. In July 1782 the Coalbrookdale partners formally consented to allow the bridge trustees to use the road along The Wharfage at a nominal rent of a guinea a year.[6] The eastern end of The Wharfage was linked to the bridge by a short, steep stretch of road built by the proprietors, and now called Tontine Hill.

During 1780 the bridge trustees built the road now called Church Hill, which leaves the open space north of the bridge by a dog-leg corner and climbs the side of the Gorge to join the old turnpike road at the top of Lincoln Hill. This was never a satisfactory route and, after a quarter of a century of procrastination, in 1806 an Act of Parliament was obtained for building the road now called Madeley Bank that ascends from the Square by the bridge to a junction with the old turnpike near the Lane Pits in Madeley, and also formally incorporated The Wharfage and Tontine Hill into Madeley turnpike network.[7] The new road was completed by 1810, and remains one of the outstanding feats of civil engineering in the Gorge. The Iron Bridge trustees donated £15 towards its costs in 1809.[8]

A turnpike road through the village of Leighton from Tern Bridge on the main road from Shrewsbury to London established access to the bridge from the county town. The road was under consideration as early as September 1775, but it was not until 21 October 1777 that a meeting of those interested was held at the house of a Mrs Francis in Buildwas (probably the *Buildwas Bridge Inn*). An Act of Parliament was obtained the following year, and Abraham Darby III's accounts show that in February 1778 he paid £50 to Thomas Addenbrooke for the solicitor's expenses in London while obtaining the Act. The trustees, who included most of the subscribers to the Iron Bridge project, first met on 8 June 1778.[9] The new road joined the Wenlock turnpike at Buildwas Bridge, from which the trustees took over the short stretch of road to the end-on junction with the Madeley turnpike road at the Birches Brook, the boundary between the parishes of Madeley and Buildwas. The road was opened in September 1779, many of its first travellers being sightseers going to view what the *Shrewsbury Chronicle* called 'that most singular curiosity, the Iron Bridge of one arch over the River Severn'.[10] Parts of the road were widened in the early 1960s to allow the passage of equipment for the Ironbridge 'B' power station, but otherwise it retains much of its original appearance. Distances were marked by cast-iron plates affixed to stones, giving distances to Shrewsbury and to the Iron Bridge. The style of lettering suggests that they date from the turnpiking of the road. The Iron Bridge proprietors granted £64 to the road trustees for improvements for improvements in Buildwas in 1783.[11]

The Madeley road trustees, of whom Abraham Darby III was one of the most active, responded to the Iron Bridge by building a new bridge over the Birches Brook in 1778, a bridge over the stream at Dale End in 1781-2, and a toll house at the Meadow Wharf in 1785. The Meadow Gate was let for £65 in 1786, for £96 in 1788 and for £138 in 1791, which suggests a steady rise in traffic-flow.[12] The pattern of roads on the north side of the river that persisted until the late 20th century was completed in 1818 when a new road over Jigger's Bank, Coalbrookdale, provided a direct link from the Iron Bridge to Wellington.[13]

The Bridge as a Spectacle

Within a few years of its completion the Iron Bridge had become a symbol of changing attitudes towards technological advance. Members of polite society were accustomed by the 1770s to view new enterprises just as they visited spas or stately homes. James Boswell went to the Soho Manufactory and to the Derby Silk Mills; while the daughters of the ironmasters of Coalbrookdale took trips on Earl Gower's canal, the first in Shropshire, and visited the porcelain factory at Caughley. The Iron Bridge seemed in the 1780s an outlandish and incredible feat, to an extent that is now difficult to appreciate. Much of the interest in the bridge was nevertheless the result of conscious promotion, first by the trustees, and then by the hotel keepers and coach-operators who stood to benefit from the interest of tourists.

The Severn Gorge was already a subject of interest to artists and to the writers of guidebooks. Samuel Simpson described the Gorge in *The Agreeable Historian* as early as 1746. Thomas Robins (1715-70) sketched views of the Severn in the area in the 1750s. In 1758 George Perry (1719-71), who had arrived in Coalbrookdale in 1736 as tutor to the children of the ironmaster Richard Ford (1689-1745), became the Coalbrookdale Company's accountant in 1749, and subsequently manager of their concerns in Liverpool, published a pair of engravings of Coalbrookdale by Thomas Vivares (1709-80), which clearly proved popular. While the Iron Bridge was being planned, the Shrewsbury artist William Williams painted two views of Coalbrookdale that were engraved and published in the autumn of 1777, and exhibited at the Royal Academy in 1778. Abraham Darby III bought five sets of the engravings.[14]

William Williams was perhaps the first artist to depict the Iron Bridge for it was to him in October 1780 that Abraham Darby III paid ten guineas for a

'drawing' of the bridge measuring 3 ft. 4 in. by 2 ft. 10 in. (1.02 × 0.87m). This painting is now owned and displayed by the Ironbridge Gorge Museum. Williams chose a downstream viewpoint showing the limestone cliffs of Benthall Edge to the left byond the bridge, which frames the chimneys of the lead smelter in the Bower Yard. The ferry boat was still plying and is shown on the south bank. A barge is moored on the north bank below the bridge, while a forest of masts is visible upstream, and a coracle bobs beneath the ribs. A carriage is shown traversing the Wharfage, while another is depicted on the Bridge itself, perhaps artist's licence, since it was not formally open when Williams made his drawing. The most striking feature of William's view of the bridge is the attitude of spectators. While the people in his Coalbrookdale paintings are turning away from the ironworks, the Iron Bridge is the centre of all attention. A punt-like vessel is shown beneath the ribs, propelled by an apparently hired boatman, from which a gentleman enthusiastically explains the structure to two seated ladies.[15]

22 The Cast Iron Bridge near Coalbrookdale (William Williams, c.1740-98).

The first print of the bridge to be published was probably a woodcut by John Edmunds, bookseller and printer of Madeley, in which the arch fills the whole width of the picture, and a barge and the hills of Broseley are visible through the centre. Its lengthy caption is an important early source on the history of the bridge. The woodcut was probably based on an anonymous watercolour, which shows the bridge from an identical viewpoint, but portrays the sailing barge and the distant hills rather differently.[16]

23 View of the Cast Iron Bridge near Coalbrookdale (Michael Angelo Rooker, 1780-82).

The best-known early view of the bridge is that by Michael Angelo Rooker (1743-1801), scenery painter at the Haymarket Theatre. On 10 June 1780 Thomas Addenbrooke announced in the *Shrewsbury Chronicle* that a 'view of the cast iron bridge engraved by a capital artist' was about to be published, and it was doubtless for this advertisement that Abraham Darby III paid 18s. on 20 June to his clerk, Mark Gilpin, 'for advertising the views'. The advertisement almost certainly refers to the work of Rooker. In January 1781 Abraham Darby III paid £29 to the painter as fee and expenses for travelling from London to draw a view of the bridge. By May 1781 Rooker's drawing, engraved by William Ellis, was on sale from Mark Gilpin (d.1805) at Coalbrookdale, or from booksellers in London and Shrewsbury. The Coalbrookdale Company published a second edition, dedicated to King George III, in 1782. Rooker's drawing must have been made before the bridge was opened, and the first edition of the engraving shows no travellers on the bridge, but several vehicles and pedestrians appear on the second version. The Rooker prints proved popular. Many copies survive, and one was purchased by Thomas Jefferson. Engravings of views of the bridge by E. Edgcombe and Thomas Burney (1765-85) were also published in the early 1780s, and in 1788 the bridge featured on three of the celebrated set of six engravings of paintings of the Severn Gorge by George Robertson (1724-88).[17]

The celebrity of the bridge was enhanced by the display of a model in London. Thomas Gregory built the model, of mahogany, during the winter of 1784-5, paying two guineas to a Birmingham metal worker for the tiny spikes used for the parapet railings. Abraham Darby bought three packing boxes in the summer of 1785 and hired a room for a period that extended into 1786, probably at the premises of J. Barclay, an ironmonger, at 183 Fleet Street.[18] In October 1787 Darby presented the model, by this time evidently damaged, to the Society of Arts. The Society proposed to honour him as builder of the Iron Bridge. One member suggested that the matter be deferred while Darby was asked to comment on the supposed 'failure' of the bridge, but on 28 November 1787 the Society voted by ballot to award Darby its gold medal. A design for a case for the model was submitted in February 1788. The model was subsequently presented, with other items held by the Society, to the Science Museum in South Kensington.[19]

By the 1790s the Severn Gorge was attracting many artists, amongst them J.M.W. Turner (1775-1851), Philip James de Loutherbourg (1740-1812) and John Sell Cotman (1782-1842), none of whom, apparently, painted or sketched the bridge itself. It was depicted in five pencil drawings by Paul Sandby Munn (1773-1845) in July 1802, in sketches made by Sir Richard Colt Hoare (1758-1838) in May 1801 and it appears in the distance in a sketch of the Gorge made by Joseph Farington (1747-1821) in September 1789. Other artists who published engravings of the bridge between 1800 and 1835 include Samuel Ireland (d.1800), W. Scarrott, Mathew Dubourg, Arthur Holdsworth (1780-1860), W. Smith, William Westwood and Cornelius Varley (1781-1873).[20]

Two of the artists whose views of the bridge were engraved and published stand out from the rest. Rooker's drawing, whose publication was sponsored by those responsible for building the bridge, epitomises the way in which attitudes to industry were changing. He drew the bridge from the same downstream viewpoint that had been chosen by William Williams. Rooker shows two gentlemen earnestly examining the ribs of the bridge, while a man in a broad-rimmed hat, a long-skirted lady and a dog view it from a distance. In the 1782 edition a poacher with dog stalks along the north bank, a barge rests at anchor on the south side, a housewife gathers river water in a pitcher, smoke pours from the flues of the Bower Yard lead smelter, and a coracle floats lightly in the centre of the river. Above the bridge is a lofty crag of terrifying aspect, but it is altogether subsidiary to the man-made structure leaping across the river. Rooker shows the bridge as the centrepiece of his picture; he does not ignore the busy-ness of the riverside, nor the ruggedness of the Gorge, but it is the bridge, the achievement of industrial man, that dominates both the landscape and the human figures within it.

In Robertson's views the bridge is less substantial, in some respects dwarfed by the overpowering mountains around it. In the view from the Madeley side of the

24 The Iron Bridge (George Robertson, 1788).

river engraved by James Fittler (1758-1835) the bridge is central, but is dominated by the lofty wooded height of Benthall Edge beyond. A man in charge of a panniered packhorse regales two travellers on horseback. In the view from the bottom of Lincoln Hill engraved by Francis Chesham (1749-1806) a horseman has stopped beneath the bridge to examine it, a rowing-boat wavers unsteadily in the river, while a barge is shown, crewed, apparently by midgets. The third Robertson view, of 'Lincoln Hill with the Iron Bridge in the distance', shows Ludcroft wharf, a flat landscape with packhorses, while the crag of Lincoln Hill rises in the background, and the Iron Bridge is distant, but curiously dominant, and without doubt the *raison d'être* of the piece.

It was through the eyes of Rooker and Robertson that people in the late 18th century and subsequently have seen the Iron Bridge and its surroundings. Their pictures are curiously ambiguous: the bridge – the achievement of Man – is dominant, yet it is set in a severe, even a terrifying landscape; it is a challenge to natural forces which are formidable opponents. The human figures are for the most part puny, yet the bridge is the creation of humans. The two painters suggest that the bridge is worthy of examination and study, that industrial activity is no longer something to be viewed as a curiosity and subsequently disregarded. In his other pictures, Robertson showed an awareness of the horrors of industry, especially in his views of the Calcutts ironworks and the interior of a casting house, but in the Iron Bridge he saw its achievements.

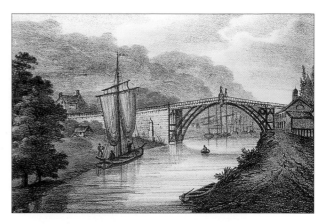

25 *(top)* Iron Bridge, near Coalbrookdale (Samuel Ireland).

26 *(above)* A View of the Cast Iron Bridge (E. Edgcombe).

In the years following the opening of the Iron Bridge the Severn Gorge attracted numerous seekers after the spectacular. For travellers from southern England it was a convenient calling point for those attracted by the mountains of North Wales. By 1800 there was a well-defined itinerary, at least for the educated visitor who could expect to be hospitably received by the ironmasters. He would go to the Coalbrookdale ironworks and try to see a blast furnace being tapped; he would climb Lincoln Hill and view the complex mixture of limestone mines and quarries and the banks of smoking kilns which so impressed J.M.W. Turner; he would explore the dark mysteries of the Coalport Tar Tunnel, and admire if not ride upon the Hay inclined plane on the Shropshire Canal; he would watch painters at the Coalport porcelain works and buy specimens of their work, and would endure the excruciating aural pain inflicted by the cannon-boring machines at Alexander Brodie's (d.1811) Calcutts ironworks. He might also try to understand the complex chemistry of Lord Dundonald's coke-ovens and tar-refineries or the intricate gearing of the Benthall corn mill with its 60 ft. (18.5m) waterwheel, which stood close to the bridge itself. Not every traveller visited all these places, but none missed the Iron Bridge.[21] The other sights were interesting, even spectacular, but it was the Iron Bridge that drew visitors to the Gorge. An anonymous writer noted in 1801 that 'the neighbourhood abounds with natural and artificial curiosities, which perhaps for variety are scarcely to be equall'd', but his real reason for visiting the area was because it was 'the place where the first Iron Bridge was cast and erected, which remains a Monument of the skill and ingenuity of its mechanics'.[22]

The Iron Bridge was depicted in popular as well as 'polite' art. Its image appeared on products of the local Caughley and Coalport porcelain factories, many of them items like tankards and single plates that were certainly not designed just for the homes of the wealthy. It adorned the bill-headings of the traders whose premises clustered at its northern end. It was depicted on the trade tokens struck in 1792 for the Coalbrookdale Company, on currency notes issued by local banks;

it appeared on the seal of the Shropshire Canal Company; and on cottage grates cast at the Coalbrookdale ironworks. The semi-circular arch became the symbol of the district.

The Bridge in its Context

The completion of the Iron Bridge stimulated the development of shops, inns and other commercial premises at its northern end that became the most consciously urban landscape in the Coalbrookdale Coalfield. Central to the development was the *Tontine Hotel*. The partners in the project included many of the Iron Bridge

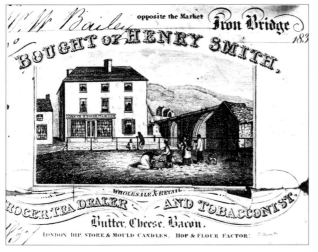

27 *(left)* The bill-heading of Henry Smith, the grocer who occupied the premises now used as the 'Shop in the Square' by the Ironbridge Gorge Museum.

28 *(right)* The bill-heading of Edward Edwards, draper, mercer and haberdasher.

29 The Iron Bridge depicted on one of the Coalbrookdale Company's trading tokens, issued in 1792.

proprietors – Abraham Darby, Samuel Darby, Edward Harries, John Wilkinson, Edward Blakeway, Sergeant Roden and Thomas Addenbrooke. Abraham Darby directed at least some stages of construction. Some travellers were told that the hotel was actually built by the bridge company: certainly it was built on the plot of land acquired from the barge owner Richard Beard for the northern abutment of the bridge, and meetings of the two groups of proprietors took place on the same days. The first phase, probably the three westernmost bays of the present building, was designed by the Shrewsbury architect, John Hiram Haycock (1759-1830), whose works included Shropshire's first Shirehall, Allatt's School in Murivance, Shrewsbury, and the workhouse at Cross Houses. It was completed by April 1784 when Haycock was discussing with the proprietors the construction of the stables, on the opposite side of the road alongside the river, and immediately downstream from the bridge. The stable block was topped by a cupola, similar to that which Haycock and his brother William added to Millington's Hospital, Shrewsbury in 1785. The two easterly bays of the hotel, with Venetian and oriel windows facing The Square, lighting the main public room on the first floor, were built to the design of the

30 *(left)* The Iron Bridge depicted on a Coalport jug dating from 1828.

31 The Iron Bridge cast on a Coalbrookdale Company fire grate.

Kidderminster architect, Samuel Wright, in 1786-7.[23]

The hotel appears to have been opened in 1784, for the bridge proprietors first met there on 16 July of that year when it was called the 'new inn'. By 3 September the bridge trustees were calling it the *Tontine*, although it was not until 22 October that the hotel proprietors formally resolved to call it by that name.[24] The surviving records of the partnership do not suggest that it was a real tontine, in the sense of a scheme under which the proprietors enjoy increasing annuities as death reduces their number, till the last survivor receives the whole income. The first of the minute books relating to the project is lost, however, and the building passed into other hands while most of the shareholders were still living. The proprietors did not make a commercial success of the *Tontine*. They let it to a tenant in 1786 and agreed in 1791 that it should be sold.[25]

32 The *Tontine Hotel*.

The *Tontine* was designed in the best provincial taste of the time, and set the pattern for the development of the market-place at the north end of the bridge. Some at least of this land was part of that purchased for the construction of the bridge. In 1784 the proprietors of the *Tontine* gave instructions for the levelling of the ground and the following year they appear to have taken responsibility for the

33 The Iron Bridge *c.*1900 showing the shop buildings on the upstream side.

stonework and steps that supported the raised area where open markets took place.[26] It is no longer evident precisely who was responsible for the other principal buildings around The Square, the three-storey, five-bay block on the northern side, with its arcaded shops on the ground floor, the market hall on the northern side which originally had an open undercroft, and the magnificent retail premises on the south side that now house the shop of the Ironbridge Gorge Museum Trust. Six properties, one a grocer's shop, had been laid out near the Iron Bridge before 1793 by Michael Hodgkiss, a collier, as a means of providing for his children. The long-term success of the urban development was nevertheless limited, and the shops on the fringes of Ironbridge, along the Wharfage and Waterloo Street, are

domestic in scale, and have the appearance of cottages even if they were intended when built to be premises for retailing.[27]

Nevertheless, in the decades after the building of the bridge urban development was pursued with vigour. The ancient market in Madeley, dating from the reign of Henry III, had lapsed before 1700, but was revived in 1763, and subsequently transferred to The Square by the Iron Bridge. In 1799 a cattle market was proposed for the area, and trading in grain and pigs began in June 1805.[28] This venture did not flourish, but retailers and professional men appear to have prospered in Ironbridge, taking custom both from Broseley and Madeley. In the 1830s Charles Hulbert, the Shrewsbury topographer, described it thus:

> ... the merchantile part of the town of Madeley ... here is the focus of professional and commercial pursuits. The Weekly Market, the Post Office, the Printing Office,

34 A panorama of the town that grew up at the northern end of the Iron Bridge.

principal inns, Drapery, Grocery and Ironmongery, Watch Making, Cabinet Making, Timber and Boat Building establishments; the Subscription Library, Subscription Dispensary, Branch Bank, Subscription Baths, Gentlemen of the Legal and Medical Professions, Ladies' Boarding School &c &c.[29]

Coach Services

The Iron Bridge soon attracted travellers from Shrewsbury, Lancashire, North Wales and Ireland heading towards London, Bristol and Bath. For those passing through Bridgnorth the route from the county town through Atcham, Tern Bridge, Leighton, the Iron Bridge and Broseley was scarcely longer than the direct turnpike road through Much Wenlock, although it involved the payment of six tolls rather than one. In 1786 an advertisement for the *Tontine Hotel* claimed that it had been built for those choosing to take the new road through Leighton and over the Iron Bridge to Bridgnorth, which, it was claimed, provided 'as many agreeable prospects as any road of the same extent in the kingdom'. The hotel's landlord gave an assurance in 1802 to 'families that wish to stop and see the Manufactories in Coal-brookdale' that 'they may depend upon having good rooms with well-aired beds and every accommodation that can be produced from a well-stored cellar and larder'.[30] In 1807-08 there were disputes between the landlords of the *Tontine* and the *White Hart* at Much Wenlock over the comparative distances between Shrewsbury and Bridgnorth by the two routes, and it was alleged that some post (i.e. private hire) coaches disobeyed their clients' instructions, and took them to Wenlock instead of to the Iron Bridge.[31] The *Tontine* also faced competition as a calling point for stage-coaches from the *White Hart* on the Wharfage at Ironbridge.

The first stage-coach service to cross the Iron Bridge was the *Diligence*, a Shrewsbury to London service, running three days a week, and travelling onwards through Bridgnorth, Stourbridge, Bromsgrove, Stratford and Oxford. It first ran on 4 October 1781, and left the *Unicorn* in Shrewsbury at 5 a.m., taking over 24 hours for the journey to London, for which a single fare of £1 15s. 0d. was charged. The proprietors of the bridge agreed with the coach operators to compound for the toll due for the use of the bridge, but the latter were not diligent in meeting their obligations, and by March 1783 had accumulated a considerable debt.[32]

In 1785 the *Balloon* coach from the *Raven & Bell* in Shrewsbury began to travel to London by way of the Iron Bridge, Bridgnorth, Wolverhampton, Birmingham and Oxford, but by November 1786 it was taking a more direct route through

Shifnal.[33] In September 1786 a coach from the *Raven & Bell* became the first regular service to Bath to cross the Iron Bridge. Two years later it was travelling to Bridgnorth via Much Wenlock, but a competing service from the *Lion* was using the Iron Bridge.[34] In 1798 the *Marquis Cornwallis*, a new and expensive service from the *Elephant and Castle* in Shrewsbury to London began to travel to Shifnal by way of Ironbridge, but not crossing the bridge. Its proprietors advertised that their passengers would be able to see 'that striking specimen of art and so much admired object of travellers'.[35] From 1815 two coaches from the *Talbot* in Shrewsbury passed through Ironbridge, a daily service, the *Duke of Wellington*, and the *Union*, which ran three days a week and appears to have been re-named the *Royal Telegraph* in 1817.[36] A service from the *Talbot* to Cheltenham and Bath was also crossing the Iron Bridge by the summer of 1817.[37] Coach services continued to pass and cross the Iron Bridge during the first four decades of the 19th century, the most celebrated being *L'Hirondelle*, which ran from Liverpool to Bath, accomplishing the whole journey in less than ten hours in May 1833, although by 1841 it was operating only between Shrewsbury and Cheltenham.[38] Details of itineraries changed from time to time. In 1828 the services comprised the *Old Worcester* from Shrewsbury to Cheltenham which called at the *Tontine* three days a week, the *Emerald*, from Shrewsbury to Birmingham which called at the *White Hart*, and the *Prince* running to and from Shifnal, connecting with London services.[39] Stage coach services declined with the opening of main line railways, and by the mid-1840s travellers between Merseyside and the West of England could use the Grand Junction and Birmingham & Gloucester railways, avoiding Shropshire altogether. The bridge nevertheless remained a focus for local transport facilities and in 1851 two omnibus services ran daily from the *Tontine* to Wellington and two to Shrewsbury.[40]

Subsequently a standard gauge railway became part of the landscape of Ironbridge. Several schemes were proposed during the 1840s, but that which materialised was the Severn Valley Railway from Worcester to Shrewsbury, planned in 1845-6, authorised in 1853, and opened in 1862. The following year it became part of the Great Western Railway. Ironbridge & Broseley station was situated at the south end of the Iron Bridge, whose approach road was crossed by the railway tracks on a level crossing. The opening of the railway proved beneficial to the bridge proprietors since every cart and wagon conveying goods between works and shops on the north bank of the river and the freight depot, and every passenger from Ironbridge bound to or from the station, had to pay tolls. The bridge thus remained prosperous, although its tolls were often criticised.[41]

The Nineteenth- and early Twentieth-Century Resort

By the mid-19th century the Iron Bridge had ceased to be one of the marvels of the age; tourists in search of spectacular engineering monuments could go to the Menai Straits to view Thomas Telford's suspension bridge of 1826 and Robert Stephenson's tubular Britannia Bridge, completed in 1850, or to Newcastle to see the latter's High Level Bridge, opened the previous year. The Severn Gorge, while

35 The *Tontine Hotel* during the time when Thomas Wilson was landlord.

still tolerably prosperous, was becoming less attractive, partly as a result of the expanding brick and tile industry that was lining the riverbanks with cliffs of tile waster scree. The author of a guide book published in the year of the Great Exhibition simply noted that from the Great Western's station at Wellington a visitor could take an omnibus to Coalbrookdale, 'where the first iron bridge was built over the Severn'.[42] When the Yorkshire-born tile manufacturer H.P. Dunnill (1821-95) first visited Jackfield, where he was subsequently to manage a large and successful company, he found that the area was not the world 'but a very poor bit of the fag end of it … made up of old pit shafts, pit mounds, rubbish heaps, brick ends, broken drain and roof and paving tiles, dilapidated houses, sloughy lanes and miry roads'.[43] In October 1878 the Prime Minister, Benjamin Disraeli (1804-81), recently ennobled as the Earl of Beaconsfield, visited Ironbridge. A newspaper commented that he had 'shed the illuminating rays of his presence upon dingy Ironbridge'.[44] The author of the most authoritative guidebook of the time wrote in 1870 that the sides of the river in the Severn Gorge were 'terribly spoilt by the forges and foundries, the banks of slag and refuse that run down to the water's edge'.[45]

A few years later Ironbridge was being promoted as a resort. Thomas B. Wilson, landlord of the *Crown*, Hodge Bower, whose beer garden still offers a spectacular view of the Severn and of the Iron Bridge, began to develop the land attached to his pub as the Hodge Bower Pleasure Gardens. He was certainly entertaining parties of visitors during the summer of 1874, and in subsequent years acted as host to many church, Sunday School and works outings from the Black Country, who arrived either in horse-drawn brakes or by train.[46] In July 1876 he told a group from St Peter's Church, Wolverhampton, of 'his determination to utilise every opportunity, believing that by judicious care and spirited enterprise the neighbourhood of Hodge Bower might become the "Brighton" of the Midland counties'. As well as providing food, music and sports facilities, Wilson arranged itineraries for his guests, encompassing various places between Buildwas Abbey and Coalport, but all including 'the famous old iron bridge'. Most of Wilson's visitors came from the Wolverhampton area, but in July 1877 he entertained the choir of Rushbury church from the depths of rural Shropshire. Perhaps as a result of Wilson's enterprise the Iron Bridge became an attraction for people from the Black Country on bank holidays, first observed in 1871.[47] Subsequently Wilson moved from the *Crown* to the *Tontine*, from which he continued to promote the attractions of the Severn Gorge. Nevertheless, the centenary of the erection of the ironwork of the bridge in 1879 was celebrated only by the placing of a few flags on the parapet railings.[48]

A topographical writer passing through Ironbridge in 1913 called for the 'removal' of 'the dirty, mean and ugly town', and recorded that he saw no beauty in the Iron Bridge but that 'a bridge of the local stone, such as the monks would have built, would be in agreeable harmony with the scene, and growing grey with age, would not force its unwilling attention on the traveller'. He acknowledged that the structure was the first of its kind, and that it was a wonder in its day, but concluded, 'How distant seems that day! Now people have ceased to wonder at it or at anything else'.[49]

Not everyone had ceased to wonder at the Iron Bridge. The railway historian T. R. Perkins was impressed by 'the old veteran', and amused that he had to pay a toll when crossing it in 1927, as he hurried to see the plateway that remained at Dale End.[50] In 1925 a local newspaper remarked that the riverbanks were untidy and that the Square was littered with loose stones, but concluded, 'It only needs enterprize to turn Ironbridge into a holiday resort'.[51] It is remarkable that after a century of almost continuous neglect of the landscape of the Severn Gorge, when Thomas Cook & Co. published the first post-World War II edition of their *Holiday Guide* in 1946, Coalbrookdale appeared within a list of 57 inland resorts in England, alongside Stratford-upon-Avon, Buxton, Chester and Ambleside.[52]

V

Decay and Reconstruction

The sides of the Severn Gorge are unstable, the river having forced its way through the coal measures long after those measures had been laid down. Throughout the Gorge evidence can be seen of landslips and subsidence. In 1773, the year in which the Iron Bridge project was first discussed, part of the hillside on the north bank of the river at The Birches in Buildwas parish slipped downwards, altering the course of the Severn, and destroying part of the turnpike-road. The landslip was made famous by the sermon preached on the site by the Rev. John Fletcher (1729-85) of Madeley.[1] It is unsurprising that the history of the Iron Bridge since 1781 as recorded in the trustees' minutes is a narrative of repairs and maintenance.

The effects of geological instability upon the bridge were first evident in July 1783 when the trustees decided to erect a 35-yard wall on the north bank on the downstream side, to prevent ground from slipping into the river, and to make good the towing-path destroyed when the bridge was built: similar measures were taken in precisely the same spot during the restoration of 1972-3. In December 1784 some 'cracks in the arch' on the Benthall side were observed – probably in the stone land arch. Orders were given for them to be measured and examined.[2] In 1787-8 the rails were varnished with a clear preparation from Lord Dundonald's (1749-1831) British Tar Company. The varnish was probably supplied from the tar company's works at Benthall, only a short distance from the bridge.[3] More substantial repairs were undertaken in 1791-2, when the trustees instructed Sergeant Roden that the 'ironwork at the bridge be improved by finishing out the back Iron Ribs to support the Crosspieces and Strengthen the Bridge'. In December 1792 the abutment on the Benthall side was causing concern, and orders were given for it to be repaired.[4] The Iron Bridge stood up well to the pressures it sustained during the great flood on the Severn of February 1795 that damaged every other bridge on the river.[5]

The stone abutment on the south bank nevertheless continued to trouble the trustees. Simon Goodrich observed in 1799 that it had been carried up too perpendicularly, without sufficient width at the base or strengthening buttresses, that it had been damaged by floods, and that it had been clamped together with iron tie-rods.[6] The trustees commissioned further repairs in 1800, and ordered 2,000 ft. (616m) of three-inch planks. Several engineers were associated with the ensuing programme of repairs that extended over several years. In the spring of 1801 Thomas Thomas reported that the ironwork on both sides of the river had moved, and that parts of it, probably some of the radials, were broken because of the pressure of the abutments. Thomas Thomas was probably the same engineer who in 1805 designed the Swinney corn-mill at Coalport, with its 70 ft.

(21.5m) waterwheel. Temporary wooden scaffolds were erected to replace the abutment on the Benthall side, and the soil was excavated from beneath it and dumped in the river.[7]

Sir Richard Colt Hoare (1758-1838), who was visiting the area on 13 May 1801, gained the impression that the foundations had given way. The same month a scheme for stabilising the bridge was put forward by Henry Williams, once steam-engine erector for Boulton & Watt, the designer of the inclined planes on the Shropshire Canal, and a future partner in the Ketley Ironworks. A timber platform was to be put down between the two abutments, beneath which the river bed was to be consolidated. It was found that piles could not be driven into the river bed with the equipment then available, and the proposal was dropped, but Williams's proposal to create a solid barrier to keep the two abutments rigidly apart was finally achieved in reinforced concrete, and with the help of 20th-century pile-driving equipment, in 1973-4.[8]

36 The Iron Bridge (Paul Sandby Munn), inscribed 'Coalbrook, July 11th 1802', showing work in progress on the repair of the bridge.

When Williams's scheme was abandoned more timber was purchased, including planks to cover the space between the ironwork and the 'back wall of the dry arch', presumably the land arch on the Benthall side. In September 1801 one John Parry recommended that both ends of the bridge should be lightened, the walls taken down on the Benthall side, and a timber platform built to carry the road on the Madeley side. In November 1801 a committee was appointed to supervise the repairs, but there is no detailed record since no minutes were taken of trustees' meetings during 1802. Paul Sandby Munn sketched the bridge on 11 July 1802, showing that the side walls of the south abutment had been demolished, but that the arch by which the towpath passed through it was still standing. A timber roadway along the line of the abutment was supported by three trustles, and timber struts propped up the face of the abutment.[9]

The work was incomplete in February 1803 when the trustees affirmed that it was to be finished. Later in the year John Simpson (1755-1815) replaced Parry as engineer in charge of the work. Simpson was a mason who frequently worked with Thomas Telford, and was principally responsible for the erection of the piers of the Pontcysyllte aqueduct. His memorial, in St Chad's church, Shrewsbury, records that he was born at Stenhouse, Midlothian, and that 'lasting monuments of his skill and ability will be found in the building of this church, which he super-intended, the bridges of Bewdley, Dunkeld, Craigellachie and Bonar, the aqueducts of Pontcysyllte and Chirk, and the locks and basins of the Caledonian Canal'.[10]

37 Iron Bridge, Coalbrook Dale (Arthur Holdsworth), showing the wooden land arches on the south side, installed in 1801-4, and replaced by iron land arches in 1821-3.

In August 1803 orders were given for two piers to be built as quickly as possible, and for the temporary bridge across the space created by the demolition of the south abutment to be secured. Instructions were issued for the fabrication of a timber platform, to be erected as soon as the piers were ready. This 'platform' was a wooden roadway carried on two timber land arches on the Benthall side of the river. At the same time pits were sunk, presumably to aid the drainage of the area. While the Iron Bridge was erected without any accidents to the workmen, it appears that a fatality did occur during this programme of repairs, for in January 1804 the trustees paid the funeral expenses of one Richard Wheale. The timber for the roadway and the wooden arches consisted of 120 ft. (37m) of oak scantlings, 55 planks, 117 rafters, 54 sleepers, and 336 ft. (103m) of elm boards. The work was apparently completed by July 1804 when spare timber was sold off, and the new structure was coated with coal tar.[11]

In June 1807 the trustees paid a gratuity of £25 to John Simpson and Thomas Telford. This may have been for some subsequent minor repairs, or it could have been an acknowledgement that the work done in 1803-4 had been successful. Telford was probably consulted during the re-building of the south abutment, his only known direct connection with the Iron Bridge.[12]

The condition of the bridge continued to cause concern, and in the first tract on the subject of iron bridges, published in 1812, Charles Hutton (1737-1823) was pessimistic about its future, venturing his opinion that the bridge was celebrated simply because it was the first of its kind, that its construction was 'very bad', and that while the cast iron was well-preserved, there were several cracks in the stonework. He forecast that it would probably not last for very long, but affirmed that there were no deficiencies in the ironwork.[13]

The timber arches of 1803-4 were evidently unsatisfactory, for in December 1818 the trustees asked the Coalbrookdale Company to give estimates for iron plates and railings on the Benthall side of the bridge. This they did, but it was not until December 1820 that they were authorised to proceed with the work. The project was observed in August 1821 by the engineer Joshua Field (c.1787-1863), who noted that the wooden side-arches had decayed, and that the road had been contracted to half its normal width while the new iron land arches were installed. The work was apparently completed in the summer of 1823 when the trustees gave instructions for the new ironwork to be painted.[14]

It is probable that a tollhouse was built before the bridge was opened to traffic. None appears on the earliest illustrations, but a building that appears to be a tollhouse can be seen on one of the Robertson engravings published in 1788. The tollhouse was enlarged in 1835. Four years later, when a gas supply became available in Ironbridge, two gas-lamps were erected on the bridge, and in 1843 the proprietors of the gas-works were allowed to lay a main taking gas over the bridge to Broseley.[15] Further repairs became necessary at intervals during the 19th century. In 1845, £95 17s. 6d. was paid to the Coalbrookdale Company for repairing the land arches, which again required attention in the early 1860s and in 1879.[16]

The peace of the evening of Sunday 24 August 1902 was broken by the thunderous sound of about 30 ft. of the parapet of the bridge crashing into the river, which brought many local residents to the riverside fearing that the whole structure had collapsed. It appears that the laying of a water main across the bridge caused one of the deck plates to snap. A further section of a deck plate weighing about 5 cwt. fell from the bridge in July 1903. Part of the ironwork that fell off was recovered during repair work in the 1990s and is now displayed in the Museum of Iron at Coalbrookdale. The bridge proprietors ordered new castings for the parapet from the Coalbrookdale Ironworks, which brought to the attention of the management the patterns for the Iron Bridge, which were kept in the pattern store. In order to create more space, the patterns were burned in the loam foundry, but that for the central roundel on the parapet, bearing the date 1779, was saved by an 18-year-old employee, W.H.Moore, and is now held by the Ironbridge Gorge Museum.[17]

38 The pattern for the central roundel on the parapet of the Iron Bridge that was saved by W.H. Moore when the remainder of the patterns for the bridge were burned at the Coalbrookdale Ironworks in 1902-3. Mr Moore, who left Coalbrookdale in 1909, presented the pattern to the Coalbrookdale Archives Association in 1958, and it is now held by the Ironbridge Gorge Museum.

Sir Benjamin Baker (1840-1907), celebrated for his role in the construction of the Forth Bridge, examined the Iron Bridge at the turn of the century and was perturbed by the dead weight of the accumulated road metal.[18] In 1904 the trustees supplied to the tollkeeper a list of tolls to be applied to motor vehicles crossing the bridge. During 1906 they were concerned as to whether their powers enabled them to charge tolls to horseless carriages, but eventually determined that, as the bridge remained a private concern, they were empowered to levy tolls. Further concerns arose in 1908 when the completion of a new concrete bridge over the Severn was imminent. Most of those crossing the bridge would have to use the road of 1828 on the south bank of the river that was managed by the Iron Bridge trustees, and for a time the trustees contemplated charging tolls at a gate in Ladywood.[19] The new bridge, financed by a public appeal, and aided by gifts of land on either side of the river, was duly completed in 1909. It was a reinforced concrete structure, one of many built to the design of L.G. Mouchel and Partners, and erected by the Liverpool Hennebique Ferro-concrete Contracting Co. at a cost of only £1,600.[20]

No tolls were charged to users of the new concrete structure that soon gained the name of the 'free bridge'. Nevertheless the Iron Bridge continued to be used both by vehicles and pedestrians. A report by the engineers Mott, Hay & Anderson in 1923 found that while the ironwork of the main span was in good condition, although it needed painting, there were causes for concern in the condition of the abutments and the ironwork of the land arches on the southern side, and that the thickness of the road metal produced a dangerously heavy dead load. They recommended that the bridge should be closed to vehicles and crowds of people while the road metal was removed, and that when it re-opened it should be restricted to vehicles of no more than two tons, which should be confined to the centre of the roadway by widening the pavements.[21]

No significant action was taken, although vehicles of more than four tons were prohibited from using the bridge, and problems increased as a result of the housing boom of the mid-1930s. In 1931, in the depths of the Depression, only 120,000 houses were completed in Great Britain, but the number rose quickly to 336,000 in 1934, and remained at over 350,000 in the following four years. Many of the

houses of that period, for example those between the Porthill and Copthorne islands on the Shrewsbury by-pass, built after 1933, were roofed with ceramic tiles, and Jackfield on the southern side of the Ironbridge Gorge was a principal source of such tiles. Drivers delivering tiles to builders working on timed contracts were insistent that they should be able to take their vehicles over the bridge, and the trustees decided that the only way to prevent danger was to close it to traffic, with effect from 18 June 1934. The

39 The Iron Bridge sustaining a heavy load at the time a circus was visiting the area in the 1920s.

County Council insisted that 'they were all proud of the old iron bridge', and affirmed that it would be retained in order to provide pedestrian access to the railway station, but the County Surveyor was instructed to make plans for a new bridge for vehicles in the vicinity.[22] The Iron Bridge was scheduled as an ancient monument during the same year. It remained a privately-owned pedestrian bridge, on which tolls were still charged, until the trustees passed responsibility for it to the County Council on 12 October 1950.[23] Toll income from pedestrians had been scarcely sufficient to cover costs of collection. No money had been available for conservation, and the County Council inherited a bridge that had been neither cleaned nor painted for many years. Scarcely any technical data was available about the structure, and after an examination of cracks in the ironwork it was concluded that the bridge was adequate for pedestrian traffic, and that complete restoration at some time in the future should be the ultimate objective.[24] At about the time the bridge passed to the County Council its setting was changed by the demolition of the tall buildings that previously framed the north abutment.

The Iron Bridge in 1950 appeared to have been neglected, but it had long outlasted many of the most significant iron bridges built during the half-century following its completion. Restoration work was to show that its northern abutment had not been well-constructed – it had none of the elaborate cross-walls that were a feature of the abutments of Thomas Telford's iron bridges. Nevertheless this was not a factor that threatened the bridge's stability. It would have been equally at risk from the pressures of the banks had the abutment been soundly-built. The iron arch itself had survived more than a century and a half of vehicular traffic remarkably well.

By 1965-6 negotiations about the restoration of the bridge were taking place between Salop County Council (as it then was), the Ministry of Works, then responsible for ancient monuments, and the Ministry of Transport, which had agreed to treat the bridge as if it carried a classified road, and to pay grants towards routine maintenance. Engineering opinion on effective ways of stabilising the bridge was divided, but moved gradually towards consensus, and a programme was agreed by the spring of 1972. Meanwhile in 1963 a new town, then called Dawley, had been designated in the southern part of the Coalbrookdale Coalfield, under the New Towns Act of 1946. In 1968 the new town was re-named Telford and its area extended to include the whole of the Coalfield north of the Severn. The earliest plans for the new town envisaged that the scenery of the Severn Gorge would be one of its principal attractions. Many were concerned about the future of the industrial monuments in the Gorge and, in response to public pressure, the development corporation formally constituted the Ironbridge Gorge Museum Trust in 1967.[25] Funding an expensive programme of conservation was beyond the normal resources of the County Council and the government departments concerned, and it had always been acknowledged that a public appeal would be necessary to raise the required money. The Museum Trust took the lead in the appeal, and in November 1971 secured a single donation of £50,000, conditional upon a matching contribution from national government, and a contribution of at least £20,000 from the county. What was to prove a lengthy programme of work began on 15 April 1972.[26]

The responsible authorities, together with the consulting engineers Sandford, Fawcett, Wilton & Bell, finally determined upon a strategy of inserting a heavy reinforced concrete invert slab between the two abutments of the bridge. It was to be placed in a trench excavated in the river bed, between and over the whole width of the abutments, and heavy reinforced-concrete facing walls in the form of 'brackets' were to be inserted, rising from this slab up the faces of the abutments themselves. The inverts and facing walls together would form a substantial trough-section, functioning together as a strut to prevent further sliding at the level of the foot of the abutments, while the monolithic facing walls would reduce any tendency for the abutments to tilt forward or twist above foundation level.

The construction of the slab was only one phase in a complex series of operations. First, it was necessary to stabilise the north abutment, a task carried out by the county council's direct labour force during the summer of 1972. The filling material within the abutment was to be removed, thus eliminating a considerable dead weight, so that the abutment would henceforth be a hollow masonry block. The roadway on the bridge was to be carried on a concealed concrete deck, and the brick archway through the abutment was to be encased in

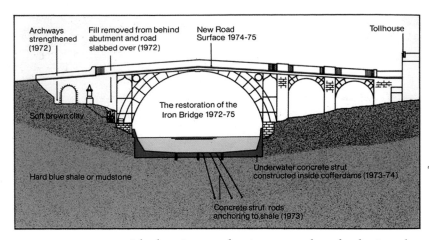

40 The restoration of the Iron Bridge 1972-75.

concealed reinforced concrete. The work proceeded smoothly, although the engineers were surprised by the poor standards of construction of the abutment.

The contract for the construction of the invert slab was placed with the Tarmac Construction Company, who commenced operations in the spring of 1973. It was agreed with the river authority to work only during the summer months, since the project involved the construction of coffer dams which might aggravate any flooding. Difficulties were encountered in driving sheet piles through the mudstone rock beneath the bridge, and, once the rock was exposed to air, it degenerated into a glutinous mud. The southern half of the invert was constructed first, and while the coffer-dam protecting the workings was in place the river was allowed to flow over the northern half of its bed. The bridge was in considerable danger while the excavations for the invert were taking place, and meticulous attention was therefore paid to the temporary steel strutting supporting the abutment while the work was in progress. The Severn proved unusually prone to flood during 1973, and on 7 August of that year there occurred the highest summer flood known on the river, before or since. The river authority provided sufficient warning for materials and equipment to be removed, but the waters flowed over the coffer-dam, and forced the project well behind schedule, frustrating the hopes of the engineers and contractors that they would be able to complete the invert in a single summer's

41 The River Severn in flood on 8 August 1973 over the coffer dam installed to enable the invert slab to be constructed between the abutments of the Iron Bridge.

42 The construction of the coffer dam on the north bank in progress during the summer of 1974.

work. The contractors ceased work in the autumn of 1973, and returned to complete the northern half of the invert in April 1974.

Other tasks continued during the next few years. The accumulated road metal was removed, and replaced by a special macadam, bound by a colourless resin-based liquid, that was both waterproof and lighter. The stonework of the abutments was renewed, and the parapet railings repaired. The Museum Trust rebuilt the tollhouse, and it was opened as an information centre towards the end of 1975.

Remedial work was suspended during the summer of 1979 when the centenary of the construction of the ironwork of the bridge was celebrated,[27] but in 1980 the whole structure was enveloped in scaffolding, and, apparently for the first time in the 20th century, the ironwork was painted. Restoration was therefore complete for the bicentenary of the opening of the bridge, which was celebrated with a pig roast

43 *(right)* The deck plates of the Iron Bridge revealed during the renewal of the road surface, 25 November 1975.

44 *(below)* The concluding phase of the restoration of the Iron Bridge during the summer of 1980.

45 *(below)* The celebration of the bicentenary of the opening of the Iron Bridge, New Year's Day, 1981.

46 The last pieces of scaffolding await removal from the Iron Bridge at the end of a programme of repairs, repainting and recording, 26 April 2000.

on 1 January 1981, a sunny winter's day, when the size of the crowds on the bridge made engineers who understood its problems rather apprehensive.

The bridge was again encased in scaffolding in the summer of 1999 to enable English Heritage to assess the need for future repairs and to enable it to be repainted. The opportunity was taken to carry out further archaeological recording. Only relatively minor repairs were needed before a new top coating of paint was applied.

The setting of the Iron Bridge changed considerably in the last two decades of the 20th century. The opening of the Ironbridge by-pass in 1989 removed most through-traffic from the roads on the north bank of the river.[28] Developments elsewhere in Telford have drawn away many of the local services that developed in the town of Ironbridge, whose economy now centres around cafés and shops selling souvenirs and antiques rather than banks and the establishments of grocers and drapers.

Nevertheless, the celebrity of the bridge has drawn increasing numbers of visitors to the area. The site of the railway station on the south bank of the river is now an extensive car park, and scarcely a daylight hour passes when the bridge is not recorded by a photographer.

The Iron Bridge has been recognised internationally as a symbol of the 'Industrial Revolution' that is, with parliamentary democracy, the feature that most distinguishes the history of Britain from that of other countries. The bridge was visited in 1973 by delegates to the First International Congress on the Conservation

47 The restored Iron Bridge carries a heavy load at the conclusion of a duck race in 1986.

of Industrial Monuments. Plaques recording the recognition of its significance by the professional engineering associations in the United States were inaugurated during the bicentenary celebrations in 1979. In 1986 the Ironbridge Gorge was designated a UNESCO World Heritage Site. The bridge is now effectively protected as a scheduled ancient monument within a managed environment.

VI

The Next Generations

Contexts

Our understanding of the development of constructional techniques in iron in the half-century after the completion of the Iron Bridge has grown since the first edition of this book was published. Much has been learned about developments in continental Europe.[1] In the first edition of this book we listed some 80 iron bridges built before 1830, of which 69 were in the British Isles. As will become evident in this chapter, it is no longer practicable to attempt a definitive list, but we can now positively identify more than 130 bridges that were built in the British Isles before 1830 – nearly twice as many as were recognised in 1979 – quite apart from small structures that were produced in series.[2] We cannot discuss every iron bridge in detail, but propose to examine bridge-building in a series of contexts, in the hope of bringing some order to the developments that began with the Iron Bridge. The chronological sequence of construction was significant for about 15 years, but after 1795-6 iron bridges became numerous and the order in which they were built ceased to be of prime importance. We can gain a greater understanding by setting the bridges built between 1796 and the beginning of main-line railways within a series of overlapping typologies which sort like from unlike, and enable the broad patterns of change to be appreciated.

The development of constructional technology is one obvious context in which bridge-building between 1780 and 1830 can be interpreted. This was a time when engineers came to appreciate the advantages and disadvantages of iron as a constructional material. Some of the most talented architects, engineers, and ironmasters, in an era of mighty talents, Charles Bage (1751-1825), William Jessop (1745-1814), John Nash (1752-1835), John Rennie (1761-1821), William Reynolds (1758-1803), Thomas Telford (1757-1834), concerned themselves with iron construction. Arches with spans considerably greater than the 100 ft. 6 in. (34m) of the Coalbrookdale structure were constructed in cast iron, and multi-span bridges and aqueducts were built across wide rivers and valleys. Iron became a credible alternative to conventional masonry arches for major bridges, and continued to be so during the first half-century of main-line railway construction. The careers of leading engineers, and the histories of the principal iron-making companies most effectively illuminate the main stream of technological development.

Some properties of cast iron were utilised in bridges that were not part of that main stream. The decorative qualities of the metal, long appreciated by architects, were exploited in bridges that adorned gentlemen's parks and pedestrian routes in fashionable cities. Small iron bridges could be constructed quickly, and iron arches carrying limited loads could be much flatter than their masonry equivalents. Such qualities made cast iron a suitable material for modest structures on canals and within dock complexes, and, in South Wales, on primitive railways. By 1830 iron bridges were being manufactured in what was in effect series production by at least one engineering company, and several small and obscure foundries cast one-off decorative bridges.

The Immediate Successors

The first question about the proliferation of iron bridges necessarily relates to chronology. The Coalbrookdale bridge was extensively publicised, yet no evidence survives of the construction of any other iron bridges in Britain during the 1780s. During that decade 11 or 12 iron bridges were built in the park of the Empress Catherine the Great at Tsarskoe Selo (or Pushkin), near St Petersburg. Most of the bridges were the responsibility of John Busch (c.1730-95), a German-born landscape architect recruited in England, and were made at the state munitions works at Sestroretsk, but whether they were of cast iron or wrought iron seems uncertain. The Scot, Charles Cameron (1743-1812), designed two bridges in the Chinese style. Eleven bridges remain at Tsarskoe Selo, none of them spanning more than 30 ft. (9m).[3] Two small-scale replicas of the Coalbrookdale structure were built at about the same time. The first, known only from a watercolour dated 1788, was in the park laid out for the Duke of Orleans by the Scottish landscape architect

48 Le pont de fer, parc de Raincy (Carmontel, 1788). The iron bridge in the park of the Duke of Orléans at Raincy.

49 The replica of the Iron Bridge in the park of the Prince of Anhalt Dessau at Worlitz.

Thomas Blaikie (1750-1838) around the chateau at Raincy, north-east of Paris, and was probably of iron but it could have been fabricated in wood.[4] The bridge has been demolished, but the park in the English style of which it formed part is now a protected site. The second, a wrought-iron replica with a span of 25 ft. (7.75m), stands in the grounds of the former summer palace of the Prince of Anhalt Dessau on the banks of the River Elbe at Worlitz, and was built in 1791.[5] In the same year the Coalbrookdale Company cast an iron bridge 'to be thrown over one of the canals in Holland' that appears to have been the first iron bridge exported from Great Britain.[6]

It is probable, nevertheless, that some small iron bridges were built in Britain in the 1780s. Thomas Bowdler, in a letter to the Royal Society in 1797, remarked that before the great bridge at Sunderland was contemplated, 'Iron *Bridges* were built at Coalbrookdale and other places'.[7] The likeliest candidate is the bridge that formerly crossed an arm of the Upper Furnace Pool below the houses of the ironmasters at Coalbrookdale. This was a footbridge spanning about 30 ft. (9m), with rings of diminishing size in its spandrels. It was standing by 1801, but was unmentioned in any of the descriptions of the flurry of bridge-building at Coalbrookdale in the mid-1790s, which suggests an earlier date. The bridge was demolished in 1849, and replaced by a timber structure, but the stub of one of its ribs remains beneath a further wooden replacement of the 1970s.[8]

The next bridge that can be precisely documented was cast by the Coalbrookdale Company and erected across the River Trent in the park of Granville Leveson-Gower (1721-1803), 1st Marquess of Stafford, at Trentham in 1794. The Marquess held extensive lands in the Shropshire Coalfield, including iron ore mines that supplied the furnaces of the Coalbrookdale Company, and his agents were acquainted with William Reynolds and other partners in the company. Trentham was a fashionable estate. The great house, re-designed by Henry Holland (1745-1806), was surrounded by pleasure grounds laid out by Lancelot Brown (1715-83), which included an orangery, 'like a mystic temple', adjacent to the bridge. The Marquess's agent broached the project with the iron company on 1 July 1793, and two weeks later the principal clerk despatched to Trentham three alternative designs, and a 1:24 scale model in wood. A single-arch design with three ribs was chosen, and constructed between May and December 1794. It spanned about 90 ft. (27.7m), was about 6 ft. (1.8m) wide, had diminishing circles in the spandrels, and bore the inscription 'Marquess of Stafford' and the symbol of the Garter on the rib below the central section of the parapet. The estate became a public pleasure park in the 20th century, and bridge was demolished about 1931 when a concrete bridge was constructed to give access to a new ballroom. Stubs

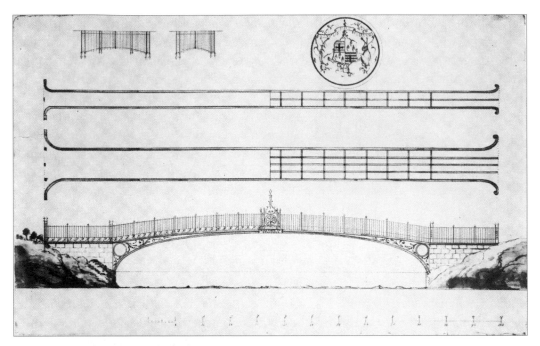

50 *(top)* The design that was most probably used for the iron bridge in the park of the Marquess of Stafford at Trentham in 1794.

51 *(far left)* A fragment of one of the ribs of the bridge over the Upper Furnace Pool at Coalbrookdale.

52 *(left)* A fragment of one of the ribs of the Trentham Bridge.

of the ribs remain beneath the concrete. The Trentham bridge is the earliest documented parkland iron bridge, but the ease with which the Coalbrookdale Company produced alternative designs suggests that it may not have been the first of its kind.[9]

Before the bridge at Trentham was contemplated, between January and July 1793, Watkin George, engineer at the Cyfarthfa ironworks at Merthyr, constructed across the River Taff a king-post truss in cast iron, known as Pont-y-Cafnau (the bridge of troughs), carrying on its deck an edge railway, conveying limestone to the blast furnaces. A trough beneath the deck took water to provide power in the ironworks, and at its central point the bridge supported one of the trestles that carried the high and lengthy wooden aqueduct taking water to *Aeolus*, the celebrated 50 ft. (15.4m) waterwheel that powered the furnace bellows. The bridge is 24 ft. 5 in. (7.5m) long, precisely the span of the cast-iron trusses that roofed the old forge at Cyfarthfa that was built at the same time.[10]

Pont-y-Cafnau was the first of a series of railway bridges in South Wales, and the first structure to use an iron trough to carry water, but it also embodied constructional principles that were influential elsewhere. William Reynolds placed a drawing of Pont-y-Cafnau made in 1794 in his sketchbook, and a similar form of construction, using diagonal cast-iron beams to support a trough, was employed on the aqueduct at Longdon-on-Tern on the Shrewsbury Canal that was cast at his ironworks at Ketley. Josiah Clowes (1735-94), engineer to the canal company, proposed to carry the waterway over the Tern by means of a conventional masonry aqueduct, but he died in December 1794, and on 10-12 February 1795 floods damaged the preparatory works. Thomas Telford was appointed to succeed Clowes, and on 14 March the canal proprietors agreed to construct an iron aqueduct. The 187 ft. (57m) long trough is flanked by a brick abutment, on the eastern side, that appears to have been designed as part of Clowes's masonry structure, while that on the western side, of sandstone, appears to have been built by Telford on foundations provided by Clowes. The aqueduct was opened to traffic on 14 March 1796.[11] A week or so earlier Benjamin Outram's (1764-1805) 44 ft.

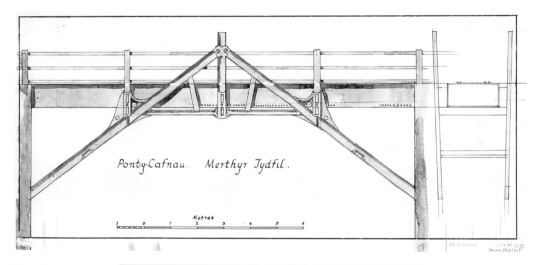

53 Drawing of Pont-y-Cafnau (the late Douglas Hague).

54 Pont-y-Cafnau.

55 Portrait of William Reynolds (William Hobday, 1796). He is holding the plan for 'the first iron aqueduct'.

56 The drawing of the aqueduct at Longdon published in the Canals section (written by Thomas Telford) of Joseph Plymley's *A General View of the Agriculture of Shropshire* (1803).

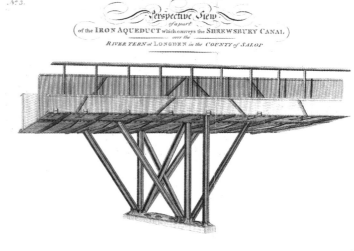

57 The aqueduct that carried the Shrewsbury Canal over the River Tern at Longdon, Shropshire.

58 The trough and towpath of the aqueduct at Longdon.

(16.7m) aqueduct taking the Derby Canal over the Markeaton Brook at Holmes was completed. The Holmes Aqueduct appears to have been the first iron aqueduct for navigational purposes. It was demolished in 1971.[12]

Architects and engineers were taking an increasing interest in iron structures while the Trentham bridge and Pont-y-Cafnau were being built. John Rennie designed two bridges for the island of Nevis in the West Indies in 1791 and 1794. Neither was built but at least two other bridges were despatched from England to the Caribbean in the following decade.[13] A small iron foot-bridge was built in Sheffield in 1795, crossing the River Don at the end of Nursery Street. It was swept away in the great flood of 1864.[14] The architect John Nash, the political philosopher Thomas Paine and the Durham landowner, Rowland Burdon, with his architect Thomas Wilson, were all involved at much the same time in devising plans for using small sections of iron to build up arches, rather than to cast half-ribs, as was done at Coalbrookdale in 1779.

Tom Paine

The practical achievements of Tom Paine (1737-1809) were the least of the three, but his ideas were influential. Born at Thetford of Quaker parents, he was dismissed from his post as an exciseman in 1773 after calling for better treatment of his profession. The following year he went to America and, after supporting the colonists in the War of Independence, returned to his scientific interests, setting himself the task of designing a bridge to span the River Schuylkill in Philadelphia, a demanding problem, since the presence of ice-floes in spring dictated a structure with a single span of about 400 ft. (123m). Paine's account of his research is eloquent:

> The natural mightiness of America expands the mind and it partakes of the greatness it contemplates. Even the war, with all its evils, had some advantages. It energised invention and lessened the Catalogue of Impossibilities. At the conclusion of it every man returned to his home to repair the ravages it had occasioned, and to think of war no more. As one among thousands who had born [sic] a share in that memorable revolution, I returned with them to the enjoyment of quiet life and that I might not be Idle, undertook to construct a bridge of a single arch for this river.

A distinguished American historian of bridges has remarked that bridging America's deep, fast-flowing rivers needed new materials and new design principles, concluding that 'Paine was the first person in the New World to recognise iron's potential to fill this need ... by providing a glimpse of what could be, Paine showed the way to a technology that would make possible the nation's great westward expansion during the nineteenth century'.[15]

Paine proposed a bridge of 13 ribs, one for each of the United States, each weighing 40 tons, and sent a model in June 1786 to Benjamin Franklin. A second model was built to carry the weight of three men. In 1787 Paine left America for Europe where his design was approved by the French Academy of Sciences. The following year he was in England and took out a patent (1788 No. 1667) for 'A method of constructing of arches … either in iron or wood, on principles new and different to anything hitherto practised'.[16]

Paine persuaded Walkers of Rotherham, whose foundry was celebrated for its cannon, to make for him an experimental arch. Its span, restricted by the dimensions of the foundry buildings, was 90 ft. (27.7m). There were four ribs, rising to a height of 5 ft. (1.5m). The arch was erected in April 1789, using a steel furnace and a workshop as abutments. The space between them was rather greater than 90 ft., and the distance was shortened by filling up with 'chunckes of wood'. Centring was erected, and construction began, contrary to the practice of building a masonry arch, with the placing of the keystone. The arch bore a load of six tons of pig iron. Paine claimed that the components making up the four ribs weighed only three tons.[17]

In June 1789 Walkers agreed to make a five-rib bridge of 110 ft. (33.9m) span that could be erected across the Thames. Paine was in France the following winter, but in May 1790 the parts were shipped to London and displayed at the *Yorkshire Stingo* public house in Lisson Grove. The bridge spanned 110 ft. (34m), and consisted of six ribs each made up of 105 cast-iron voussoirs, held together with wrought-iron ties, with tubes providing lateral spacing. The cast-iron components weighed 13 tons. 13 cwt., and those of wrought-iron 22 tons 16 cwt. Soon afterwards Peter Whiteside, Paine's American patron, who had witnessed the patent application in 1788, was declared bankrupt, which, with the changing political situation in England and France, led to the abandonment of the project. The first part of Paine's *The Rights of Man* appeared in May 1791, the second part in February 1792, and in May of that year he was charged with sedition. He crossed to Paris in September 1792, and was imprisoned until September 1794, when he returned to America. The parts exhibited at Paddington were returned to Rotherham from October 1791. Pieces remained at the works for several decades

59 Design for an iron bridge by Tom Paine.

and some of the wrought-iron strapping appears to have been re-worked and used in the Sunderland Bridge.[18]

The principles on which Paine's bridge was constructed are neither stated clearly in his patent nor are they evident from the surviving drawing.[19] Paine claimed that the principle was taken from 'a spider's web of which it resembles a section, and I naturally suppose that when nature intended that insect to make a web she taught it the best method of putting it together'. Another concept taken from nature was that of 'increasing the strength of matter by dividing it and combining it and thereby causing it to act over a larger space than it would occupy in a solid state as is seen in the quilts of birds, bones of animals, reeds, &c.' The drawing shows a structure of three spans whose ribs are composed of short, perforated segments.[20]

The exhibition of Paine's bridge may have stimulated thinking about iron construction. John Nash, architect of the Regent's Park terraces and the Royal Pavilion at Brighton, was practising in the Welsh borders, when in 1795 he was commissioned by Sir Edward Winnington (1749-1805) of Stanford Court to replace a masonry bridge over the River Teme that had been damaged by flooding. The bridge was completed in the autumn of 1795, but shortly afterwards subsided into the river, so slowly that a little boy who was crossing it escaped unhurt. The gradual collapse suggests that the bridge was made up of iron voussoirs. The Coalbrookdale partners affirmed in the Midlands press that they had not been involved with the bridge. Nash subsequently moved to London, where, in February 1797, he took out a patent (1797 No. 2165) for his design for a new bridge at Stanford, made up of cast-iron voussoirs that could be filled with ballast, with hollow iron sections in the spandrels. The bridge was opened during 1797, having been cast at the Coalbrookdale foundry, to which in 1799 Nash returned an assortment of constructional materials.[21] It was replaced in 1911 by a ferro-concrete arch, the contract for which mentioned the cast-iron boxes of the previous structure.[22]

The Sunderland Bridge

The next iron bridge to gain the celebrity of the structure at Coalbrookdale linked Sunderland to Bishop's and Monks' Wearmouth, on the north bank of the River Wear. Its construction was due principally to Rowland Burdon (c.1756-1836), a member of a gentry family in Co. Durham, a banker, and Tory MP for the county from 1790 until 1806. He studied architecture with Sir John Soane (1753-1837) in his youth, but devoted his life to promoting the port of Sunderland, where coal shippings doubled between 1750 and 1790. Although so prosperous, Sunderland was notoriously 'a town on the road to no place', and a bridge that would not be an obstacle to shipping was needed to replace the existing ferry on the coast road towards South Shields and Newcastle.

The Act of Parliament for the bridge was obtained in 1790. Work began in December 1792 when two men ventured out in a boat to measure the width of the river. The foundation stone was laid in September 1793, and in 1795 Burdon, who apparently knew the Coalbrookdale bridge, but disapproved of its principles of construction, took out a patent (1795 No. 2066) for a system of bridge-building using cast-iron boxes as voussoirs. Engravings of the bridge under construction show the centring, held up by two towers of wooden scaffolding, with vessels passing on the river. The components were cast by Walkers at Rotherham whose works Burdon visited three times in the early months of 1793. A rib was erected there as a trial, and taken down in December 1793.[23] Thomas Wilson (c.1750-c.1820), a Sunderland architect, supervised the construction.

The inscription on the foundation stone revealed that Burdon's political views were the antithesis of those of Tom Paine:

> At the time when the impetuosity of the French nation eager for what was wrong disturbed the nations of Europe with iron war, Rowland Burdon, Esq., desirous of better things, determined to join together with an iron bridge the rocky and steep banks of the Wear.

Prince William, Duke of Gloucester (1743-1805) opened the bridge with masonic rituals on 9 August 1796. Its span was 236 ft. (72.7m), much larger than any previous iron bridge.[24] It was 32 ft. (9.8m) wide, and at low tide was 100 ft. (31m) above water level. It was formed of six ribs, spaced 15 ft. (4.62m) apart, and each made up of 105 iron voussoirs, 5 ft. (1.54m) in depth, and tapering from 4 in. × 2 ft. 4½ in. (0.1 × 0.74m) at the top to 4 in. × 2 ft. 4 in. (0.1 × 0.72m) at the bottom. The voussoirs were fixed together by wrought-iron tie rods, 3 in. × 1 in. in section, and the ribs joined to each other by iron tubes. The spandrels were filled with iron circles. The ironwork in the bridge weighed only 260 tons, much less than the Iron Bridge. It cost £32,424 19s. 7d., of which Burdon himself subscribed £30,000. The cost of stone and lime at £5,450 exceeded that of the iron, which was £4,018. Wages for masons and labourers cost more than £10,000, the purchase of land over £700 and timber £1,966.

Burdon retired from public life in 1803 following the collapse of the Surtees Bank in which he was a partner, and he was declared bankrupt in 1806. Other names have been linked with the Sunderland Bridge, although Burdon's part in the project was fluently explained by his son in 1859.[25] Thomas Wilson built other bridges on similar principles, but his role at Sunderland was defined by a visitor in June 1796 who, after drinking tea with him and dining with Burdon, noted that 'Mr. Burdon erected the bridge at his sole expence and invented the blocks which were an essential part of its construction, but that Mr. Wilson had the management of the whole project'.[26] Tom Paine has also been linked with the bridge, and the wrought-iron strapping that held together the voussoirs may have been salvaged by Walkers from Paine's Lisson Grove bridge.[27] It does not diminish Paine's achievement to assert that he had no other connection with the Sunderland Bridge. John Nash claimed to have designed the Sunderland Bridge, and was acquainted with Burdon, but while the constructional principles he used at Stanford were similar to Burdon's he had no active role in the project,[28] nor was John Rastrick I (1738-1836) responsible for the bridge, although he claimed that Burdon had plagiarised some of his ideas.[29]

60 Sunderland Bridge under construction.

61 West view of the Sunderland Bridge.

62 Sunderland Bridge after the restoration by
Robert Stephenson in 1859, but before its
replacement by the present steel bridge in
1929.

Sunderland Bridge became an icon in the North-East. Its image appears on engravings, and on ceramic- and glass-wares. A Swedish visitor commented in 1802 that he had come across views of the bridge all over England, even on the bill of the inn where he was staying.[30] Burdon showed that iron could be used to create a colossal arch, substantially longer than any single-arched masonry bridge then existing. The bridge was rebuilt in 1859 under the direction of Robert Stephenson, who replaced the diminishing circles in the spandrels with diagonal bracing. It was demolished in 1928-9 when Sir William Arrol & Co. built the present steel bridge.

Several patterns of iron bridge-building were established by the end of 1796. The Coalbrookdale Company and Walkers of Rotherham were the pre-eminent suppliers of castings. Within the main stream of structural development, Nash, Paine, Burdon and Wilson had shown that ribs of considerable span could be assembled from voussoirs, while Watkin George had developed different principles analogous to those used in the construction of roofs, and he, Outram and Telford had shown that iron could be used to carry flowing water. The bridge at Trentham demonstrated the decorative qualities of cast iron. Those at Raincy and Worlitz showed that the fame of the Iron Bridge had spread to continental Europe. These various patterns will be explored in the remainder of this chapter.

Walkers and Wilson

The origins of one pattern were at Sunderland. After the completion of Burdon's bridge, Thomas Wilson lived in an adjacent house. He continued to collaborate with Walkers, and took out his own patent in 1802 (1802 No. 2635) for the construction of arches from connecting metallic blocks. One traveller observed, with some exaggeration, that he 'very properly enjoys nearly the exclusive advantage of designing and superintending iron bridges'.[31] The ironworks at Rotherham was established by Samuel (d. 1782), Jonathan (d. 1778) and Aaron Walker (d. 1746) alongside the Don Canal and moved to Holmes (SK 410924) in 1757. By 1782 the company had three blast furnaces blown by a Boulton & Watt engine. They began to manufacture cannon in 1773, and some of their products remain on H.M.S. *Victory*.[32]

Wilson's name and the date 1800 are inscribed on a four-rib bridge cast by Walkers, with a span of 81 ft. 9 in. (25m), that was constructed in Spanish Town, Jamaica in 1801.[33] The following year he appears to have designed a 40 ft. (12m) bridge crossing the River Loddon on the Stratfield Saye estate in Berkshire, then owned by George Pitt, Baron Rivers (*c*.1722-1803), whose family's fortune was derived from coal-mining in Co. Durham.[34] Subsequently the estate formed part of the endowment granted by Parliament to the 1st Duke of Wellington (1769-1852). Wilson's other designs were less successful. In 1800 he agreed with the magistrates of Surrey and Middlesex to build an arch with a 181 ft. (56m) span to replace the old bridge at Staines. A visitor to Walker's foundry in the following year watched the production of components 'upon a construction superior to any hitherto cast'. When the centring was removed in 1803 the bridge began to subside and was closed after about a week's use. The weight of iron in the arch had exerted too great a lateral thrust for the abutments. Nevertheless, a German visitor had found it 'high and audaciously vaulted', and observed that it was attracting sightseers from London. A wooden replacement was hurriedly erected, which was succeeded by George Rennie's (1791-1856) bridge in 1832.[35] Wilson also designed a bridge with a span of 180 ft. (56m) to carry the road from York to Durham over the River Tees at Yarm, authorised by an Act of Parliament of 1802. Walkers supplied 250 tons of castings that were erected remarkably quickly, but at about midnight on 12 January 1806 the bridge collapsed, one newspaper remarking that the concussion was felt all over the town.[36] As at Staines, the abutments were unable to resist the lateral pressure of the arch, and travellers continued to use the 15th-century bridge erected by Bishop Walter Skirlaw.

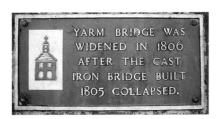

63 Inscription recording the collapse of Thomas Wilson's bridge at Yarm.

Wilson and Walkers shared responsibility for two other bridges. An Act of Parliament (42 Geo.III c.96) was obtained in 1802 for a bridge over the River Witham at Boston, a project on which Wilson collaborated with John Rennie, and disagreed with him about the details, the latter favouring vertical struts rather than diminishing circles in the spandrels. Walkers completed the castings during 1806, and the bridge, of 86 ft. (26.5m) span, with six ribs each of 11 segments, was opened the following year. Wilson and Rennie disputed responsibility over cracks that appeared in the ironwork and in the abutments, but they combined to withstand complaints by the borough corporation. The bridge was replaced by a steel structure on the same foundations in 1912-13.[37] Thomas Wilson worked with Henry Provis (1760-1830), on the Tickford Bridge over the River Lovat at Newport Pagnell, for which an Act of Parliament (49 Geo.III c.144) was obtained in 1809. Walkers cast six 60 ft. (18.5m) ribs each of 11 segments, and after the first stone was laid in June 1810 construction proceeded rapidly. After restoration, it remains in use, the only Wilson bridge carrying a public road in Britain that survives in the 21st century.[38]

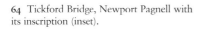

64 Tickford Bridge, Newport Pagnell with its inscription (inset).

Aqueducts

Pont-y-Cafnau was the origin of several lines of development. The most consequential was the use of iron troughs to convey water, in the form of leets feeding waterwheels, navigable canals, or natural streams crossing newly constructed transport routes. Pont-y-Cafnau appears directly to have influenced the design of the aqueduct that carried the Shrewsbury Canal over the River Tern at Longdon. Soon afterwards Robert Fulton (1765-1815) proposed to use a similar

trough at Marple on the Peak Forest Canal, a project that was eventually realised by Benjamin Outram in stone.[39] Subsequently Outram recommended a cast-iron trough as a replacement for a damaged aqueduct carrying the Huddersfield Canal over the River Tame at Stalybridge. The 47 ft. (16.75m) long trough, sometimes called the Stakes Aqueduct, was completed in 1801. A stone arch sustained the towpath.[40] After two centuries the structure remains as Outram left it, apart from some tie bars added about 1870. In 1801 Thomas Telford used cast-iron plates to seal the bottom of the stone aqueduct at Chirk carrying the Ellesmere Canal over the River Ceiriog from England into Wales – the cast-iron sides that give the impression that the canal runs through a trough were added later.[41]

65 Benjamin Outram's aqueduct on the Huddersfield Canal at Stalybridge.

A cast-iron trough forms part of one of the most extraordinary creations of the Industrial Revolution, the 1000 ft. (308m) long, 127 ft. (39m) high aqueduct, opened in 1805, that carries the Ellesmere Canal across the valley of the River Dee at Pontcysyllte. It is ironic that such a structure should be a component of a waterway that was never completed as planned. Its strategic purpose was in any

66 The Pontcysyllte Aqueduct carrying the Ellesmere Canal over the River Dee.

case doubtful, for a route from Merseyside to Bristol that depended on the fitful navigation of the upper reaches of the River Severn was unlikely to prosper. Pontcysyllte differs in several respects from Pont-y-Cafnau and Longdon. The trough is supported on cast-iron arches rather than diagonal struts, while the towpath runs over the trough. Historians debated at some length in the last three decades of the 20th century who was responsible for designing and building the Pontcysyllte aqueduct, and it became evident that it is no longer possible to give all the credit to Thomas Telford, in the manner of his biographers of the 1940s and '50s. Charles Hadfield showed that Telford himself, and John Rickman (1771-1840) who edited his autobiography, ignored or diminished the achievements of the great engineer's equals, notably William Jessop, engineer to the Ellesmere Canal, while lavishing praise on those he acknowledged as subordinates. Contemporaries were aware that Pontcysyllte was not Telford's work alone. The contributor of the article on canals in Rees's *Cyclopaedia,* written about 1805, observed that 'a most stupendous work ... has been undertaken by Mr Jessop on the Ellesmere Canal and is now nearly or quite completed across the Dee river at Pontcysyllte'. It is evident from Hadfield's analysis that William Jessop conceived the idea that a high aqueduct at Pontycysyllte was feasible, and that it was he who established the project in such a way that Telford could complete it.[42] Pontcysyllte is not diminished by such arguments. The waterway in the sky in the Vale of Llangollen, particularly when viewed in an early morning mist, appears to be an heroic defiance of conventional thinking, a monument of the Romantic Movement as well as the Industrial Revolution.

An arch-reinforced iron trough carries the Grand Junction Canal over the River Ouse at Wolverton in Buckinghamshire. It replaced a three-arch masonry aqueduct that collapsed on 18 February 1808. The canal company's engineer and secretary recommended an iron structure after inspecting Longdon, Chirk and Pontcysyllte, and in April 1809 gave an order to William Reynolds & Co. of Ketley,[43] for a trough 101 ft. (31m) long, supported by a central masonry pier. Benjamin Bevan (*c.*1773-1833) supervised the construction, and the aqueduct was opened to traffic on 22 January 1811.[44] The Uttoxeter branch of the Trent & Mersey Canal also opened in 1811, incorporating an iron aqueduct over the River Tean. The branch closed to traffic in the face of railway competition in 1847.[45]

Three iron troughs were built on the southern section of the Stratford on Avon Canal between its junction with the Warwick & Birmingham Canal at Kingswood, and the River Avon at Stratford, built between 1812 and 1816.

67 The Wolverton Aqueduct on the Grand Junction Canal.

The most substantial, usually called the Edstone Aqueduct, is near Bearley, a 520 ft. (158m) long trough, supported by 12 brick piers, which carried the canal over a lane. The Stratford-Henley in Arden railway subsequently passed beneath it. The aqueduct crossing the Birmingham-Stratford road at Wootton Wawen carries a plaque recording its construction in October 1813, together with the names of William James (1771-1837), deputy chairman and inspiration of the company, and William Whitmore (c.1748-1816), the engineer. The third and shortest aqueduct, across a stream at Yarningdale, is a trough fabricated in 1834 by the Horseley Company, to replace an original structure damaged by a flood.[46] On the Edinburgh & Glasgow Union Canal, constructed under the direction of Hugh Baird (1770-1837) in 1818-22, are three substantial aqueducts, at Slateford, and over the rivers Almond and Avon, all iron troughs supported by hollow masonry arches.[47]

Civil engineers who had to build aqueducts in subsequent decades could choose between iron troughs or masonry arches lined with puddled clay, and their choices reflect no particular pattern. Telford's plan of 1825 for the Macclesfield Canal required the construction of 10 aqueducts, but only one, at Congleton, was built in iron.[48] On the Birmingham & Liverpool Junction Canal, opened in 1835, he opted for iron troughs to carry the waterway over Watling Street at Stretton and at Nantwich across the road to Wrexham, but at Berrisford Road, Market Drayton (SJ 685384) and Shebdon (SJ 758261) he employed monumental masonry arches. The same options are illustrated on the new stretch of the Oxford Canal near Rugby, completed in 1834 as part of the programme of improvements devised by

68 *(top left)*
The Bearley or Edstone Aqueduct on the Stratford Canal.

69 *(top right)*
The aqueduct carrying the Stratford Canal over the Birmingham – Stratford main road at Wootton Wawen.

70 *(above left)*
Thomas Telford's aqueduct carrying the Birmingham & Liverpool Junction Canal over Watling Street at Stretton, Staffordshire.

71 *(above right)*
Thomas Telford's aqueduct at Congleton on the Macclesfield Canal.

Charles Vignoles (1793-1875), for which William Cubitt (1785-1861) was consulting engineer. The canal crosses the old road to Leicester in an iron trough, supported on six iron arches, but a few yards to the east it is carried over the River Swift on three blue brick arches. The trough was probably designed by James Potter (1801-57), and cast by Parkes & Otway of the Capponfield Ironworks, Bilston. It was restored by British Waterways in 1991 to something like its original condition.[49]

Two later aqueducts merit particular mention. In the closing years of his life, Thomas Telford created a new line for the Birmingham Canal through its summit at Smethwick. He employed an iron trough passing between 21 short iron columns, themselves mounted on ribs of the kind that he used in his shorter road bridges,[50] to carry a feeder from the Rotton Park reservoir, known as the Engine Arm, across the new line of the canal to join the old line at the top of the Smethwick lock flight. It was cast by the Horseley Company in 1830 and is the most elegant of the smaller British aqueducts.[51] The most innovative aqueduct of that generation carried the Aire & Calder Navigation over the River Calder at Stanley Ferry, and opened to traffic in 1839. George Leather (1786-1870) and his son John W. Leather (1810-1887) suspended

72 (top) The aqueduct carrying the new line of the Oxford Canal over the old road to Leicester at Rugby.

73 (above left) Thomas Telford's Engine Arm Aqueduct on the Birmingham Canal Navigation at Smethwick.

74 (above right) The aqueduct at Leamore (or Birchills) carrying the Wyrley & Essington Canal over the Cannock branch of the L.N.W.R.

75 (right) George Leather's Stanley Ferry Aqueduct carrying the Aire & Calder Canal over the River Calder near Wakefield.

the trough and its towpaths between two iron arches, ornamenting the whole structure in the classical style.[52]

Iron troughs were used to replace damaged aqueducts on the Montgomeryshire Canal, at Birthdir in 1819, and across the Lledan Brook at Welshpool in 1836, and several were built to carry canals across railways. At Brownhills, the Anglesey Arm of the Wyrley & Essington Canal crosses the railway from Walsall to Lichfield in a trough built in 1849-50, and a similar structure built by Lloyds Foster & Co. of Wednesbury in 1856 takes the main line of the same canal over the Cannock branch of the London & North Western Railway at Leamore (Birchills). An iron trough was built at Leahurst to take the Cromford Canal across the Ambergate-Matlock line of the Midland Railway opened in 1849. Perhaps the best-known aqueduct of this kind is the Windmill Bridge (Three Bridges) at Hanwell carrying the Grand Junction Canal under Windmill Lane and over the Brentford branch of the Great Western Railway that was opened in 1859.[53]

A Bridge-building Tradition in South Wales

Pont-y-Cafnau was also significant as the first of a sequence of small iron bridges in South Wales. The next stood nearby, was made from the same set of castings and carried a tramway constructed in 1795 over the River Taff into the Cyfarthfa ironworks, immediately east of the blast furnaces that still stand. It was photographed in the 1920s, but appears to have been removed in the following decade, although the abutments survived to be recorded in the 1970s.[54] At the south end of the works a tramway crossed the river on a bridge also designed by Watkin George, but of A-frame design, with the deck supported by and suspended from a cast-iron arch. J.M.W. Turner (1775-1851) drew the bridge in 1797, but no trace remains.[55] A little further downstream the Taff was spanned by a 66 ft. (20.1m) road bridge of 1799-1800, whose deck was supported by a subtle combination of arch and cantilevers, also, apparently, designed by Watkin George. In the course of time it was named the 'Old Iron Bridge', having been closed to traffic and adapted for pedestrian use in 1880. In 1963, in spite of having been scheduled and in the face of eloquent protests, it was demolished, and the parts dumped pending re-erection that has yet to take place.[56] Less than a mile to the south at Rhyd-y-Car a 24 ft. (7.3m) parapet truss bridge of similarly early date carried the road from Merthyr to Waunwalt over the Glamorganshire Canal. It was dismantled in the 1970s and re-erected outside the birthplace of the musician Joseph Parry (1841-1903) in Chapel Row (SO 046066), Cyfarthfa.[57] Thus five iron bridges, all probably designed by Watkin George, had been built by 1800 or soon afterwards within a distance of little more than a mile, near the Cyfarthfa ironworks. Watkin George, a carpenter by trade, was evidently an engineer of imagination and skill. His abilities secured him a

76 The Rhyd-y-Car Bridge displayed outside the birthplace of Joseph Parry in Merthyr.

partnership in the ironworks but he left in 1807, with £30,000 as his share of the capital, and became a manufacturer of tinplate.

Watkin George established a tradition of building bridges in iron. Between 1798 and 1802 two iron bridges were built in the western part of the South Wales Coalfield near Llanelli by the coal- and ironmaster Alexander Raby. They carried tramways over the River Lleidi, and were probably cast at Raby's Cymddyche furnace.[58] In Merthyr a four-rib structure spanning 28 ft. (8.6m) was constructed in 1813 to carry a road over the Morlais Brook.[59] South of Merthyr, the Waterloo Bridge stood near the Penydarren Ironworks. It was replaced in 1903 but some components, including that inscribed '1815', survived to be salvaged in the 1990s and displayed outside the birthplace of Joseph Parry.[60]

The Rhyd-y-Car bridge appears to have been the prototype for a succession of small truss bridges of varying and uncertain dates, but apparently of identical design, taking roads or tramways over the Glamorganshire Canal, including bridges at Capel-y-Craig and Quay Row, Abercanaid, the Hen Tai bridge a little further south, and the Hafod Tanglwys Bridge at Aberfan. Another bridge to this

77 (above left)
The Robertstown Bridge at Aberdare, built in 1811 to carry a tramway.

78 (above right)
Aaron Brute's Bridge at Blaenavon, of *c.*1813.

design, carrying a tramway over a watercourse within the Penydarren works, had been built by 1813.[61] Two further iron bridges of early date have been identified further south on the Glamorganshire Canal: the Pont Haiarn bridge at Goitre-coed, north of Abercynon, was erected before 1814; the bridge near North Road Lock on the edge of Cardiff, known as Lord Bute's Bridge, was an elegant structure of cast iron with a wrought-iron parapet in the Regency style that was demolished in 1949. The Pentyrch Bridge of 1815 across the River Taff at Melingriffith might also be regarded as part of this tradition.[62]

Tramway systems serving ironworks in South Wales proliferated in the early 19th century. Their builders, following the precedent set by Watkin George at Pont-y-Cafnau, in many instances used iron bridges. It is likely that the surviving bridges represent only a small proportion of those constructed. The Robertstown Bridge carried a tramway, serving the Abernant Ironworks and built by George Overton, over the River Cynon. It is a four-rib structure, spanning about 24 ft. (7.2m), bearing the date 1811 on its central parapet member. The bridge now stands in the shadow of the A4059 roundabout north of Aberdare.[63] Aaron Brute's bridge at Blaenavon is an arched structure that carried a tramway leading from an adit driven between 1812 and 1818.[64] At Llanfoist the extension of Hill's Tramroad, opened in 1822, crosses the Brecknock & Abergavenny Canal on a bridge with a cast-iron deck laid on T-section cast-iron beams.[65] Smart's Bridge, adjacent to the Clydach Ironworks has four ribs, springing from stonework set in an iron frame, spans about 25 ft. (7.5m), bears the date 1824, and has Gothic ornamentation suited to the kind of bridge erected in a landscaped park.[66] A bridge built by 1832 that carried Mr. Hill's Tramroad across the River Taff near the Plymouth Iron-works south of Merthyr may have been a pioneering wrought-iron latticework structure.[67]

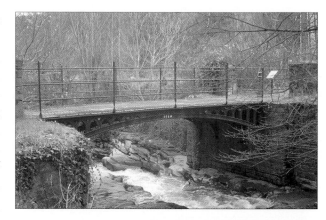

Several constructional techniques in iron developed from Pont-y-Cafnau in the region that became the principal iron-producing area in Britain in the early 19th century. The bridges were of modest dimensions, but they included some of the first iron structures to carry flowing water or iron rails, and early examples of truss construction and series production. This flower-ing of Welsh technology was scarcely recognised outside the Coalfield, apart from its influence on the development of iron trough aqueducts, and curiously there is no evidence before 1820 of the supply by a company in South Wales of an iron bridge to a customer outside the Valleys.

79 (top)
Smart's Bridge at Clydach, a structure in the Gothic style that carried a tramway into the Clydach Ironworks.

80 (above)
The under side of Smart's Bridge, showing the iron frame in the abutment.

Progress at Coalbrookdale

After following the lines of development that stem from Sunderland and Pont-y-Cafnau it is appropriate to return to the Coalbrookdale ironworks, the original source of thinking about cast-iron construction. The capital structure of the Coalbrookdale Company was confused during the early 1790s following the indebtedness and death of Abraham Darby III. After a restructuring of the company's capital in 1797 the Coalbrookdale works was wholly the concern of the Darby family, while the Reynolds family took control of the Madeley Wood and Ketley concerns. William Reynolds was active in the Coalbrookdale works in the early 1790s, offering opinions, for example, on the design of the Trentham Bridge, and appears to have retained an influence there after 1797.[68]

The company's bridge-building business received a two-fold stimulus from the flood on the River Severn that reached its peak on 12 February 1795. At Shrewsbury the quays, timber-yards and warehouses were swept clean of all that was in them, and many graves in the Abbey churchyard fell in. In the Severn Gorge water flowed three feet deep in the rooms of the *Swan*, *White Hart* and *Meadow* inns, and barrels floated out of the cellars. The Shropshire Canal and the Severn were united at Coalport, where the wooden counting house used by the coal-factors sailed away down the river. The keepers of the Madeley Wood furnace were able to extinguish it just before the rising water reached it, ultimately to lie several inches deep in the hearth. The medieval bridge at Buildwas was swept away, and the Preen's Eddy Bridge at Coalport was severely damaged. Two arches of Bridgnorth Bridge collapsed; Bewdley Bridge and Pritchard's bridge at Stourport were damaged beyond repair.[69]

The Iron Bridge survived:

> the noble arch … exulting as it were in the strength of its connected massy ribs, reared its lofty head triumphantly above the mighty torrent, and would have given an undaunted and generous reception to double the quantity; neither huge logs of timber nor parts of houses which came with such mighty force, made any impression. It firmly stood and dauntless braved the storm.[70]

This was an illusory impression, for it was not long after the flood that repairs to the Iron Bridge became necessary, and one of the objectives of the work carried out in 1801-04 was doubtless to relieve the abutments from the pressures of future floods.[71] Nevertheless the Iron Bridge remained, and it was believed, mistakenly, that its survival demonstrated the superiority of iron construction. The flood created simultaneously a market for new bridges, and a perception that they should be of iron.

The Preen's Eddy Bridge, two miles downstream from the Iron Bridge, became an iron bridge as a result of the great flood. The project to build a bridge at Preens Eddy was launched in the autumn of 1775 when the Iron Bridge subscribers were preparing to obtain their act of Parliament. The petition calling for the bridge was presented to the House of Commons on 31 January 1777, and the Act (17 Geo. III c.12) was obtained within two months. Supporters of the project included landowners from Broseley, among them Edward Harries, Edward Blakeway and John Wilkinson, who were also trustees of the Iron Bridge. The leading figure was Daniel Onions, an innkeeper and farmer, father of an ironmaster, and a man accorded some credit for his participation in the construction of the Iron Bridge.[72] The first meeting of trustees was held on 2 May 1777, and a wooden structure of two spans was erected by Robert Palmer (d.1780), a local timber merchant, to the design of William Hayward (d.1782), a Shrewsbury architect who had worked with Thomas Farnolls Pritchard and subsequently with John Gwynn on the English Bridge in Shrewsbury between 1766 and 1774, and on the Severn bridge at Atcham. He designed the bridge that carries the Holyhead Road over the River Tern at Atcham, and died at Henley, while building the bridge over the Thames.[73]

81 A reconstruction drawing of the Preen's Eddy Bridge based on a sketch by Joseph Farington of 1789.

The Preen's Eddy Bridge was completed in the spring of 1780, and was the first to carry traffic over the Severn in the Gorge. A drawing made by Joseph Farington (1747-1821) in 1789 suggests that considerable repairs had already proved necessary, and the bridge was sold in 1791 to a new body of trustees. Edward Blakeway became the principal shareholder, with eight shares, and William Reynolds held five. The bridge was repaired during 1792, but after the flood of February 1795 the central pier was removed, and the wooden superstructure was sustained by a single arch of three cast-iron ribs, each cast in two halves. This hybrid structure had a short life. One of the half-ribs cracked in December 1817, and during the following year it was replaced, two complete outer ribs were added, and the wooden superstructure was replaced with iron bearers and plates, topped by a stone surface, together with a cast-iron parapet bearing the initials of the contractor, John Onions. The scheme was completed by May 1819, and, following the growth of the nearby settlement, which had been fostered during the 1790s by William Reynolds, it came to be known as Coalport Bridge. It remained a toll bridge during the 19th century, but passed to Salop County Council in 1922.[74]

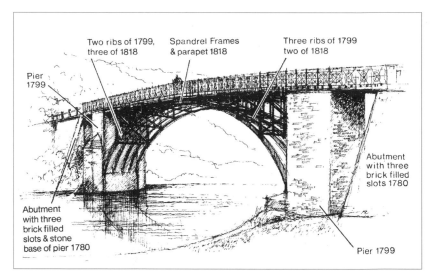

82 The phasing of Coalport Bridge.

The flood also changed the nature of the Severn crossing upstream from the Iron Bridge. The medieval bridge at Buildwas, adjacent to the ruins of the Cistercian abbey, consisted of four short spans with refuges above each of the piers. By the 18th century it was the responsibility of Quarter Sessions and a cause for concern. After toying in 1790 with the prospect of a new bridge, the county authorities decided the following year to spend £1,600 on repairs under the supervision of Thomas Telford, by this time county surveyor. The artist Samuel Ireland recorded the rebuilding of the northernmost arch. Nevertheless, two arches were swept away in the flood of February 1795. The Coalbrookdale Company proposed a replacement similar to the Iron Bridge, but on the advice of William Reynolds and John Wilkinson, the magistrates opted for a design by Telford, his first for an iron structure.[75] It was opened for traffic in 1796.

By July 1795 the ribs for the new Buildwas Bridge were being made at Coalbrookdale, alongside castings for several other bridges. One, designed by John Dodson, carried the Shrewsbury-Much Wenlock road over the Cound Brook. Little is known of the structure, save that it had a span of 40 ft. (12.3m); it was replaced in 1818.[76] Another was an arch of 75 ft. (23m) to cross the River Parrett at Bridgwater, Somerset, which was completed in 1798 at a cost of £4,000. The spandrels were filled with diminishing rings and 'other fanciful figures'. When it

83 *(right)* Coalport
Bridge in the setting
of William
Reynolds's new town
of the 1790s.

84 *(below)* A
drawing of Coalport
Bridge showing its 10
half-ribs, five of 1795
and five of 1818.

85 *(bottom)* The
Cound Arbour
Bridge in Shropshire,
built by the
Coalbrookdale
Company in 1797.

was demolished in 1883, the casting of the
town's coat of arms was placed above the
entrance to the nearby *Royal Clarence Hotel.*[77]
In 1796-7 the Coalbrookdale works produced
castings for John Nash's second bridge over the
Teme at Stanford,[78] and for the Cound Arbour
Bridge, a 36 ft. (11m) structure carrying a lane
over the Cound Brook, that bears the inscription
'Cast at Coalbrookdale 1797', and is perhaps the
oldest iron bridge that remains in use for vehicular traffic, although it has been strengthened
with concrete.[79]

Evidence of the boom in bridge-building at
Coalbrookdale in the mid-1790s comes only
from newspapers, visitors' journals and the
records of customers. A surviving settling book
for the years 1797-1808 shows that the bridges
provided occasional rather than regular business.[80] Two bridges were provided in 1800 to
cross the Kennet & Avon Canal in Bath.[81] In
1806 the company fulfilled an order for the
Bristol Dock Company, including a 10 h.p. steam
engine, and sets of castings for two bridges to
the design of William Jessop. The Harford
Bridge on the road to Bedminster lasted until

1882, while Hill's Bridge, carrying the Bath Road, continued in use until it was hit by a steamer in 1855. Thomas Thomas, who had been involved in the repair work on the Iron Bridge several years earlier, supervised the construction.[82] In 1807 castings weighing 50 tons 10 cwt. for a bridge to be erected in Jamaica were shipped down the Severn from Coalbrookdale.[83]

The company's records from the rest of the 19th century have been destroyed, and evidence of bridge-building activities comes only from other sources. The next known Coalbrookdale bridge was an elliptical arch of 27 ft. (8.4m) span erected in the park at Egginton Hall, Staffordshire, which bears the name 'Coalbrookdale' and the date 1812. The company experienced a surge of orders for bridges after the peace of 1815. The Halfpenny or Wellington Bridge, a graceful single arch of 140 ft. (43m) span that carries pedestrians over the Liffey at Dublin, was designed by John Windsor, a works foreman, and erected in 1816.[84] The librarian to the King of Prussia, who saw the castings being made in 1815, observed that the company was also making a 40 ft. (12.3m) bridge for the estate near Carlow of a Mr Brewing.[85] In 1817 the company completed a substantial bridge in the city that was becoming the symbol of the new industrial age, linking Manchester with the Salford bank of the River Irwell at Strangeways.

86 The Wellington or Halfpenny Bridge in Dublin.

The company's workmen erected the single 120 ft. (37m) arch in only eight months.[86] In 1823 Coalbrookdale produced the castings for Thomas Telford's county bridge over the River Onny at Stokesay.[87] Subsequently the company built two bridges for Staffordshire Quarter Sessions, to the design of Joseph Potter (c.1755-1842), county surveyor, who had worked for Telford on the Harecastle Tunnel. The Chetwynd (or Salter's) Bridge at Alrewas was built in 1824, and the High Bridge at Mavesyn Ridware in 1830.[88] The only other known Coalbrookdale bridge of the 1820s carries the Severn towpath over the mouth of the Borle Brook near Highley, and is documented only by the inscription 'Coalbrookdale Company 1828'.

Subsequently the Coalbrookdale Company built several monumental cast-iron arched railway bridges across the Severn, the Belvidere Bridge of 1849 in Shrewsbury (SJ 520125), the Albert Edward Bridge at the western end of the Severn Gorge (SJ 661038) and the Royal Victoria Bridge near Arley (SO 766793), both of 1862. Nevertheless, the company that was one of two principal suppliers of castings from bridges in the 1790s, was one amongst many by 1830, and it seems not to have built any significant railway bridges in distant parts of Britain. It was only when the Simpson family, former employees of the company, took over the Horsehay Works from 1886 that the Coalbrookdale Coalfield once more began to supply bridges throughout Britain and indeed throughout the world.

Thomas Telford and William Hazledine

Thomas Telford, 30 years of age, a skilled mason and an aspiring architect, settled in Shropshire in 1786 or 1787 with a commission to rebuild Shrewsbury Castle as an appropriate setting for the realisation of the political ambitions of his patron and fellow Scot William Pulteney (1729-1805). He soon gained other commissions and from 1788 was employed as county surveyor of bridges, for which he had no regular salary but received a percentage of each contract for which he was responsible.[89] His appointment to succeed Josiah Clowes as engineer of the Shrewsbury Canal, and the damage caused by the flood of February 1795, provided him with the opportunity to build the Longdon Aqueduct in iron, and to produce a design that appears to have been wholly his own for a new bridge at Buildwas. In 1793 he became general agent to the Ellesmere Canal, and in due course took responsibility for the erection of the Chirk and Pontcysyllte aqueducts.[90]

Telford's design for Buildwas was for a structure radically different from the Iron Bridge, based on the wooden bridge erected in 1754 over the Rhine at Schaffhausen in Switzerland by the brothers Grubenmann, and destroyed by the French army in 1799.[91] The outer ribs rose to the top of the parapet railings and were connected with the lower ribs by dovetailed king posts, thus avoiding too great an elevation of the roadway. The arch, spanning 130 ft. (40m), used 170 tons of iron compared with 378 tons in the Iron Bridge. The cost, over £6,000, proved greater than had been expected. The masonry contractors went bankrupt and the Coalbrookdale Company lost over £700 on the project.[92]

Buildwas Bridge stood at a spot where the banks of the Severn are unstable and was subject to damaging pressures throughout its existence. In 1819 the spandrel-boxes were filled with ballast in an attempt to increase the outward thrust of the arch on to its slipping abutments. Sir John Fowler (1817-98) reported in 1888 that the condition of the bridge needed no special action, but by 1905 Salop County Council found it necessary to replace Telford's iron arch with a Pratt truss, resting on rollers, and later slides, at the north end to allow for earth pressure against the abutments. After many adjustments, the truss was replaced in 1992. The stone abutments and iron base plates of Telford's bridge remain, and a portion of one of the ribs bearing the date 1796 is displayed at the north end of the new structure.[93]

Buildwas Bridge and the Longdon Aqueduct were completed in 1796. In the decade that followed Telford was involved in the construction of the Ellesmere Canal, and of the two great aqueducts in particular. He built no other iron bridges, but he was involved in discussions about a new London Bridge. The proposal arose from congestion in the port of London, where all ocean-going ships were loaded and unloaded on riverside quays downstream from the ancient London Bridge. One solution was the construction of wet docks, and Acts of Parliament enabled William Jessop to begin building the West India Docks in 1800, and John Rennie to start work on the London Docks in 1801. Sir Frederick Morton Eden (1766-1809) proposed that a new London Bridge, allowing the passage of ships of up to 200 tons, could extend the port as far as Blackfriars. A parliamentary select committee was set up to review the situation. Thomas Wilson put forward a design for a three-arch structure, while Telford in collaboration with James Douglass published alternative proposals for a three-arch or a five-arch bridge. William Jessop raised the possibility of a single arch, and in the autumn of 1800 Telford and Douglass produced a design for such a bridge, drawing attention to it by the publication of a superb engraving. Telford devoted much time in 1800-01 to calculations relating to the form of the ribs and the spandrel frames, which influenced the design of his subsequent iron bridges. In April 1801 the select committee sought the views of authorities on structural matters, including John Wilkinson, William Reynolds, James Watt (1736-1819), William Jessop, John Rennie, Charles Bage, designer of the Ditherington flax mill, and Charles Hutton (1737-1823) of the Royal Military Academy, Woolwich, author of the first pamphlet on iron bridges. The project was not pursued. While the arch may theoretically have been feasible, it would have been difficult to establish secure abutments, a problem that had been highlighted by the failure of Wilson's bridge at Staines. A high-level bridge would also have required access routes, that would have involved disruption of densely inhabited parts of the capital. Furthermore the success of the wet docks removed the impetus for extending the port upstream, and when London Bridge was replaced in 1831 it was by the masonry bridge designed by Sir John Rennie and completed by his son.[94]

The London Bridge enquiry is evidence of Telford's involvement in the scientific appraisal of iron structures. His pocket memorandum book records that experiments were made on the ribs of Buildwas Bridge, and on the vertical columns of the Longdon aqueduct. The results of the latter were utilised by Charles Bage in the design of the iron-framed Ditherington flax mill. John Banks, the peripatetic lecturer on scientific subjects, employee of the Yorkshire iron-founders, Aydon & Elwell, and designer of the elliptical cast-beam for steam engines, described experiments made to test the strength of cast iron in an essay published in 1803. Some were carried out at Ketley in March 1795, and were probably concerned with the Longdon aqueduct. Others were made at Coalbrook-dale in April 1795. One was on an iron rib with a span of 29 ft. 6 in. (9m), 11 inches (0.28m) high in the centre, which carried a load of 99 cwt. but broke when its supporting abutments were removed. Another was on a rib spanning 29 ft. 3 in. (9m) that was a segment of a circle reaching a height of three feet (0.92m) in the centre. This supported a load of five tons, but similarly broke when the abutments were removed. These experiments, known also to Telford, convinced Banks of the importance of accommodating the lateral thrusts exerted by cast-iron arches by building abutments strong enough to contain them. Doubtless the Coalbrookdale partners absorbed this lesson, for, in contrast to the record of Thomas Wilson and Walkers, none of their bridges collapsed through design faults. By 1800 engineers and ironfounders were no longer using the empirical methods of the builders of the Iron Bridge, but were making calculations and testing to destruction the components they intended to use. The Reynoldses specifically requested Banks to make known the results of the Ketley tests, and the readership that he enjoyed shows how such knowledge could be spread.

Subscribers for one of his pamphlets in 1795 included John Dalton (1766-1844), Sir Robert Peel (1750-1840), Joseph Priestley, John Rastrick, John Rennie and John Wilkinson.[95] Analysis of the structural properties of iron was developed in the publications of Charles Hutton in 1812, and Thomas Tredgold in 1824, and later in the work of Eaton Hodgkinson (1789-1861) and William Fairbairn (1789-1864).[96] Understanding grew slowly, but the principle of scientific enquiry was already established by 1800-01 and Telford was one of those who upheld it.

Telford's thinking on iron bridges was aided and influenced by the views of William Hazledine (1763-1840), the ironfounder who cast the arches and the trough for Pontcysyllte. Hazledine, son of a millwright, grew up in the Shropshire iron trade, and was established as a millwright in Shrewsbury by 1789, shortly after Telford's arrival in the town. Within a few years he established a foundry in Coleham, on the banks of the Severn, where he cast the frame of the Ditherington flax mill. In the late 1790s he leased the Plas Kynaston estate near Wrexham, and built the ironworks that provided the ironwork for Pontcysyllte. He also worked Upton Forge, four miles east of Shrewsbury, and about 1817 leased the Calcutts Ironworks in the Ironbridge Gorge.[97]

Pontcysyllte was opened in 1805. Neither Hazledine nor Telford appears to have been concerned with the construction of another iron bridge for another six years, but by 1811 they were using two basic designs that, with modifications, they continued to employ for the remainder of their working lives. The first, for structures that spanned no more than about 100 ft. (31m), consisted of pairs of half-ribs, castings that incorporated ribs, spandrel-frames and deck-bearers in a grid pattern, that rested in stone abutments splayed out from the base. The first erected on this principle, a county bridge across the Rea Brook at Meole Brace, Shrewsbury, was a 55 ft. (17m) structure, whose castings were provided by Hazledine in 1811. Telford, as county surveyor, was responsible for the bridge, but Thomas Stanton, who succeeded him as general agent to the Ellesmere Canal Co. and operated from the company office, did the detailed design, as he did for most of Telford's county bridges from 1805.[98] Meole Brace Bridge lasted until 1933 when the construction of the first Shrewsbury by-pass necessitated its removal. Hazledine supplied the ironwork in 1812 for a similar bridge of 28 ft. (8.6m) span at Long Mill near Wellington, that lasted until 1883. In 1812-13 a 31 ft. (9.6m) span bridge was built at Aston Cantlop, that is now the only Telford cast-iron arch bridge in its original condition. Responsibility for the bridge, on the road from Shrewsbury to Acton Burnell, was only assumed by Quarter Sessions after it had been completed, so that the designer and contractor are undocumented. In 1818 the same basic design was used for a 55 ft. (17m) iron arch that replaced John Dodson's bridge of 1795 at Cound. This was a county bridge inscribed with Telford's name, for which Hazledine provided the castings. The inner ribs were

87 Aston Cantlop Bridge, Shropshire.

encased in concrete in the 1920s. It was replaced in 1967, and the outer ribs now form a footbridge in the centre of Telford.[99]

The largest and most celebrated bridge of this pattern is the least easily recognised as such, since its outer ribs are gloriously ornamented with iron roses, shamrocks, leeks and thistles, symbols of a road from London to Dublin through Wales built by a Scotsman. The Waterloo Bridge at Betws-y-Coed was constructed on one of the stretches of road to which Telford

gave priority after his appointment as engineer to the Holyhead Road Commission in 1815. The bridge spans 105 ft. (32.3m) and was sensitively rebuilt by Mouchel & Partners in 1923, with cantilevered footpaths and the central ribs encased in concrete. The inscription 'This arch was constructed in the same year the Battle of Waterloo was fought' is well-known but inaccurate. It was not until August 1816 that the castings, made at Plas Kynaston, were shipped from Chester, presumably to the head of navigation on the River Conwy. The bridge bears the names of William Hazledine and William Stuttle (d. 1827), his foreman.[100]

Telford employed this pattern of bridge through the 1820s. The Coalbrookdale Company provided the castings for his 55 ft. (17m) county bridge at Stokesay in 1823. The bridge remained in use until 1965, and a half-rib is displayed at Ironbridge. The Icknield Street Bridge across the Birmingham Canal, now demolished, was completed in 1828, and was chosen as an illustration in Telford's *Autobiography*.[101] Telford built several similar bridges for the company. The Engine Arm aqueduct on the Birmingham Canal, a structure that for flamboyance ranks with the Waterloo Bridge, follows the same basic design.

Larger bridges by Telford and Hazledine had ribs made up from segments, with the deck-bearers supported by vertical or inclined struts in the spandrels. The rib and spandrel strut castings were designed to avoid weaknesses caused by uneven cooling in the moulds, while the rib-segments were flanged to facilitate joining. The first of the kind was built at Bonar in 1811-12, uniting the counties of Ross and Sutherland, across the Dornoch Firth. Telford planned two iron spans of 150 ft. (46.2m), but the foundations proved less secure than had been predicted, and a three-span structure was built by William Stuttle, with only the longest 150 ft. span in iron. The castings were made at Plas Kynaston, where they were displayed in May 1812, before despatch by the Ellesmere Canal over Pontcysyllte to the port of Chester. The bridge was demolished after the main span cracked in January 1892. The successor had a shorter life than Telford's bridge. An elegant bowstring truss replaced it in 1973.[102] While Bonar Bridge was under construction, Telford put forward plans for cast-iron arched bridges across the Menai Straits, one of them for a 500 ft. (154m) single span, with nine ribs, each cast in 23 pieces. This was essentially an enlarged version of Bonar Bridge. The Holyhead Road project was delayed, and Telford never came near to achieving such a span with a cast-iron arch.[103]

88 *(above)* The Waterloo Bridge at Betws-y-Coed.

89 The bridge at Eaton Hall, Cheshire, constructed by William Hazledine in 1824.

90 Thomas Telford's Mythe Bridge across the River Severn at Tewkesbury.

91 Craigellachie Bridge.

Telford and Hazledine's next segmental arch links Banffshire with Moray across the River Spey at Craigellachie and bears the date 1814. Again the span was 150 ft. (42.6m), achieved by an arch of four ribs each made up of seven segments, cast at Plas Kynaston, and erected by William Stuttle. Telford created a Romantic image for the bridge by constructing pairs of crenellated towers at each end. Robert Southey (1774-1843) described it as 'something like a spider's web in the air'. The bridge was sensitively restored in the 20th century.[104] The third bridge of this type was erected in 1820 over the River Esk north of Carlisle, about two miles south of the Scottish border on the road to Glasgow. It had one span of 150 ft. (46.2m), flanked by two of 105 ft. (32.3m), and Hazledine again supplied the castings. It

was declared unsafe in 1911, and demolished five years later. Its nameplate and a lamp bracket are held in Tullie House Museum, Carlisle.[105]

Together or separately, Telford and Hazledine built more bridges with segmental iron arches during the 1820s. In 1824 Hazledine supplied castings for a 150 ft. (46.2m) arch across the River Dee on the Eaton Hall estate near Chester, for Robert, 2nd Earl Grosvenor (1767-1845). This, the most ambitious parkland iron bridge, bears the names of its builders: 'William Hazledine, Contractor; William Stuttle, Clerk of Works, William Stuttle, Junr., Founder; William Crosley, Surveyor'. Telford had links as a consultant with the three-span iron bridge at Windsor (TQ 986772) opened in 1823. It was designed by Charles Hollis who was also responsible for the iron bridge over the River Wye at Bigsweir (SO 539051), opened in 1827.

In 1823 Telford began the construction of the Mythe Bridge over the Severn at Tewkesbury, made up of six ribs, assembled from segments cast at the Coleham foundry from the best Shropshire No.2 iron. The span is 170 ft. (42.4m), the longest of Telford's cast-iron arches. It was completed in April 1826 at a cost of £14,500, of which the ironwork cost £4,500. The Gothic land arches, the trefoil detailing on the stonework, and the curious tollhouse combine with the elegant lines of the arch to make the Mythe Bridge a product of the Romantic Movement that ranks with Pontcysyllte and Craigellachie. Hazledine's construction team moved upstream from Tewkesbury to Holt Fleet, Worcestershire, where a 150 ft. (46.2m) iron arch

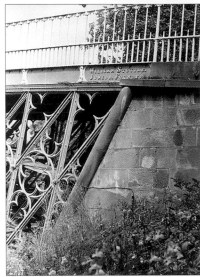

to Telford's design was completed in 1827. Many of the components of these two great bridges over the Severn were identical with those in the Scottish bridges.[106]

Hazledine supplied the ironwork, probably from the Calcutts Ironworks, for the five spans of the bridge spanning the estuary of the River Plym at Laira east of Plymouth, a private venture of John Parker, 1st Earl of Morley (1772-1840), designed by James Meadows Rendel (1799-1856), a civil engineer who had worked with Telford until he set up his own practice in Plymouth in 1822. An Act of Parliament (4 Geo.IV c.10) was obtained in 1823, but construction of the ironwork did not begin until the autumn of 1826. William Stuttle was taken ill while supervising the erection of the bridge, and died on 23 February 1827, his task passing to his son. The bridge opened on 14 July 1827, passed into the ownership of Plymouth Corporation in 1897, and was demolished in 1962.[107] In 1827 Hazledine provided the castings for the Cleveland Bridge at Bath, spanning 110 ft. (33.9m), with seven ribs, each made up of five segments. Its width, over 36 ft. (11.1m), and its tollhouses in the classical style, make it an imposing structure. Telford's last major iron bridge was the Galton Bridge over the Smethwick cutting on the new line of the Birmingham Canal, erected in 1829 with castings for a 150 ft. (46.2m) span supplied by the Horseley Company.[108] Telford died in 1834; Hazledine in 1840. The last iron bridge on which they collaborated appears to have been the Stretton Aqueduct of 1832 on the Birmingham & Liverpool Junction Canal. Already during the 1830s there were signs that Hazledine's foundries were declining and none of them provided castings for any substantial bridge after his death. Nevertheless between 1811 and 1834 Hazledine's association with Telford had made him the leading supplier of iron bridges in Great Britain.[109]

William's brother John Hazledine (1760-1810) was also concerned with bridge-building. He is best-known as a mechanical engineer, whose foundry in Bridgnorth built engines for Richard Trevithick (1771-1833). John Urpeth Rastrick (1780-1856) succeeded him as managing partner for about five years between 1811 and 1816. John Hazledine is credited with the design of the bridge completed about 1808 to replace, somewhat belatedly, Pritchard's bridge at Stourport that had been damaged in the flood of 1795. Estimates for an iron arch to be erected on stone abutments already being built were sought in April 1802, but it was not for another year that the trustees considered the tenders that had been put forward. Hazledine constructed a single arch, made up of half-ribs and spanning 165 ft. (51m). The

92 The inscription in the classical style recording the role of William Hazledine as contractor and ironfounder for the Cleveland Bridge at Bath.

93 The inscription in the Gothic style recording the role of William Stuttle, Junior, as iron founder for the bridge at Eaton Hall, Cheshire.

94 The bridge over the River Wye at Chepstow.

superstructure was wooden, but was replaced by J.U.Rastrick with iron deck plates in 1821. The present cast-iron arch replaced Hazledine's bridge in 1870.[110] The Bridgnorth foundry provided the castings for the five-arch bridge across the Wye at Chepstow, linking Monmouthshire with Gloucestershire, which bears the date 1816. John Rennie produced plans for the bridge in 1812, and contractors were sought in 1813 to build stone piers and iron arches 'according to Mr. Rennie's plans and specifications'. The construction was supervised by J.U. Rastrick, who was seeking barge-owners to bring stone for the project early in 1815. Whether the design of the bridge as built was Rennie's or Rastrick's remains uncertain. The bridge, strengthened with steel and concrete since 1889, remains in use.[111]

Rennie, Outram and Butterley

The place of iron bridges in the context of civil engineering in the opening decades of the 19th century is further illustrated by the careers of two other engineers and by the progress of the company in which one was a partner. John Rennie was born near Edinburgh, and worked as a millwright before studying at Edinburgh University between 1780 and 1783. He was offered employment by Boulton & Watt and, after erecting the Watt steam engine at the Albion Mills in London, established his own practice in the capital. He was subsequently a consultant on many civil as well as mechanical engineering projects, and wrote about structural theory. As early as 1791 he produced designs that were never realised for iron bridges on the island of Nevis. The same year he was appointed engineer of the Kennet & Avon Canal, and in this capacity was responsible in 1800 for the iron bridges in Sydney Gardens, Bath, although he did not design them. He was consulted after the collapse of Wilson's bridge at Staines in 1803. In 1804 he ordered iron swing bridges for the London Docks, and in 1809 designed a similar structure at Leith, as well as a parkland bridge at Brentwood, Essex.

95 One of the two bridges supplied by the Coalbrookdale Company in 1800 to cross the Kennet & Avon Canal in Sydney Gardens, Bath.

Rennie's first involvement with a major iron bridge was at Boston in 1802-8. He was responsible from 1801 for the drainage of the East, West and Wildmore fens, an area of more than 40,000 acres (16,200 ha) in the vicinity of Boston, and in 1811 built three elegant footbridges crossing the fen drains, of which two survive. The castings were supplied by the Butterley Company, whose name they bear. His other designs included a bridge for Lucknow, cast by Butterley and despatched to India in 1816, although its construction was delayed, a bridge that was erected at Naples, and possibly the bridge at Chepstow. Rennie's principal structure in iron was Southwark Bridge, designed in 1811 and opened to traffic in 1819. Its central span of 240 ft. (74m), the longest cast-iron arch erected in Britain, was flanked by two arches of 210 ft. (64.7m). Steep gradients restricted its usefulness, and it was demolished in 1913, its replacement opening in 1921. For all his involvement with iron construction, Rennie is best remembered as a builder of stone bridges and aqueducts, as the designer of the Waterloo Bridge in London, the Lune Aqueduct at Lancaster and the Dundas Aqueduct at Bath. Civil engineers were well aware of the potential of iron arches, but circumstances often dictated that masonry was the preferable option.[112]

Southwark Bridge marked the end of more than two decades of bridge-building by Walkers' ironworks at Rotherham, where the 240 ft. arch was exhibited in the closing weeks of 1815. Some of the work was sub-contracted to the Gospel End Ironworks, Tipton, that Walkers subsequently took over.[113]

The Butterley Company, whose deed of partnership was sealed in December 1792, followed the pattern of the ironworking companies in Shropshire. Its partners leased land in the Erewash Valley in Derbyshire for mining coal and iron ore and for quarrying limestone, produced pig iron in blast furnaces and subsequently wrought iron at forges, and used their castings and forging to supply bridges and other structures. The most active partner in the company, Benjamin Outram, was himself a civil engineer, who was responsible for the Holmes Aqueduct in 1796, and recommended the use of iron in the Stalybridge aqueduct five years later. Another partner was William Jessop, who employed Butterley rails in the construction of the Croydon, Merstham & Godstone Iron Railway completed in 1805. Jessop spent his last years before his death in 1814 at nearby Butterley Hall, and four of his sons worked for the Company.[114]

It was probably through Jessop's activities at Croydon that the Butterley Company came to build the Hack Bridge that crossed the River Wandle at Carshalton. The company ledger shows payments relating to the bridge during 1805 and 1806. The bridge spanned about 40 ft. (12.3m), each rib consisting of about 30 voussoirs, in a form that was probably derived from Thomas Wilson's bridges. The Hack Bridge was replaced by a concrete structure that bears the date 1914.[115]

The Butterley Company provided the castings for John Rennie's three bridges over the fen drains in the Boston area, for some of those for the Magdalene Bridge in Cambridge of 1823, and for the bridge at Lucknow. The company also provided iron for James Walker's Vauxhall Bridge in London, opened in 1816. The bridge had nine spans of 78 ft. (24m), and remained in use until 1898.[116]

James Walker (1781-1862) figures prominently in the history of iron bridges in the capital. In 1809 he secured the contract to design a bridge to cross the River Lea near the East India Docks. The bridge, probably completed in 1812 or 1813, comprised a series of five semi-circular arches springing from columnar piers. In

96 The iron bridge crossing a Fenland drain at Cowbridge near Boston, built in 1811, designed by John Rennie and cast by the Butterley Company.

97 The Butterley Co. inscription on John Rennie's bridge near the Maud Foster Mill in Boston, Lincolnshire.

was frequently damaged by boats and was succeeded by a new bridge in 1896.[117] Walker also designed the Haw Bridge (SO 844278), built in 1824-5 that crossed the Severn upstream from Gloucester until it was hit by an oil barge in 1958.

Docks and Waterways

Many small iron bridges were built on and around canals and navigable rivers, and in the wet dock complexes that from 1800 were constructed in most of the principal British ports. Iron had advantages over traditional methods of construction. Relatively flat arches offered greater clearance for boats passing beneath. Such structures could be erected quickly, and could be multiplied in series production. Loadings on most bridges of this kind were likely to be insubstantial. The use of small iron truss bridges on the Glamorganshire Canal in the years after 1800 has been discussed above.

The earliest bridges of this kind were possibly the cantilevered 'split' or 'divided' structures that serve as turnover and accommodation bridges on the Staffordshire & Worcestershire Canal, which may even pre-date the Iron Bridge. The canal, opened in 1772, extends for 46 miles (74 km.) from Great Heywood near Stafford to Stourport on the Severn. James Brindley (1716-72) settled its route, but his assistants Samuel Simcock and Thomas Dadford were responsible for the detailed design and construction. The cast-iron cantilevered bridges, extending

98 The split bridge at Marsh Lock near Swindon (Staffs.) on the Staffordshire & Worcestershire Canal.

from masonry abutments, with gaps between the two halves allowing tow-ropes to be slipped through, have long been recognised as a feature of the canal, but the waterway lacks a detailed history and their origin has not been investigated. Five split footbridges remain on the canal. Bridge No.12 by Cauldwall Lock, Kidderminster, which has now been replaced, was wide enough to take vehicles.[118] The Stourbridge Canal, opened in 1779, joined the Staffordshire and Worcestershire at Stewponey, and included at least one cantilevered split

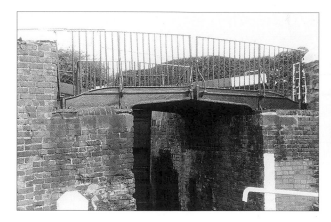

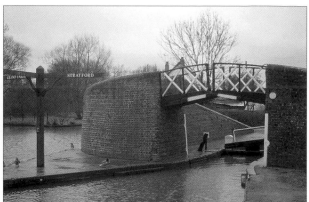

bridge, by the locks at Wordsley.[119] It is not currently possible to be certain whether the split bridges are original features of the Staffordshire & Worcester and Stourbridge canals, but archaeological study could establish whether this is likely.

Similar cantilevered bridges were built on the Stratford Canal. There are two on the Lapworth lock flight, on the section of the canal from King's Norton to Kingswood Junction that was opened in 1802, and many more on the section from Kingswood to Stratford that was built under the direction of William Whitmore between 1812 and 1816.[120]

Curiosities amongst canal bridges are three on the Ellesmere Canal, built to Telford's design or with his approval. The bridges appear to be conventional masonry arches, but iron ribs sustained timber baulks, which supported filling material on which the road was laid. One carries the former turnpike road from Oswestry over the canal at Chirk Bank, and has been rebuilt as a mass concrete structure without altering its appearance. The others are at Trevor Basin on the north side of Pontcysyllte.[121]

Several channel bridges of cast iron were built on the part of the Shrewsbury Canal which was completed before the death of Josiah Clowes. There were at least four, one at Wrockwardine Wood (SJ 699126), one at Wombridge (SJ 689123), one at Longdon-on-Tern (SJ 615156) near the aqueduct, and one at the wharf at Long Lane (SJ 635156) that has been re-located by the Ironbridge Gorge Museum at Coalport (SJ 695025).

The earliest iron bridges over canals that can be precisely dated were a pair, each spanning 23 ft. (7m), that cross the Kennet & Avon Canal in Sydney Gardens, Bath, built in 1800 at a cost of £456 for the two. The designs were chosen from several sent by the Coalbrookdale Company to the proprietors of the Sydney Gardens pleasure-grounds, who included George Stothert (1755-1818), an ironmonger. Subsequently Stothert set up his own foundry, and in 1815 he cast two further iron bridges that cross the canal in Bath.[122]

99 (*top left*) The split bridge at Wordsley on the Stourbridge Canal.

100 (*top right*) The split bridge at Kingswood at the beginning of the southern section of the Stratford Canal.

101 (*above*) The Quay Bridge across the River Avon at Tewkesbury.

John Rennie was responsible for the installation of five cast-iron swivel bridges in the London group of docks between 1804 and 1819, and for a bridge at East Old Dock, Leith, while Telford installed a 45 ft. (13.9m) cast-iron turning bridge over the entrance lock of St Katharine's Dock. The Horseley Company supplied similar bridges for the East India Docks in 1816. The principal suppliers of bridges of this kind in the first two decades of the 19th century appear to have been Aydon & Elwell of the Shelf Ironworks, Bradford, who may have produced as many as twenty between 1804 and 1824.[123]

The proprietors and engineers of inland waterways used iron bridges in many ways. John Rennie's elegant footbridges over the fen drains near Boston can be regarded as structures of this type. The trustees of the towpath along the River

102 (below) The iron bridge built for the Wiltshire & Berkshire Canal at Abingdon, Berkshire, in 1824.

103 Gallows Bridge on the Brentford line of the Grand Junction Canal built by the Horseley Co. in 1820.

Severn were responsible for two bridges over the mouths of tributaries during the 1820s, that over the Mor Brook being cast by the foundry of John Onions in 1824, and that over the Borle Brook by the Coalbrookdale Company in 1828. A bridge of 1811, cast at the foundry of William Evans at Paulton, crossed the Somerset Coal Canal at Monkton Combe, and a century later was re-erected to span the Limpley Stoke-Camerton railway. It was demolished in 1960, but one of its inscribed plaques is preserved at the nearby school. The Quay Bridge at Tewkesbury, built in 1822, spans the Avon and for a time carried railway tracks. It was restored in 2001 and bears the weight of trucks serving the adjacent flour mills. The Wiltshire & Berkshire Canal Company built a bridge, cast by Acraman's foundry of Bristol in 1824, across the River Ock at its confluence with the Thames at Abingdon.[124] Thomas Telford noted in 1813 that he and William Jessop had decided to use iron bridges for turnover and accommodation purposes on the Caledonian Canal. Just one of the bridges they built, a 30 ft. (9.5m) structure at Moy, cast at Plas Kynaston in 1812, remains in use.[125]

The Horseley Company constructed many iron bridges across canals. A road bridge crosses the Wyrley & Essington Canal adjacent to the site where the Pelsall Ironworks flourished between 1832 and 1888, on the edge of Pelsall North Common by the *Free Trade* public house. It has six ribs, bears the inscription 'Horseley Coal & Iron Co. 1824', and has wing walls composed largely of iron slag. The best-known Horseley Co. bridges are footbridges across junctions. Each bridge consists of two main castings incorporating the handrail sections, which are joined by central locking plates, the decks being formed of cast-iron flanged plates. Many are ornamented with Gothic quatrefoils or crosses. The prototype appears

to have been Gallows Bridge on the Grand Junction Canal near Brentford that bears the date 1820.[126] The majority of such bridges were built for the Birmingham Canal Navigation between 1824 and 1836, when the company replaced earlier wooden swivel and draw-bridges. Not all the replacements were iron structures – many were conventional brick arches – but eight Horseley Company bridges constructed before 1850 have been identified on the Birmingham Canals. The canal company continued to develop its network, and similar bridges, made by Horseley and other Black Country ironworks, were installed on new stretches, at Windmill End near the western portal of the Netherton Tunnel, for example.[127] Horseley supplied bridges for the reconstruction of the northern section of the Oxford Canal carried out under the direction of C.B.Vignoles in the early 1830s. At least five remain in the Rugby area, and two bridges span the old and new lines of the canal at Braunston.[128]

104 (top left) Pelsall Works Bridge, built by the Horseley Company across the Wyrley & Essington Canal in 1824, next to the site where the Pelsall Ironworks was established eight years later.

105 (top right) A Horseley Company footbridge carrying the new line of the Oxford Canal, completed in 1834, over a junction with a by-passed loop of the old line, at Cathiron, near Rugby.

106 (above) A Horseley Company footbridge of 1828 at Smethwick Junction on the Birmingham Canal Navigation.

Parkland and Estate Bridges

The parkland bridge, utilising the decorative properties of iron to create an aesthetically pleasing feature of a planned landscape, can be regarded as a particular type of iron bridge. Robert Southey disliked such structures commenting 'to look at these iron bridges which are bespoken at the foundries, you would actually suppose that the architect had studied at the confectioner's, and borrowed his ornaments from the sugar temples of a dessert'.[129] Some bridges of this type were built on minor country roads, either by subscription or by the philanthropy of an individual landowner. Some canal bridges, like those in Bath, and even the tramway bridge at Clydach, might merit inclusion in this category. The earliest documented bridge designed to ornament a park is the wrought-iron structure at Kirklees,[130] and wrought-iron bridges fabricated by blacksmiths were erected on several great estates. John Busch, the landscape architect who was responsible for building iron bridges at Tsarskoe Selo, settled in 1789 at Syon Park, Isleworth, on the estate of Hugh Percy, 2nd Duke of Northumberland (1742-1817). He doubtless had some influence on the three wrought-iron bridges in the park, designed in 1790 by the architect James Wyatt (1746-1843), of which one three-span structure remains. In 1812 a wrought-iron bridge of three spans was built on another estate of the Duke of Northumberland, at Hulne Park, Alnwick.[131] Several wrought-iron bridges designed by a Ledbury architect, T. Holland, and made by a Mr Sealy, probably a local blacksmith, were built at Eastnor Castle, Herefordshire in the 1820s.[132]

The Trentham and Upper Furnace Pool bridges show the involvement of the Coalbrookdale Company with cast-iron parkland bridges in the 1790s, and a letter to a Norfolk landowner of December 1795 offers to provide a bridge of four arches for £1,470, delivered to King's Lynn, ready for erection.[133] Two early parkland bridges are of particular technological interest. Stratfield Saye is the only Thomas Wilson bridge to remain in its original condition. The bridge at Culford House, Suffolk, appears to follow the patent of Samuel Wyatt (1738-1807) for structures with hollow iron ribs. Samuel Wyatt regarded himself as an 'engineer-architect', and amongst his acquaintances were Matthew Boulton, James Watt and Josiah Wedgwood. Wyatt's brother, the architect James Wyatt, directed alterations at Culford Hall, home of Charles, 1st Marquess of Cornwallis (1738-1805), in the 1790s. The bridge dates from 1803, spans 60 ft. (28 m), and has six ribs, each consisting of five segments, with a stone parapet. The Gateshead foundry of William Hawks & Son provided the castings.[134]

This is a category of bridge for which records are certainly incomplete, and further examples are likely to come to notice in the future. John Rennie's Rochetts Bridge at Brentwood, Essex, built in 1809 for John Jervis, 1st Earl of St Vincent (1735-1823) was identified through the Historic Engineering Works project. A small iron bridge at Dolforgan Hall, Kerry, built between 1807 and 1818, came to official attention in 1996. It consists of four ribs, each in two sections, bolted at the centre, with open ring spandrels, and a timber deck.[135] Only

107 (below) One of the iron bridges in the park of the Empress Catherine the Great at Tsarskoe Selo (or Pushkin) near St Petersburg.

108 (bottom left) The bridge at Syon Park, Brentford, probably built c.1790, under the direction of John Busch, who had been responsible for the iron bridges at Tsarskoe Selo.

109 (bottom right) The iron bridge at Culford, Suffolk.

inscriptions reveal that the elliptical arch at Egginton Hall, Staffordshire, was cast by the Coalbrookdale Company in 1812, and that the three-rib bridge over the River Goyt at the northern entrance to Brabyn's Park, Marple was supplied by the Salford Ironworks in the following year. The two ornamental bridges in the grounds of Shugborough Hall were built in 1813-14, with castings by John Toye of Rugeley. The 'Red Bridge' of 1814, by the celebrated Chinese House of the 1740s, is a single parabolic arch of two ribs. The 'Blue Bridge' of 1813 consists of three shorter arches. At the approaches to the bridges are iron posts capped with coronets.[136] At Walton Hall near Wakefield an elegant bridge of 1828 crosses a lake to give access to an island on which the mansion of 1767-8 was built by Thomas Waterton, father of Charles Waterton (1782-1865), the naturalist and explorer.

Some bridges in the same style carry minor public roads. At Horsforth, north of Leeds, a four-rib bridge built by John Pollard of Newlay House carries a lane over the River Aire. The bridge which gives its name to the hamlet of Barrington-bridge in Co. Limerick, is a 57 ft. (17.4) span structure, ornamented with trefoils, and inscribed 'Erected in 1818 by Mr. Barrington' and 'J.Doyle, Fecit'. The tasteful structure in the Gothic style, built at Hampton Lucy by the Horseley Company in 1829, was the gift of the rector, the Rev. John Lucy, and carries the road eastwards from the village towards his family's seat at Charlecote Park. The most spectacular structure of this type was the Eglinton Tournament Bridge in Ayrshire, built in 1839, which survived until the 1960s.[137]

110 *(top left)* The iron bridge at the northern end of Brabyn's Park, Marple, Cheshire, built by the Salford Iron Company in 1813.

111 The iron bridge at Egginton, Staffordshire, showing (inset) its inscription.

112 *(below left)* The Red Bridge at Shugborough, Staffordshire.

113 *(below right)* The Blue Bridge at Shugborough, Staffordshire.

115 (*above*) The bridge in the Gothic style built by the Horseley Company at Hampton Lucy, Warwickshire, in 1829.

116 (*left*) The bridge of 1832 near the west door of the Abbey at Bourne, Lincolnshire.

114 (*above*) The bridge that gives its name to Barringtonbridge, Co. Limerick, with (inset) the inscriptions recording the erection of it and the ironfounder who made the castings.

The urban footbridge is a similar type of structure, offering opportunities for ornamentation while requiring to be designed for only modest loadings. The Sheffield bridge of 1795, the Pont des Arts in Paris and the Halfpenny Bridge in Dublin fall into this category. The bridge in the cathedral close at Exeter bears the date 1814 with the names of the officials responsible for its construction. Two small bridges of this kind remain in Bourne, Lincolnshire. The Bourne Eau threads its way mysteriously through and sometimes under the town, and at its southern margin provided a navigable connection to the sea. It emerges into daylight to run parallel with the west front of the abbey of St Peter and St Paul, and is crossed

117 The bridge of 1834 in the Cathedral Close at Exeter.

outside the church by two gated iron bridges giving access to nearby villas. The longer of the two, a two-rib structure with a span of about 15 ft. (4.6m) and about 7 ft. (2.2m) wide, has bosses in the centre inscribed with the letter 'M' and the date 1832. The smaller, only about 20 yards away, has diminishing circles in the spandrels, and could only have served as a footbridge. The iron-arched viaduct is a sub-species of the urban bridge, of which there are two notable examples. The Spa Bridge at Scarborough consists of four arches of 66 ft. 6 in. (20.5m) span, on stone piers, and was built in 1827 to the design of John Outhett, with castings supplied by Stead, Snowden & Buckley. The North Street

118 The iron bridge at Avington Park, Hants., which consists of three T-section, semi-circular cast-iron ribs to which the cast-iron treads and risers of the stairs are attached, together with a sinuous wrought-iron parapet. The bridge is undocumented but thought to be of early 19th-century date.

viaduct at Exeter (SX 917927) consists of six 40 ft. (12.2m) arches cast by Russell & Brown of the Blaina Ironworks in 1834-6.[138]

Bridge-building Regions

Some iron bridges were supplied by companies from distant parts of the country – the Laira bridge by William Hazledine from his ironworks in the Severn Gorge, and Culford by a foundry from Gateshead – but many were provided by local foundries, which created regional concentrations, such as the bridges by Coalbrookdale and Hazledine in Shropshire, the bridges in South Wales, and the

119 (below) The St Miles (or Coslany) Bridge of 1803 in Norwich.

120 (bottom) The Duke's Palace Bridge of 1822 in Norwich, as re-erected over the entrance to the Castle Mall shopping centre in 1992.

profusion of Horseley Company structures on the canals of the Black Country. Between 1780 and 1850 mechanical engineering works, using cupola furnaces for melting pig iron or scrap, machine tools supplied by manufacturers in London or Manchester, and making use of the inland waterway system for their supplies of iron and coke, were established in most English towns of consequence, and some of them occasionally made an iron bridge.

The significance of foundries to urban economies was summarised by a Norfolk newspaper that, when a new bridge in Norwich was contemplated in 1803, commented, 'for the sake of the Norwich foundries [it] ought to be of iron'.[139] East Anglia has a concentration of early iron bridges. Six bridges were built in the Norwich area between 1804 and 1844. The first, now called St Miles' Bridge, designed by James Frost (c.1774-1851) and opened on 15 November 1804, remains in use as a footbridge. The Duke's Palace Bridge of 1822 was dismantled in 1972, but the best ends of its outer ribs have been combined since 1992 to

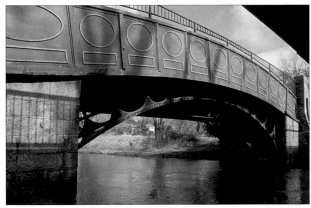

121 Hellesdon Bridge of 1818-19 over the River Wensum on the outskirts of Norwich.

span the Market Avenue entrance to the Castle Mall shopping centre. The other bridges in the city centre have been replaced, but a lane at Hellesdon to the west is carried over the River Wensum by a bridge of three solid ribs, with circular and elliptical perforations, also designed by James Frost. The outer ribs rise to form the parapet, in the manner of a through truss. The town bridge at Thetford dates from 1829, and was cast at the nearby St Nicholas works of the Burrell family, later celebrated for their showmen's engines. Magdalene Bridge, Cambridge, was opened on 12 December 1823, and was designed by Arthur Brown, who was also responsible for the short-lived Carrow Bridge in Norwich of 1810. Benjamin Bevan supervised its construction. The Burtterley Company provided the main structural members but other castings came from the local foundry of Charles Finch. The Ipswich firm of J. & R. Ransome constructed several iron bridges to the design of William Cubitt in the second decade of the 19th century, the Stoke Bridge at Ipswich of 1818, now demolished, the bridges at Brent Eleigh and Clare, which both bear the date 1813, and Saul's Bridge at Witham in Essex which was built in 1814. The three latter bridges have much in common. The spandrels are solid castings, while

122 (above) The bridge at Clare, Suffolk, designed by William Cubitt and cast by J.&.R. Ransome in 1813.

123 (above right) The Town Bridge at Thetford, of 1829.

124 (right) The Gasworks Bridge at Sowerby Bridge, Yorkshire, of 1816.

125 The Newlay Bridge at Horsforth, of 1819, with details of the inscription recording its construction and the inscribed 'keystone'.

126 The bridge of 1828 at Walton Hall, Yorkshire.

the ribs support timbers behind which it appears that there were fillings of rubble stone.[140]

There is also a significant concentration of early iron bridges in West Yorkshire. Aydon & Elwell of the Shelf Ironworks were specialists in the supply of swivel bridges for docks and canals, but also built the Gasworks Bridge at Sowerby Bridge in 1816, and at least two estate bridges, the Mearclough Bridge at Norland of 1816, and the Newlay Bridge at Horsforth of 1819, which still remains. The Milton Ironworks provided castings for several bridges including the Walton Hall Bridge in 1828. Two substantial iron arched bridges of slightly later date remain in Leeds, the Victoria Bridge of 1837-9, and the Crown Point Bridge of 1832, both designed by members of the Leather dynasty of engineers, whose founder, George Leather (1787-1870), was also responsible for the Monk suspension bridge in Leeds of 1827-8, and the Stanley Ferry Aqueduct of 1836-9.[141]

The Iron Arch in Continental Europe

The possibilities of using wrought iron in bridges were much discussed in France in the late 18th century, and some French engineers disparaged the Iron Bridge because it was made of cast iron which they regarded as 'treacherous'. French interest in British foundry techniques related to the manufacture of cannon rather than to the potential structural uses of cast iron. Apart from the bridge at Raincy, the first iron bridges in France were built as a result of the demands of the Consulate in 1800-01, the Pont des Arts over the Seine in the centre of Paris, with its nine spans of 60 ft. (18.5m), which still stands in a modified form, and the Pont d'Austerlitz, designed on a system derived from the Sunderland Bridge, with five spans of 106 ft. (32.6m). Construction commenced in 1802 and it took its name from Napoleon's victory of 1805. The ironwork suffered many fractures and it was replaced with a stone bridge in 1854. A parkland bridge, le pont Napoleon, across the canal de l'Esplanade at Lille in 1809, was the only other iron bridge built in France during the First Empire.[142]

127 The Pont des Arts, Paris.

The building of 11 iron bridges in the park at Tsarskoe Selo in the 1780s was followed by the construction of two further small bridges in St Petersburg itself in the early 1790s. The first substantial iron bridge in Russia, a structure of 63 ft. (19.4m) span, with ribs of 11 segments, was cast by the Scots foundryman Charles Baird (1766-1843) and built near the Tallow Wharf in the city in 1805-06. Another Scot, the architect William Hastie (1755-1832), was responsible for the Police Bridge of 70 ft. (21.6m) span, built in 1806. Ten bridges of this type were built in St Petersburg by 1830, of which eight remain, and the practice of building parkland bridges also continued in Russia.[143]

Apart from the replica of the Coalbrookdale bridge at Worlitz, the first iron bridge in the German-speaking lands was erected in 1796, in Silesia, then part of Prussia, but now in Poland. It was cast at the Malapanew (Malapane) ironworks in Ozimek, probably under the direction of the Scot, John Baildon (1772-1846). It consisted of five ribs spanning 13 m (40 ft.), with the spandrels filled with diminishing circles, and crossed the Strzegomka river (Striegauer Wasser) at Lazany (Laasan), 42 km (27 miles) south-west of Wroclaw (Breslau) on the road to Strzegom (Striegau). Silver and bronze medallions commemorated its construction. The bridge was demolished in the 1930s.[144] The Malapanew ironworks also made the castings for a footbridge over the Kupfergraben in Berlin in 1798, and bridges erected in Potsdam in 1801, Charlottenburg in 1803 and Paretz in 1804. A canal bridge with a span of 22 ft. (6.61m) was produced in 1800 by an ironworks in Gliwice (Gleiwitz), which provided castings for a bridge designed by Karl Friedrich Schinkel (1781-1841) in Berlin in 1819, and during the 1820s advertised its bridge-building capacity by a large-scale model of an arch bridge, parts of which remain on display at the works. In 1822 the Royal Bridge over the city moat in Wroclaw was constructed, spanning 50 ft. (15.08m), with segmental arches, and the spandrels filled with diminishing rings. It remained in use until 1866. The celebrated foundry outside the Oranienburg gate of Berlin, the pioneer in the production of art castings, built several bridges in the city during the 1820s. The ironworks in Hronce (Rohnitz), now in Slovakia, built several small bridges in 1810-13, one of which remained in use until 1962. Parts are displayed in the town.[145]

In Europe, as on a smaller scale in Britain, concentrations of iron bridges arose more from the availability of foundries that could provide castings than from the work of theoreticians. In some continental countries as well as in Britain iron arch bridges in the 1820s became too numerous to itemise. At the same time their limitations were being realised and engineers were turning to other forms of iron structure, the suspension bridge and the truss. The long-term significance of the Iron Bridge is best considered in the context of such developments.

VII

Beyond the Arch

An overview of the history of iron bridge construction in Britain suggests that a peak of optimism was reached in 1800-02, when the London Bridge project was being seriously discussed and Pontycysyllte was under construction. One writer listed 'iron bridges *of any span or height*' amongst the products of the Coalbrookdale ironworks, and a visitor to Walkers' foundry concluded 'no doubt remains that iron bridges will supersede those of stone entirely, as they are put up with a fifth part of the expense, a tenth part of the time, and will be found to be equally if not more durable'.[1] Such optimism was dispelled by the well-publicised collapses of the bridges at Yarm and Staines, and perhaps also by excessive costs. Buildwas cost more than £6,000, compared with an estimate of £3,700, while Burdon was ruined when he had to find £30,000 to complete the Sunderland Bridge. Engineers were also, as a result of experiments and publications described above, coming to realise the limitations of cast iron as a structural material.

The limitations of the cast-iron arch were recognised from 1809-10 when the government prepared to improve the road from London to Holyhead. Reports were commissioned, and the opinions of engineers were sought as to means of bridging the Menai Straits. John Rennie proposed schemes for an iron bridge of three arches, and for a single arch of 450 ft. (139m), which he thought could be built for £268,500. Telford contemplated a larger arch, of 500 ft. (154m) span, with nine ribs, each cast in 23 pieces.[2] The proposals failed to progress because the Holyhead Road Commission was not set up until 1815. Between 1814 and 1817 iron structures were among the designs put forward for a crossing of the Mersey at Runcorn. William Turner of Whitchurch, who had proposed a masonry aqueduct at Pontcysyllte, favoured a 500 ft. (154m) cast-iron arch, while Edward Lloyd Rowland recommended a wrought-iron bridge with a total length of 1,000 ft. (308m). The Runcorn project led Thomas Telford to contemplate suspension bridges, and to make contact with Samuel Brown (1774-1852), builder of the Union Bridge (NT 934511) over the River Tweed at Hutton, Berwickshire, which was opened in 1820.[3]

The suspension bridge by which Thomas Telford carried the Holyhead Road over the Menai Straits (SH 556714) was opened in 1826 and was an affirmation that cast-iron arches 'of any span or height' were not practical propositions. The tides of the Menai Straits, coupled with the Admiralty's demand that there should be clearance for warships beneath any bridge erected there, presented formidable problems to civil engineers. By the time that Telford came to plan the Menai

128 John Rennie's design of 1812 for a three-span iron bridge across the Menai Straits.

129 Thomas Telford's suspension bridge across the Menai Straits, opened on 30 January 1826.

crossing after 1815 he had decided to build a suspension bridge. The Menai Bridge was an iron bridge, but it depended upon the tensile strength of wrought iron, not the strength in compression of cast iron. William Hazledine provided the iron, although most of it came from his forge at Upton Magna and not from his foundries. It spanned 579 ft. (178m), by far the longest suspension bridge up to that time, and a much greater distance than any single iron arch that was ever completed. It was a demonstration of the potential of the suspension bridge at a time when many engineers were interested in its possibilities. Telford was aware that it was a venture beyond the frontiers of proven technology. Its weakness was that the bridge deck was insufficiently stiff. Only a week after the opening six suspension-rods were broken in a storm, and in January 1839 it was so severely damaged that it had to be closed for five days, a period which would have been extended if Telford had not ensured that a supply of spare rods was stored in the house on the Caernarfonshire side of the bridge. Nevertheless Menai provided the pattern that has been followed, with many modifications, in the design of road bridges of lengthy span up to the present day.[4]

The Liverpool & Manchester Railway was opened in 1830, and in the 20 years that followed a network of railways grew up which extended to almost every town of consequence in Britain. The first iron bridge of consequence to carry standard gauge railway tracks was the Gaunless Viaduct at West Auckland (NZ 186266) on the Stockton & Darlington Railway, opened in 1825. It is displayed at the National Railway Museum, York, where it can be seen from passing trains. It was designed by George Stephenson in collaboration with the ironfounders, John and Isaac Burrell of Newcastle-upon-Tyne. Each of the five spans consisted of a pair of fish-belly shaped girders of which the curved members were round, wrought-iron bars. These were held together by five cast-iron uprights and were joined in cast-iron bosses.[5]

Cast iron could readily be pre-fabricated, which enabled railway bridges, particularly small structures crossings country lanes or minor streams, to be built quickly. Many iron-arched or girder bridges of this kind were built. The outer members of many of them remain, bearing the names of such concerns as the Brymbo Ironworks, the Butterley Co. or the Lilleshall Co., masking the strengthening of the structures with steel or concrete. Many such railway bridges of the 1830s and '40s consisted of cast-iron members strengthened with wrought-iron ties of various kinds. One type that was widely used by the early 1840s was the trussed girder in which wrought-iron bars were used to joint and reinforce castings. Robert Stephenson's Dee Bridge (SJ 396659) at Chester, which collapsed while a train was

130 Robert Stephenson's tubular bridge, designed to carry the Chester & Holyhead Road across the estuary of the River Conwy, under construction.

passing across it on 24 May 1847, was a bridge of this kind. Five people were killed in the accident and such was public disquiet that a parliamentary commission was appointed to investigate the disaster. The commission provided a thorough survey of the state of knowledge of iron construction that led to the proliferation on Britain's railways of truss bridges of wrought-iron or of composite wrought-iron and cast-iron construction.[6]

Only one of the heroic structures of the first decades of railway construction, Robert Stephenson's (1803-59) High Level Bridge across the River Tyne between Gateshead and Newcastle (NZ 252637), opened in 1849, was a cast-iron bridge. In this extraordinary structure six cast-iron arches sustained by stone piers carry the deck of the railway bridge, while a road bridge is slung between them.[7] After the Dee Bridge accident, when iron was used in large railway bridges it was usually wrought iron. Robert Stephenson used box girders fabricated from wrought-iron plates in the Britannia Bridge, opened in 1850, that carried the Chester & Holyhead Railway, opened in 1850, across the Menai Straits (SH 542710), and in the structure that carries the same line over the River Conwy (SH 785775).[8] I.K. Brunel (1806-59) devised a form of wrought-iron truss which he first used in a road bridge of 1849 across the entrance lock to the Cumberland Basin in Bristol (ST 570723), and then, on a larger scale, in the railway bridges across the River Wye at Chepstow (ST 539941), completed in 1852, and the Royal Albert Bridge over the River Tamar at Saltash (SX 435588), opened in 1859.[9] Such designs were ingenious but elaborate and expensive, and many more large railway bridges consisted of wrought-iron lattice girders of relatively simple design, like that used by Brunel to carry the Great Western Railway's branch line to Windsor over the River Thames (SU 961773), or William Baker's viaduct of 1863 that lifts the Weaver Junction-Liverpool line of the London & North Western Railway over the River Mersey at Runcorn (SJ 509835). Some of the most spectacular iron railway bridges were the viaducts modelled on T.W. Kennard's bridge at Crumlin (ST 212986) that carried the Taff Vale extension of the Newport, Abergavenny & Hereford Railway over the Ebbw Vale. The lattice beams were supported by iron piers made up of circular cast-iron columns braced with horizontal and diagonal wrought-iron ties. Crumlin Viaduct was opened in 1857, but was demolished in the 1960s, as were Thomas Bouch's Belah (NY 839105) and Deepdale (NY 017162) viaducts, both opened in 1859, on the South Durham & Lancashire Union line between Penrith and Darlington. The viaduct at Meldon (SX 565923) in Devon, built in 1874, still carries ballast trains, and Bennerley Viaduct (SK 470437), that from 1876-7 carried the Derby branch of the Great Northern Railway over the River Erewash, the Midland Railway and the Nottingham Canal, has survived many threats and remains a landmark within a much-altered industrial landscape. Ironically the outstanding cast-iron arched railway bridge of the late 19th century was constructed on the same line. The bridge constructed in 1878 that carried the Great Northern Railway over Friargate (SK 352372) was cast at the local foundry of Andrew Handyside, and bears the city's coat of arms. It was not the last cast-iron arched bridge to be built but it was the last of any consequence, and was completed almost exactly a century after the Iron Bridge.

131 Bennerley Viaduct on the Great Northern Railway's line from Nottingham to Derby (Friargate).

132 The bridge carrying the Great Northern Railway across Friargate in Derby, built by the local ironfounder, Andrew Handyside, in 1878.

The Dee Bridge accident was the cause of much concern amongst the engineering profession and the political classes, but the collapse of Thomas Bouch's Tay Bridge in 1879, the year after its opening, created a public outcry. The precise cause of the collapse remains a matter of debate, but it is clear that the workmanship of the cast-iron piers supporting the wrought-iron girders was faulty, that Bouch had been negligent in his inspection of the castings, as well as in his assessment of the foundations, and that the North British Railway had allowed trains to exceed recommended speed limits. The bridge was replaced by a structure designed by W.H. and C. Barlow and opened in 1887, in which wrought-iron lattice girders were placed between brick piers (NO 395263 – NO 392293). The construction of a bridge designed by Bouch over the Firth of Forth had already commenced in 1879, but the project was suspended after the Tay Bridge disaster. Bouch's plans were discarded, and a new design by John Fowler and Benjamin Baker was adopted using a cantilever structure in mild steel. The new bridge (NT 138782 – NT 131809) was opened in 1890 and became one of the most readily recognised symbols of the British railway system, while steel – in the form of girders, fabricated arches, suspension rods or reinforcing bars in concrete – became the characteristic bridge-building material of the 20th century.

A survey of the first generation of large railway bridges helps to place in perspective the tradition of the cast-iron arch that began on New Year's Day 1781 with the opening of the Iron Bridge. There were some substantial cast-iron railway bridges, and, before the Dee Bridge accident, many of lesser consequence.

Nevertheless, some large railway bridges were constructed in timber, the Willington and Ouseburn viaducts (NZ 262647) on the Newcastle & North Shields Railway of 1837-38, the original Etherow (SJ 998938) and Dinting Vale (SK 019944) viaducts on the Sheffield, Ashton-under-Lyne & Manchester Railway of 1842 and 1844, I.K. Brunel's bridge of 1840 over the River Avon at Bath (ST 752642), and his numerous yellow pine structures on the railways linking Exeter with Penzance.[10] However, the majority of the great bridges of the first generation of main line railways were masonry arches, Joseph Locke's Dutton Viaduct of 1837 on the Grand Junction Railway (SJ 592874), Brunel's Wharncliffe Viaduct at Hanwell (TQ 150805) of 1838 and his elliptical arches over the Thames at Maidenhead (SU 491810) of the following year, J.U.Rastrick's Ouse Viaduct near Hayward's Heath (TQ 323278) of 1840 with its architectural embellishments by David Moccata, John Miller's Ballochmyle Viaduct (NS 480329) near Cumnock of 1848 with one of its arches spanning 180 ft. (55.4m) and Robert Stephenson's Royal Border Bridge (NJ 992530) of 1850 were all structures on an heroic scale, but none employed iron, and none embodied principles unknown to the Romans. Indeed, one of the outstanding bridges of the period, although not the best-known, the Victoria Bridge in Co. Durham (NZ 320546) of 1838, was consciously modelled on the bridge over the River Alcantara built in honour of Trajan, the Roman Emperor, about A.D.105. The cast-iron arch was used to carry railways in the first generation of railway-construction, but it was not the dominant form.

A similar pattern can be observed in the construction of road bridges. The Grosvenor Bridge at Chester SJ 402655), with its segmental arch spanning 200 ft. (61.6m), was built between 1827 and 1834 to the design of the architect Thomas Harrison (1744-1829). Until the completion of the Cabin John Bridge in Washington DC, with a span of 218 ft. (67.1m) in 1864, the Grosvenor Bridge appears to have been the longest spanned masonry arch in the world. The most important new road bridges in Britain built after 1830 were in big cities. Some were iron arches, such as Thomas Page's (1803-77) Westminster Bridge, the Sean Heuston Bridge of 1821 in Dublin, and the North Parade Bridge in Bath (ST 754656). Some were suspension bridges, such as the Hammersmith, Lambeth, Chelsea and Hungerford bridges in London, and the Clifton Bridge in Bristol (ST 564730). Others, for example Sir John Rennie's London Bridge and the Waterloo Bridge, were masonry arches. A few iron arches like those at Abermule (SO

133 The Forth Bridge.

162952) and Buttington (SJ 246088) in Montgomeryshire were built in rural areas, but elsewhere engineers chose to cross rivers on masonry structures.

The Iron Bridge at Coalbrookdale was a symbol of the most productive and most innovative ironmaking region in Britain of the second half of the 18th century. Alongside the Duke of Bridgewater's canal and coal mines at Worsley, Richard Arkwright's Cromford Mill, Josiah Wedgwood's potworks at Etruria, and Boulton & Watt's Soho Manufactory it was seen as a harbinger of an industrial new order that future generations called the Industrial Revolution. In a more narrow sense it was less influential. Its form was not copied by subsequent builders of iron bridges, except for the designers of the small-scale replicas at Raincy and Worlitz. Several of the second generation of iron bridges were unsuccessful, and the optimistic forecasts made in about 1800 for the future of cast-iron arches were never realised. However, some large iron bridges have proved long-lived, and some, like Mythe and Craigellachie, have combined longevity with elegance. Particular qualities of cast iron were utilised by the designers of many waterways bridges, and by some landscape architects creating ornamental parks, but in both cases stone and timber structures continued to be employed. The failings of cast iron when used in tension were quickly appreciated in the era of main-line railways, particularly after the Dee Bridge accident of 1847, but the use of iron bridges of modest size was a factor in the rapid creation of a network of 6,000 miles of main-line railways between 1830 and 1851, and some large cast-iron railway bridges were notable for their ingenious design or aesthetic qualities. The Iron Bridge was therefore the direct ancestor of a dynasty of iron arches that extended for about a century, but which was always just one choice for engineers, who, with the possible exception of Jessop and Telford at Pontcysyllte, could always have chosen other means of construction.

In another sense the Iron Bridge had a profound and lasting effect on the history of the world. It was a structure that had an influence like that of the contemporary War of Independence in America, which, in Tom Paine's words, 'energised invention and lessened the Catalogue of Impossibilities'.[11] While some of the much-trumpeted 'firsts' claimed to have been achieved at Coalbrookdale in the 18th century, the forging of wrought iron in a reverberatory furnace by the brothers Cranage in 1766, and the casting of the first iron rails in 1767 for example,[12] prove on close examination to be very modest steps in mankind's progress, it is clear that the Iron Bridge impressed and inspired all who saw it. In all but the most direct senses it was the beginning of a process that continued through Sunderland, whose builder reacted to its constructional principles by devising different ones, through Longdon to Poncysyllte and to Telford's great iron bridges in Scotland and across the Severn in Worcestershire and Gloucestershire. The bridge was known to Charles Bage of Shrewsbury, whose Ditherington Flax Mill of 1796-7 was the first wholly iron-framed building. The inadequacies of the cast-iron arch led Samuel Brown and more particularly Thomas Telford towards the suspension bridge. Many accounts of the great railway bridges acknowledge their origins in the Iron Bridge at Coalbrookdale, and through such structures as the Britannia Bridge and the Royal Albert Bridge at Saltash it can be linked to the

Forth Bridge and to steel construction. There is no space to catalogue in a work of this kind the advances in constructional science of the 20th century, but it is pertinent to notice that in the visitor centre that interprets the Honshu-Shikoku Bridges, the amazingly ambitious project linking the southern islands of Japan that opened in 1988, there is a model of the Iron Bridge at Coalbrookdale.

Before 1970 the Iron Bridge appeared rusty and neglected, and visitors had no source of information on its history at hand. That it is now smartly painted and interpreted to visitors is a measure of the increased awareness of the significance of the industrial

134 The Honshu-Shikoku bridges linking the southern islands of Japan, completed in 1988.

heritage that developed in Britain in the last quarter of the 20th century. Nevertheless, just as much remains to be discovered about the history of the Iron Bridge, so there is a continuing need to communicate to the public at large the relevance of Britain's industrial past to life in the 21st century. The semi-circular arch linking Madeley with Benthall will continue to be a lively part of that process. It is as relevant in 2002 as it was in 1979 to assert that 'For the legacy of the Gorge to have a future requires an understanding in depth as well as breadth, a detailed archaeological, historical and ecological appreciation of why the Gorge is like it is, an ability to stand by principles, a conscious exercise of restraint, but above all a sense of humility'.[13] Understanding the significance of the Iron Bridge is, like the understanding of the industrial past in general, a continuing and ever-changing process. We trust that this new edition will take the process forward, and are conscious that it will go further still in future generations.

The Iron Bridge in America

Eric DeLony

Nearly a decade passed since completion of the original Iron Bridge in 1779 before the next notable spans. Both were small-scale replicas of the famous original. One, erected in 1788, at Raincy near Paris, is known only from a watercolor rendering. The other, built in 1791, still stands in its miniature glory at 25 ft. in the restored park of Worlitz, near Madgeburg, now part of the unified Germany. What ensued after these modest attempts at emulation was a frenzy of iron bridge building that fed off the English precedent throughout France, Prussia, Russia and, eventually, the United States.

Though American cast-iron arch bridges never achieved English numbers or flourish, there was a brief spurt of cast-iron arch bridge construction that I will summarise here. The story starts with an Englishman, Thomas Paine, who was neither engineer nor builder. (Paine's bridge-building activities are covered elsewhere in this book, but I mention him here to establish the context for American cast-iron arch bridge building.) Though considered an inconsequential historical character by some Englishmen, to most Americans he was a patriot, who through his writings articulated just cause for freedom. While recuperating from the strains of the American Revolution, in 1786 Paine designed a 400-ft cast- and wrought-iron bridge with 13 arched ribs – one for each state in the new union – to span the Schuylkill River in Philadelphia. Paine realised that stone and wood, though excellent in compression, were poor in tension, or, in the case of wood, hard to splice in a good tension connection. He was among the first anywhere to recognise the potential of iron as bridge material. He acted on his convictions by inventing and modelling the first American design for a cast-iron arch of greater span than ever proposed. But when Paine's plans were reviewed by members of the Pennsylvania Assembly, who would have to pay for the bridge across the Schuylkill, some were impressed with his idea while others questioned whether America's iron industry could produce enough material for such a large span. At the suggestion of Benjamin Franklin, Paine took his idea to Europe where iron technology was far more advanced, especially in England. The bridge was favourably reviewed by the French Academy of Sciences and patented in England, and he actually succeeded in building a 110-ft prototype in Paddington. But, Paine's venture into iron bridge building was derailed for nearly a decade when he reverted to his old passion of politics and returned to France when ordinary Frenchmen and women revolted against the aristocracy.

The next American venture in iron bridge building occurred in 1810, when another Englishman, Joseph Joshua Dyster living in Philadelphia, received the first

American patent for an iron bridge. With a patent date of 23 February 1810, Dyster's is the earliest American iron bridge patent. This is new information in the annals of American bridge scholarship. Prior to this recent discovery, American bridge scholars for decades have attributed August Canfield's bridge patent of 1833 as the first iron bridge patented in America. Dyster allegedly constructed a model bridge of 150-ft span to show its advantages over other types. He claimed the usual attributes for iron bridges – less expense, accelerated erection time, greater durability, and superior appearance. He described his span as a single arch, much wider than comparable bridges of wood or stone, with sufficient length to span most navigable rivers without intermediate piers. He went on to claim that the arches were of sufficient height for its length and could easily be extended from 300-1,000ft. He further contended that the bridge would stand the test of the ages without repairs. Dyster went on to establish 'The Friends of the Establishment of Iron Bridges' in hopes of soliciting subscriptions to erect a 150-ft demonstration span. He estimated the cost at $2,000.[1]

On 20 August 1811, Dyster wrote to the Commissioners in Philadelphia requesting subscriptions for a permanent bridge over the Schuylkill at Upper Ferry, that he would contract to build '... on my patent tubular principles – elegant, stable, and in all respects what a good bridge ought to be, for $40,000 – to be done in six months.' The letter also contained a lengthy printed broadside entitled 'A Prospectus of the Newly-Discovered American Dysterian Iron Architecture, as applicable to the erection of iron bridges and various other architectural processes; such as Domes, Saloons, Halls, Vaulted Ceilings, Arched Cellars, Fire-Proof Buildings, etc.' Dyster was listed in *Kite's Philadelphia Directory for 1814* as 'Dyster, Joseph J., Tubular iron Bridge Architect, corner of 12th and Chestnut'.[2] Unfortunately, like Paine's bridge, no illustration survives of Dyster's invention. The original patent specifications and any drawings were lost during the American patent office fire of 1836.

The second American patent for an iron bridge, dated 29 June 1833, was granted to August Canfield, a West Point graduate working in Paterson, New Jersey. It was not for an iron arch, but rather a curious flat suspension structure of iron rods hooked together and anchored to abutments from which a truss was hung. Although there is no record that the bridge ever was built,

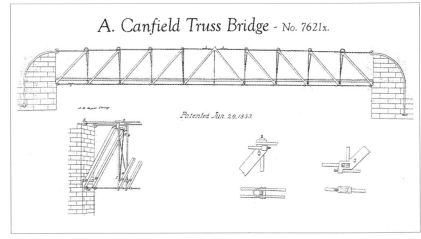

135 August Canfield's patent drawing (No.7621x, 29 June 1833) of his curious cast- and wrought-iron bridge.

this patent marked a material trend for American bridges – the combination of cast- and wrought-iron that lasted nearly fifty years until the brief interlude of all-wrought-iron construction in the 1880s, and then the advent of steel in the 1890s, the material in use today.

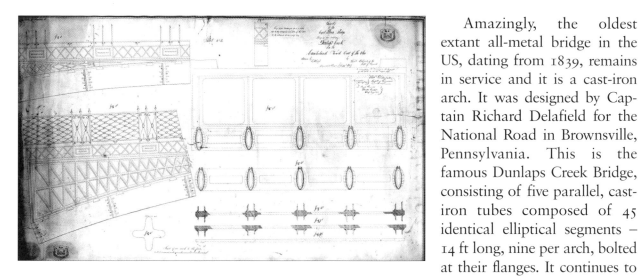

Amazingly, the oldest extant all-metal bridge in the US, dating from 1839, remains in service and it is a cast-iron arch. It was designed by Captain Richard Delafield for the National Road in Brownsville, Pennsylvania. This is the famous Dunlaps Creek Bridge, consisting of five parallel, cast-iron tubes composed of 45 identical elliptical segments – 14 ft long, nine per arch, bolted at their flanges. It continues to

136 Dunlaps Creek Bridge (1839), Brownsville, Pennsylvania.

carry Old Route 40, the National Road, on a span of 80 ft. Though Delafield claims that his idea was original, I feel that the elliptical form resembles Antoine Polonceau's Pont du Carrousel over the Seine in Paris, built in 1834. The Delafield span is not nearly as complicated as Polonceau's bridge with all its fittings, spandrel ring castings, and curious tar-impregnated wooden staves that reinforced the elliptical arch ribs. It is conceivable that Delafield, being an engineer in service with the Army Corps, could have seen an illustration of Polonceau's design in one of the engineering periodicals.[3]

137 Washington Aqueduct Bridge over Rock Creek (1860), Georgetown, District of Columbia, Montgomery C. Meigs, designer.

In 1860, another arch of cast-iron was erected by Montgomery C. Meigs over the Rock Creek as part of the Washington aqueduct system. The bridge is unique in that it served the dual purposes of carrying Pennsylvania Avenue while at the same time delivering water to the citizens of Washington. This was accomplished by two four-foot-diameter cast-iron pipe sections bolted through their flanges,

forming an arch that carried both road and water. The bridge remains intact though it has been widened and encased in stone, appearing like a stone arch in keeping with the classic style of the capital city. But looking at the underside of the arch, one can see several of the cast-iron tubular segments with the flanges of the tubes covered with decorative castings of acanthus leaves. Several historians have pointed out the similarity between the Rock Creek bridge and Dunlaps Creek and drawn the conclusion that Meigs' design must have been

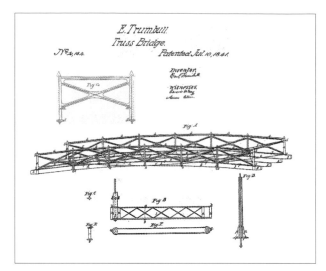

inspired by Delafield's bridge. Both engineers were familiar with each other's work through their service with the army corps.[4]

The evolutionary mainstream of American iron-bridge technology was the composite cast- and wrought-iron truss rather than cast-iron arches. The first constructed was completed in 1840. It was a composite truss (cast- and wrought-iron) carried by a self-anchoring iron suspension system consisting of wrought-iron stay rods, 1.5 in diameter, anchored to vertical end posts and then passing under the two centremost floor beams on lugs cast integrally to intermediate posts. The bridge was patented 10 July 1841 (Patent No. 2,164) by Earl Trumbull and carried a road 70 feet over the Erie Canal at Frankford, New York.

Squire Whipple's cast- and wrought-iron bowstring truss (patented 24 April 1841, No. 2,064), spanning 82 feet over the Erie Canal in Utica, NY, was the second all-metal truss bridge erected in the United States. Whipple was a mathematical instrument maker from Upstate New York who was employed briefly as a surveyor on the Baltimore & Ohio Railroad. It was during this tenure with the B&O that he probably was exposed to the need for good serviceable bridges. For his first bridge, Whipple did not claim that he invented the bowstring arch, only the cast-iron segmental arch section in combination with the diagonals to sustain the shape against the effects of unequal loadings. His specification included claims for the bottom chord casting and the elongated wrought-iron links, which he called a 'thrust tie'.

The connecting blocks and link chords are two parts of the Whipple bowstring that exemplify the craft of American cast- and wrought-iron bridges. The connection block, a complicated casting relying on the skill and collaboration between the designer, pattern maker, mould maker and foundry man, is beautifully sculpted. Eyebars eventually replaced the looped links in subsequent bridge construction.

The bowstring form proved exceptionally suitable for short highway spans, train sheds, and other curved vaults. For the last quarter of the 19th century it was one of the most generally adapted truss forms in use in America. Several dozen patents were granted for variations of the bridge. Whipple's invention also marked the transition between composite wood and iron bridges and the beginning of all-

138 (above left) Earl Trumbull's patent drawing (No. 2164, 10 July 1841) of the first American cast- and wrought-iron bridge actually constructed.

139 (above right) Detail of bottom chord connection, Whipple Truss Bridge.

iron bridge construction – a new American industry. Whipple himself operated one of the earliest bridge-fabricating companies, building hundreds of iron bridges.

Whipple also was a theoretician. In both England and America, practice always preceded science; thus structural systems were invented first before any theory was developed. For America, the first structural treatise was published in 1847, when Squire Whipple, without precedent or example, was the first American to arrive at a clear quantitative understanding of forces in members, and possibly the first in the world to publish a book on truss analysis. A 47-page essay was expanded into book length that is recognised by some as America's greatest contribution to structural mechanics.

Whipple's major breakthrough is the realisation that truss members can be analysed as a system of forces in equilibrium, assuming that a joint is a frictionless pin. Forces are broken down into horizontal and vertical components whose sums are in equilibrium. Known as the method of joints, it enables the determination of forces in all members if two forces are known. If a form is statically determinant, the forces and moments at all connection points (and all points along an arch's axis) may be determined using only force and moment equilibrium equations. This simplified design considerably. Whipple clearly outlined methods, both analytical and graphic, for solving determinant trusses considering uniformly distributed dead loads and moving live loads (200 lbs/sq.ft. for railroads, 100 lbs/sq.ft. for roads). Though ignored for years, the book constituted the scientific basis of American bridge design, marking the beginning of rational rather than empirical design, and initiated the transition of bridge building from the craft of carpenters and millwrights to the profession of civil engineering.[5]

The outstanding collection of cast-iron arch bridges in America is the group of five in New York's Central Park. Two others, Spur Rock and Outset Arch, were destroyed in 1934. Four of them separate equestrian from pedestrian traffic while the fifth, Bow Bridge, spans The Lake. On appearance, Bow Bridge looks like a cast-iron arch. However, a discerning eye can tell that the arch is much too shallow to develop arch action for a span of this length (87ft). Instead, Bow Bridge (1862) has the distinction of being one of the earliest wrought-iron girder bridges in the United States. These remarkable bridges were constructed by two British architects, Calvert Vaux and Jacob Wrey Mould, working with the landscape architect Frederick Law Olmsted. Constructed while the American Civil War was being fought, the

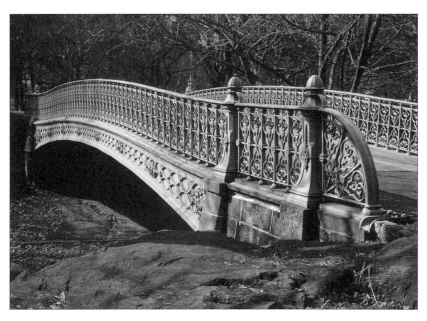

140 Pine Bank Arch (1861), Central Park, New York.

141 Chestnut Street Bridge (1866), Philadelphia, Pennsylvania, Strickland Kneass, designer.

Central Park bridges follow the European precedent of using cast-iron arches in park settings. The nature of cast iron allowed it to be moulded into intricate and elaborate naturalistic forms. The Central Park bridges seem to have grown out of the ground.[6]

The largest cast-iron bridge ever built in the United States was the Chestnut Street Bridge, completed in 1866, that spanned the Schuylkill River in Philadelphia. The bridge had two segmental arches of six parallel ribs, 185ft each, designed by city engineer Strickland Kneass. The arches were erected without false work using the method of cantilevering out from the abutments to a central pier, the segments being lifted from barges and temporarily held in place by cables until the arch ring was closed. Chestnut Street and the Central Park bridges represent the apogee of American cast-iron arch bridge construction. It took nearly half a century for American designers, craftsmen and foundries to equal the craft and skill of British decorative cast-iron bridge production.

To round out this brief summary of American cast-iron arch bridge construction, I will suggest some of the differences of American and European bridge design. Bridge engineering evolved differently in America from the way it did in Europe. In Britain, the Crown represented private enterprise, and Parliament had to approve all public works, while in France, financing and design emanated centrally from Paris. In America, engineering came to be dominated by entrepreneurs and craftsmen, largely self-taught at first and interested in doing rather than studying. Differences between American and European design can also be explained by the disparities in national needs. American engineers and builders adapted designs to address conditions of a country that was sparsely populated, with a rugged and undeveloped interior. Designs for most things, especially bridges, represented a kind of do-it-yourself mentality, simple structures easily built so that any carpenter, millwright, or mechanic by necessity became experienced and skilled though not necessarily formally trained in the building arts. Later, bridges were prefabricated in factories in the East and shipped to distant locations.

This explains the development in America of short portable cast- and wrought-iron components and pin connections that could be easily assembled in the field by unskilled or semi-skilled workmen without the need for complicated special machines or equipment. England and Europe opted for rigid riveted bridges of built-up sections that required heavy, portable boilers to drive the riveting machines, and highly skilled labour.

Another factor was that timber not only was plentiful in America, but also was well adapted to inexpensive, relatively temporary construction in a country with meagre financial resources and where the uncertainty of future requirements did not justify more permanent construction. Consequently, America first built in wood rather than iron or stone. It was left to America, where vast stands of virgin forests and a new generation of millwright/carpenter/builder, unfettered by scientific theory and a masonry tradition, took up where the Swiss and Germans left off and empirically perfected the truss bridge in forms suitable to mass production and capable of carrying railroad loads. The earliest wooden bridges were built by expert carpenters who were also the designers. These early wooden bridges were similar to ancient Roman bridges, i.e. they were built by extremely practical men of sound judgment and unusual mechanical abilities who depended on their own resources and instincts, experimenting with models and learning from previous mistakes. American builders had no accurate method of evaluating the strains in the various members produced by external forces. He would buy timber at saw mills convenient to the site and have it cut to order. The same held true for iron work. If the bridge needed rods, bolts, shoes, or straps, he would have the parts made by local blacksmiths. A local crew would be hired to erect the false work and then, under direction of the builder, the bridge would be framed, finished, and opened to traffic. Similar methods were used for iron highway bridges when they started replacing the wooden covered bridges in the 1840s and '50s. Each of these builders had his own bridge with certain often patented details. There was little competition as each builder controlled a certain territory.

It was from this wooden bridge tradition that American iron bridges evolved. In America, the cast-iron arches discussed above were an anomaly. Less than a dozen were ever constructed. Early engineers such as Canfield, Trumbull, and Whipple paid little attention to European models, instead developing their own metal truss systems independently as the previous generation of builders had done with wooden bridges. American bridge building evolved from a tradition of wooden truss forms. The successful truss forms such as the Howe, Pratt, Whipple, Bollman and Fink trusses were readily adaptable in iron, using the system of analysis developed by Squire Whipple, and possessed merits which insured their wide adoption for metal structures. The first iron bridges in America were adaptations of the wooden examples like the Howe and Pratt trusses. The earliest iron bridges were composites of cast and wrought iron with wrought iron being used in tension members, usually iron rods threaded at the ends or elongated links made of forged square rods with loop welded ends. Though eye bar links had been used by Telford on the Menai Suspension Bridge in 1826, forged eye bars were not introduced in America until Jacob H. Linville patented them in 1861.

Within the fifteen years preceding the Civil War, American metal bridge construction made very creditable progress, but became practically dormant throughout the conflict (1861-65). Afterwards, it gained remarkable impetus during the two succeeding decades.[7] Following British precedent, America had developed a strong tradition of experimental research oriented towards industry and design solutions, but a weak tradition of theoretical research in the engineering sciences. 'Practical bridge builders', or builders less theoretically accomplished dominated American bridge practice, wrote C. Shaler Smith, a prominent American bridge engineer following the Civil War. In an article he wrote comparing the Fink, Bollman, and Warren rectilinear trussing systems in 1865, he wrote, 'However ingenious and even sound the theories and complex equations may be, they are only agreeable exercises of the learned men who proposed them.' Smith is clear that he doesn't denigrate high science or the theoretical postulations of eminent men, but, in truth, they were entirely disregarded by the majority of the designers and builders of bridges. 'In the planning of trusses, the engineers can obtain full knowledge only through experimental tests and by noticing the effects of passing trains at various speeds.'[8]

Smith further explains that the use of cast iron for compression parts is sanctioned by long and satisfactory experience in America, although opposed in England. Failure results when the material is subjugated to transverse strains due to injudicious proportioning and the arrangement of parts. When cast iron is designed with the proper section and protected from cross strains, it is the safest part of the combination. Failures result from the fracture of wrought-iron tension rods, from insufficient sectional area, bad iron, or imperfect welding. In 1865, Smith clearly advocated the use of pin connected cast- and wrought-iron bridge construction and recommended against built up members of wrought iron riveted together.[9]

The modern era of American bridge design began after the Civil War. This period can be regarded as an epoch when bridges designed by Bollman and Fink came into use and the earliest iron Whipple and Pratt trusses were built. Though many engineers still used empirical knowledge and factors of safety (the number of times that a maximum load would have to be increased to break a bridge) to design a bridge, the educated engineer who relied on scientific calculation to determine the exact amount of stresses in each member began to exert his influence, and steady progress was made from this time forward. The statically determinant cast- and wrought-iron truss with pin connected, eye-bar connections became the signature American bridge for nearly half the 19th century. Eventually, this form was discarded in favour of the European method of rigid, riveted construction.[10]

Tables

Table 1: *Payments for workmen employed on the construction of the Iron Bridge (Data from SRR1987/47/1 and IGM.1993.3374)*

Date of payment	Amount L S D	Amount in pence	Supervisor
11.11.1777	2.19.6	714	Charles Hornblower
22.11.1777	3.17.3	927	
6.12.1777	4.0.6	966	
20.12.1777	4.2.3	987	
5.1.1778	2.16.0	672	Charles Hornblower
17.1.1778	4.8.6	1062	
2.2.1778	7.16.7	1897	
14.2.1778	14.5.9	3429	
28.2.1778	19.13.7	4723	
14.3.1778	19.4.5	4613	
25.3.1778	17.14.10	4258	
10.4.1778	16.10.0	3960	
24.4.1778	26.8.10	6346	
9.5.1778	45.3.0	10836	
24.5.1778	24.8.4	5860	
6.6.1778	29.15.20	7150	
20.6.1778	28.15.3	6903	
4.7.1778	30.10.11	7331	
18.7.1778	21.15.6	5946	
25.7./1.8.1778	16.11.4	3976	
15.8.1778	12.0.8	2888	
31.8.1778	11.9.9	2757	
15.9.1778	28.8.4	6820	
26.9.1778	23.16.2	5714	
10.10.1778	33.0.0	7920	George Parker
24.10.1778	24.8.9	5865	
7.11.1778	30.19.8	7436	
21.11.1778	18.9.4	4432	
4.12.1778	22.17.4	5488	
18.12.1778	20.14.0	4968	
4.1.1779	7.10.0	1800	George Parker
18.1.1779	9.4.6	2214	
31.1.1779	10.13.4	2560	
12.2.1779	13.9.10	3238	
27.2.1779	17.7.3	4167	
13.3.1779	23.1.11	5543	
27.3.1779	20.1.6	4818	
10.4.1779	41.0.3	9843	
24.4.1779	32.15.0	7860	
8.5.1779	35.12.11	8555	
22.5.1779	33.10.11	8051	
5.6.1779	42.4.1	10129	
19.6.1779	29.11.7	7099	
3.7.1779	35.2.8	8432	
17.7.1779	28.18.7	6943	
31.7.1779	34.5.0	8220	
14.8.1779	37.16.9	9081	
28.8.1779	33.9.0	8028	

Table 1: contd.

Date of payment	Amount L S D	Amount in pence	Supervisor
13.9.1779	30.16.1	7393	
25.9.1779	29.15.4	7144	
9.10.1779	31.19.1	7669	
25.10.1779	34.4.6	8214	
6.11.1779	30.15.5	7385	
20.11.1779	27.18.0	6696	
4.12.1779	19.1.9	4581	
19.12.1779	14.19.4	3592	
1.1.1780	17.6.9	4151	Thomas Gregory
15.1.1780	7.19.6	1914	
29.1.1780	10.10.5	2525	
12.2.1780	10.10.5	2525	
26.2.1780	22.4.8	5336	
11.3.1780	13.9.9	3237	
25.3.1780	18.15.3	4503	
8.4.1780	14.19.8	3596	
22.4.1780	19.8.2	4658	
6.5.1780	24.13.2	5918	
20.5.1780	20.9.0	4908	
2.6.1780	27.0.6	6386	
17.6.1780	21.18.11	5267	
1.7.1780	26.3.6	6282	
15.7.1780	26.3.11	6287	
29.7.1780	26.11.4	6376	
12.8.1780	22.15.5	5465	
26.8.1780	20.11.11	4943	
8.9.1780	16.15.4	4024	
23.9.1780	15.1.0	3612	
7.10.1780	15.7.3	3687	
21.10.1780	19.19.2	4790	
4.11.1780	10.8.7	2503	
18.11.1780	12.3.8	2924	
2.12.1780	13.4.1	3169	
16.12.1780	10.18.11	2627	
29.12.1780	9.8.3	2211	Daniel Rose
13.1.1781	11.13.11	2807	
27.1.1781	7.6.9	1761	

Table 2: Iron Bridges constructed 1781-96

	Period of construction	Grid reference	Manufacturer	Notes
11 or 12 bridges at Tsarskoe Selo, near St Petersburg	1781-90	-	Sestroretsk	May be of cast iron or wrought iron
Raincy	By 1788	-	-	Replica of the Iron Bridge, possibly of wood
Rotherham	1789	SK 410924	Walker	Temporary demonstration of Tom Paine bridge
Lisson Grove	1790-1	TQ 275822	Walker	110 ft. span designed by Paine, exhibited in London
Worlitz	1791	-	-	Wrought-iron replica of the Iron Bridge
Netherlands	1791	-	Coalbrookdale	Crossed a canal. Location unknown
Pont-y-Cafnau	1793	SO 038072	Probably Cyfarthfa	Designed by Watkin George. Railway bridge and aqueduct.
Trentham	1794	SJ 867409	Coalbrookdale	Demolished. Fragments remain.
Stanford I	1795	SO 751658	Unknown	Designed by Nash. Collapsed soon after completion
Sunderland	1792-6	NZ 396574	Walker	Designed by Rowland Burdon, construction supervised by Thomas Wilson.
Sheffield	1795	SK 357877	-	Destroyed in flood 1864
Cound I	1795	SJ558057	Coalbrookdale	In use till 1818. Designed by John Dodson.
Lazany	1796	-	Malapanew	In Silesia
Holmes Aqueduct	1796	SK 359362	-	On Derby Canal. Designed by Outram.
Longdon Aqueduct	1796	SJ 621155	Ketley	On Shrewsbury Canal. Opened 14 March 1796.
Buildwas	1796	SJ 645045	Coalbrookdale	Designed by Telford. In use till 1905.
Stanford II	1796-7	SO 751658	Coalbrookdale	Designed by Nash replacing Stanford I. In use till 1911.

Table 3: Bridges designed by Wilson and/or cast by Walkers

	Period of construction	Grid reference	Manufacturer	Notes
Sunderland	1792-6	NZ 396574	Walker	Designed by Rowland Burdon. In use till 1929.
Spanish Town, Jamaica	1900-01	-	Walker	Remains in use. Inscribed 'Thomas Wilson 1800'
Stratfield Saye	1802	SU 706624	Probably Walker	On estate of George Pitt, Lord Rivers.
Staines	1800-03	TQ 032715	Walker	Subsided before completion. Removed 1806-07.
Yarm	1802-05	NZ 418432	Walker	Opened 1805. Collapsed 12 January 1806
Boston	1803-07	TF 328440	Walker	Designed by Wilson in collaboration with Rennie. Rebuilt 1912-13.
Tickford, Newport Pagnell	1809-10	SP 878438	Walker	Designed by Wilson in collaboration with Henry Provis. Remains in use.
Southwark	1811-18	TQ 324806	Walker	Designed by Rennie.

Table 4: Tramway, canal and road bridges in South Wales 1793-1830

	Period of construction	Grid reference	Manufacturer	Notes
Pont-y-Cafnau	1793	SO 038072	Probably Cyfarthfa	Designed by Watkin George in form of a king-post roof truss, carried track and water channel to ironworks waterwheels.
Cyfarthfa I	c.1795	SO 039069	Probably Cyfarthfa	Cast from Pont-y-Cafnau patterns, carried track over Taff at Cyfarthfa Ironworks. Demolished, probably in 1960s.
Cyfarthfa II	By 1798	SO 040068	Probably Cyfarthfa	Cast-iron arch with suspended deck, carrying railway over Taff to lower part of ironworks.
Rhyd-y-Car, Merthyr	Between 1790 and 1814	SO 046063	Probably Cyfarthfa	Parapet truss bridge, possibly designed by Watkin George. Preserved at Joseph Parry birthplace.
'Old Iron Bridge', Merthyr	1799-1800	SO 047062	Probably Cyfarthfa	Road bridge of 62 ft. (20.1 m) span, designed by Watkin George. Demolished 1960s. Some parts remain.
The 'Ironbridge', Llanelli	c.1801	SN 499005	Probably Cymddyche	Carried railway constructed by Alexander Raby over Lleidi River, site covered by later standard gauge railway.
Wiselboom Bridge, Llanelli	c.1801	SN 499004	Probably Cymddyche	Carried branch of Raby's railway over Lleidi. Any remains likewise buried.
Robertstown Bridge, Aberdare	1811	SN 997056	Abernant	Bears date 1811.
Aaron Brute's Bridge, Blaenavon	Between 1812 and 1818	SO 248086	Probably Blaenavon	Arched bridge carrying track from a level driven between 1812 and 1818.
Waterloo Bridge, Penydarren	c.1815	ST 056070	Probably Penydarren	Carried track over Morlais Brook into Pen-y-darren Ironworks. Part preserved at Joseph Parry birthplace.
Llanfoist	c.1822	SO 285130	Probably Blaenavon	Carried extension of Hill's Tramroad, opened 1822, over Brecknock & Abergavenny Canal. Cast-iron deck plates laid on T-section beams.
Smart's Bridge, Clydach	1824	SO 131228	Probably Clydach	Carried track into Clydach Ironworks. Bears date. Gothic ornamentation in spandrels.

Table 5: Principal iron aqueducts

	Period of construction	Grid reference	Manufacturer	Notes
Pont-y-Cafnau	1793-5	SO 038072	Cyfarthfa	Designed by Watkin George. Combined plateway bridge and aqueduct for leet.
Holmes	1795-6	SK 359362	Probably Butterley	Designed by Benjamin Outram. On Derby Canal. Completed by February 1795. Demolished.
Longdon on Tern	1795-6	SJ 621155	Ketley	On Shrewsbury Canal. Opened for traffic 14 March 1796.
Chirk	1796-1801	SJ 287372	William Hazledine	Cast-iron plates used to seal the waterway of a masonry aqueduct.
Stalybridge	1799-1801	SJ 954982.	Probably Butterley	Recommended by Outram to replace damaged aqueduct on Huddersfield Canal.
Pontcysyllte	1795/1801-5	SJ 272422	William Hazledine	Carries Ellesmere Canal above River Dee.
Wolverton	1809-11	SP 800417	Ketley	Carries Grand Junction Canal. Replaced collapsed masonry aqueduct.
Edstone/Bearley	1816	SP 163608	-	On Stratford on Avon Canal, designed by William Whitmore.
Wootton Wawen	1816	SP 158629	-	On Stratford on Avon Canal, designed by William Whitmore.
Birthdir	1819	SJ 198022	-	On Montgomeryshire Canal, replacing earlier structure. Designed by G.W.Buck.
Avon	1818-22	NS 967758	-	On Edinburgh & Glasgow Union Canal. Iron trough in masonry aqueduct. Designed by Hugh Baird.
Almond	1818-22	NT 105706	-	
Slateford	1818-22	NT 220727	-	
Engine Arm	1827-30	SP 023889	-	Designed by Thomas Telford. Carries Engine Arm feeder.
Congleton	1831	SJ 866622	-	Designed by Telford. Carries Macclesfield Canal over road.
Yarningale/Preston Bagot	1834	SP 184664	Horseley	Replaced earlier structure on Stratford Canal
Rugby	Opened 1834	SP 503771	Parkes & Otway	Trough supported by 5 cast-iron arches. Carries Oxford Canal over road.
Stretton, Staffs.	1832-5	SJ 873107	William Hazledine	Designed by Thomas Telford. Carries Birmingham & Liverpool Junction Canal over Watling Street
Nantwich	Opened 1835	SJ 642526	-	Designed by Telford. Carries Birmingham & Liverpool Junction Canal.
Stanley Ferry	1828-9	SE 356230.	Milton	Designed by George Leather. An iron suspension aqueduct.
Welshpool, Lledan Brook	1836	SJ 227074	-	Replaces earlier structure on Montgomeryshire Canal. Designed by J.A.S.Sword.
Leahurst	Opened 1849	SK 320556	-	Carried Cromford Canal over Midland Railway.
Brownhills	Opened 1850	SK 053065	-	Carries Anglesey Arm of Wyrley & Essington Canal over Walsall-Lichfield railway.
Birchills/Leamore	1856	SK 005009	Lloyd Foster	Carries Wyrley & Essington Canal over LNWR.

Table 6: Coalbrookdale Company bridges 1791-1830

	Period of construction	Grid reference	Designer	Notes
Netherlands	1791	-	-	Crossed a canal. Location unknown.
Trentham	1794	SJ 867409	-	Demolished. Stubs remain.
Cound I	1795	SJ 558057	John Dodson	In use until 1818.
Buildwas	1795-6	SJ 645045	Thomas Telford	County bridge.
Stanford II	1796-7	SO 751658	John Nash	Replaced Stanford I. In use until 1905.
Cound Arbour	1797	SJ 555053	-	36 ft. span. Remains in use.
Bridgwater	1796-8	ST 301371	-	In use until 1885. Iron casting of town coat of arms remains on hotel.
Sydney Gardens, Bath (2 bridges)	1800	ST 758653	-	Cross Kennet & Avon Canal. 23 ft. span.
Upper Furnace Pool, Coalbrookdale	By 1801	SJ 666050	-	Perhaps built 1790 or earlier. Demolished 1849. Stubs remain.
Bristol, Bedminster & Bath roads (2 bridges)	1806	ST 590720 ST 597722	William Jessop	Demolished 1855, 1885.
Jamaica	1807	-	-	Location unknown
Egginton, Staffs.	1812	SK 254277	-	Parkland bridge. Remains in use.
Wellington Bridge, Dublin	1816	-	John Windsor	Footbridge. Remains in use.
Carlow	1816	-	-	About 40 ft. span. On estate of Mr. Brewing
Irwell Bridge, Salford – Strangeways	1817	SJ 836990	-	120 ft. span. Completed in 8 months.
Stokesay	1823	SO 438818	Thomas Telford	Demolished 1965. One half-rib preserved at Ironbridge.
Chetwynd (Salter's) Bridge, Alrewas, Staffs.	1824	SK 188139	Joseph Potter	Remains in use.
Borle Brook, Highley, Shropshire	1828	SO 753817	-	Carries Severn towpath. Remains in use.
High Bridge, Mavesyn Ridware, Staffs.	1830	SK 092167	Joseph Potter	Remains in use.

Table 7: Telford: Bridges of less than 110 ft. span

	Period of construction	Grid reference	Manufacturer	Notes
Meole Brace, Shrewsbury	1811	SJ 490106	William Hazledine	In use until 1933.
Long Mill, Shropshire	1812	SJ 616155	William Hazledine	In use until 1883. 28 ft. span.
Aston Cantlop, Shropshire	1813	SJ 517063	Probably William Hazledine, Coleham	By-passed 1974-75?. Remains in use, as footbridge, in unaltered condition. 32 ft. span.
Waterloo, Betws-y-Coed.	1816	SH 799557	William Hazledine, Plas Kynaston	105 ft. span. Bears date 1815. Remains in use in restored form.
Cound II	1818	SJ 558057	William Hazledine	55 ft. span. Remained in use until 1967.
Stokesay	1823	SO 438818	Coalbrookdale	4 ribs. 2 central ribs encased in concrete after damage 1919. Demolished 1965.

Table 8: Telford: Bridges of more than 110 ft. span

	Period of construction	Grid reference	Manufacturer	Notes
Buildwas	1795-96	SJ 645045	Coalbrookdale	In use until 1905.
Bonar Bridge	1812	NH 609917	William Hazledine	In use until 1892.
Craigellachie	1815	NJ 285452	William Hazledine	Remains in use in restored form.
Esk Bridge, near Carlisle	1820	NY 354649	William Hazledine	105 ft. and 150 ft. spans with later flood arch. Demolished 1916.
Holt Fleet near Worcester	1828	SO 824634	William Hazledine, Coleham	Remains in use in restored form.
Mythe, Tewkesbury	1826	SO 889337	William Hazledine, Coleham	Remains in use in restored form.
Galton Bridge, Smethwick	1829	SP 015894	Horseley Co.	Closed to motor traffic in 1974 but remains in use as footbridge.

Table 9: Bridges built by William or John Hazledine, other than those designed by Telford

	Period of construction	Grid reference	Manufacturer	Notes
Stourport II	1802-08	SO 808710	John Hazledine, Bridgnorth	Replaced bridge destroyed in flood of 1795. Itself replaced 1870.
Chepstow	1814-16	ST 536944	John Hazledine, Bridgnorth	Possibly designed by Rennie. Construction supervised by J.U.Rastrick.
Kington	1820	SO 307569	William Hazledine	Demolished. Carried tramway.
Eaton Hall, Chester	1824	SJ 418601	William Hazledine	On estate of Duke of Westminster.
Laira, Plymouth	1824-7	TA 044882.	William Hazledine, Calcutts.	Designed by Rendel. Demolished.
Cleveland, Bath	1827	SO 753657	William Hazledine	Remains in use.

Table 10: Butterley Company bridges 1805-23

	Period of construction	Grid reference	Designer	Notes
Hack Bridge, Carshalton	1805-06	TQ 281650	-	Crossed Wandle. Replaced c.1914.
Boston (Skirmeck)	1811	TF 331449	John Rennie	Footbridge over Maud Foster Drain, built as part of drainage scheme.
Cowbridge	1811	TF 328471	John Rennie	Footbridge, built as part of drainage scheme. Third, similar bridge demolished.
Vauxhall, London	1813-16	TQ 30782	James Walker	In use till 1898.
Lucknow	1814-16	-	John Rennie	3-span structure. Castings despatched to India 1816 but erection delayed.
Magdalene Bridge, Cambridge	1823	TL 447590	Arthur Browne	Principal castings by Butterley remainder by Charles Finch, Cambridge.

Table 11: Parkland and similar bridges

	Period of construction	Grid reference	Manufacturer	Notes
Kirklees	1769		Maurice Tobin	Ornamental footbridge, 72 ft. span, probably of wrought iron.
Tsarskoe Selo (Pushkin)	1783-88	-	Sestroretsk	11 or 12 bridges built for Catherine the Great.
Raincy	By 1788	-		Copy of Coalbrookdale bridge.
Syon Park	1790	TQ 167767	-	Designed by James Wyatt. Perhaps influenced by John Busch. For Duke of Northumberland.
Worlitz	1791	-	-	Wrought-iron copy of Coalbrookdale bridge.
Trentham	1794	SJ 867409	Coalbrookdale	Demolished. Fragments remain.
Coalbrookdale Upper Pool	By 1801	SJ 666050	Coalbrookdale	Demolished 1849. Fragments remain.
Sydney Gardens, Bath (2 bridges)	1800	ST 758653	Coalbrookdale	Over Kennet & Avon Canal.
Stratfield Saye	1802	SU 704624	Probably Walkers	Wilson principle. Remains in use on private road.
Avington Park, Hants.	c.1802	SU 532323	-	18.29 m span.
Rochetts Bridge, Brentwood	1809	TQ 563943	-	Designed by John Rennie for Earl St Vincent.
Hulne Park, Alnwick	1812	NU 163153	I & T Cookson, Newcastle	3-span, wrought-iron. Designed by David Stephenson for Duke of Northumberland.
Egginton	1812	SK 254277	Coalbrookdale	Inscribed 'Coalbrookdale 1812'. Pedestrian bridge. Remains in use following restoration in early 1990s.
Heveningham Hall	c.1812	TM 750734	-	Wrought-iron or cast-iron bridge.
Shugborough, 'Blue Bridge'	1813	SJ 988224	John Toye	Three spans: 19 ft. 3 in., 20 ft. 6 in., 19 ft. 3 in.
Brabyns Park, Marple, Cheshire	1813	SJ 903901	Salford Ironworks	Carriage bridge in cast iron.
Culford, Suffolk	1803	TL 828703	William Hawks & Son, Gateshead	Believed to be by Samuel Wyatt. Patent 1804. 60 ft. span. Hollow iron ribs.
Clare, Suffolk.	1813	TL 767448	Ransome	Designed by William Cubitt. 3-span.
Shugborough 'Red Bridge'	1814	SJ 993227	John Toye	Single parabolic arch. 42 ft. 6 in. span.
Carlow, Ireland	1816	-	Coalbrookdale Company	About 40 ft. span. On estate of a Mr. Brewing.
Dolforgan, Kerry	Pre-1818	SN 314290	-	Carries drive to Dolforgan Hall.
Newlay, Horsforth.	1819	SE 239369	Aydon & Elwell	Built by John Pollard of Newlay House
Winchbottom Farm, Little Marlow, Bucks.	1817	SU 868903	Priestfield Foundry, Bilston	Footbridge.
Barrington bridge, Co Limerick	1818	-	J. Doyle	6 miles SE of Limerick. 57 ft span, inscribed 'Erected in 1818 by Mr Barrington' and 'J. Doyle, Fecit'.
Boreton, Shropshire	1826	SJ 517068	-	34 ft span. Also known as Cliff Bridge.
Walton Hall, Yorkshire	1818	SE 364163	Milton	Built by Thomas Waterton.
Eastnor Castle	1826	SO 735368	Seaby of Ledbury	Designed by T. Holland, architect of Ledbury. 25 ft. span.
Hampton Lucy	1829	SP 258572	Horseley	In Gothic style. Built by Rev. J. Lucy.
Willey, Shropshire	1828	SJ 668006	-	Reinforced with concrete.
Acton Burnell, Shropshire	1829	SJ 536024	-	Bridge removed 1974. One rib displayed.

Table 12: Surviving iron bridges in West Yorkshire built before 1840

	Period of construction	Grid reference	Manufacturer	Notes
'Gasworks Bridge', Sowerby Bridge	1816	SE 067236	Aydon & Elwell	90 ft. span. Much altered.
Newlay	1819	SE 239369	Aydon & Elwell	Built by John Pollard of Newlay House.
Walton Hall	1828	SE 364163	Milton	Footbridge to island, built by Thomas Waterton.
Victoria Bridge, Leeds	1837-9	SE 229330	-	Designed by George Leather Junior.
Stanley Ferry Aqueduct	1839	SE 356230	Milton	Designed by George Leather. Iron suspension aqueduct.
Crown Point Bridge, Leeds	1842	SE 307322	-	Designed by George & J.W.Leather.

Table 13: Surviving iron bridges in East Anglia built before 1830

	Period of construction	Grid reference	Manufacturer	Notes
Culford	1803	TL 828703	William Hawks & Son, Gateshead	Believed to be by Samuel Wyatt. Patent 1804. 60 ft. span. Hollow iron ribs.
St. Miles, Coslany Bridge, Norwich	1804	TG 227088	-	Built by James Frost.
Clare	1813	TL 767448	Ransome	Designed by William Cubitt.
Brent Eleigh	1813	TL 932482	Ransome	Designed by William Cubitt.
Saul's Bridge, Witham	1814	TL 824139	Ransome	Designed by William Cubitt.
Hellesdon	1818-19	TG 199100	-	Built by James Frost.
Duke's Palace, Norwich	1822	TG 229089 Now: TG 231084	J. Browne, Jnr.	Removed 1972. Outer arch re-erect 1992 over entrance to Castle Mall.
Magdalene Bridge, Cambridge	1823	TL 447590	Butterley and Finch	Designed by Arthur Browne.
Thetford	1829	TL 868831	Burrell	Designed by Francis Stone.

Notes

Preface

1. The others were: W.G. Muter, *The Buildings of an Industrial Community: Ironbridge and Coalbrookdale* (1979); S.B. Smith, *A View from the Iron Bridge* (1979); *Industrial Archaeology*, vol. 3 (2) (1979), in which all the articles are related to the archaeology of the Ironbridge Gorge.
2. B. Trinder, 'The First Iron Bridges', *Industrial Archaeology*, vol. 3 (1979), pp.247-56.
3. A. Raistrick, *Dynasty of Ironfounders: the Darbys and Coalbrookdale* (1953). London: Longman.
4. J. Ionides, *Thomas Farnolls Pritchard of Shrewsbury: Architect and Inventor of Cast Iron Bridges* (1999). Ludlow: Dog Rose Press.
5. R. Labouchere, *Abiah Darby, 1716-93, of Coalbrookdale; Wife of Abraham Darby II* (1988). York: Sessions; E. Thomas, *Coalbrookdale and the Darbys* (1999). York: Sessions.

I: Perspectives

1. T. Tredgold, *A Practical essay on the strength of Cast Iron* (1824), pp.9-10.
2. The most recent account of the economic and social history of the Coalbrookdale Coalfield is B. Trinder, *The Industrial Revolution in Shropshire* (3rd ed., 2000).
3. Ironbridge Gorge Museum Trust, *A Walk Through Coalbrookdale* (1979), pp.2-11.
4. Trinder, *op.cit.*, pp.54-59; B. Trinder, *The Industrial Archaeology of Shropshire* (1996), pp.168-75; B. Trinder, 'The (Severn) Navigation', R.K. Morriss, *The Shropshire Severn* (1996), pp.77-92.
5. B. Trinder and N. Cox, *Miners and Mariners of the Severn Gorge* (2000), p.13.
6. T. Ruddock, 'William Edwards's bridge at Pontypridd', *Industrial Archaeology*, vol. 11 (1974), pp.194-208.
7. N. Cossons, *The BP Book of Industrial Archaeology* (3rd ed., 1993), pp.244-6.
8. J. Ionides, *Thomas Farnolls Pritchard* (1999), pp.206-7, 267.
9. *The Diary* (September 1789), quoted in J. Pudney, *Crossing London's Rivers* (1972), p.67.
10. B. Trinder, 'The Wooden Bridge at Cressage', *Shropshire Newsletter* No. 35 (1968), pp.1-6.
11. J.G. James, 'Some steps in the Evolution of Early Iron Arched Bridge Designs', *Transactions of the Newcomen Society*, vol. 59 (1987-88), pp.154-55; J.G. James, 'Iron Arched Bridge Designs in Pre-Revolutionary France', *History of Technology*, vol.4 (1979), pp.63-99.
12. T. Ruddock, *Arch Bridges and their Builders* (1979), p.132.
13. A. Sealey, *Bridges and Aqueducts* (1976), p.107.
14. J.S. Gardner, *English Ironwork in the XVIIth and XVIIIth Centuries* (1911), p.254; *Leeds Intelligencer* (2 January 1770); *London Chronicle* (4-6 January 1770); D. Northcliffe, 'A Preliminary Report on the Kirklees Iron Bridge of 1769 and its builder' (1979).
15. E. Ruddock, *Arch Bridges and their Builders* (1979), p.135.
16. A. Nimmo and T. Telford, 'Bridge', *The Edinburgh Encyclopaedia* (1830), vol. 6, p.539.

II: The Project

1. J. White, 'On Cementitious Architecture, as applied to the construction of bridges, with a prefatory note on the first introduction of iron as the constituent material for bridges of a large span by Thomas Farnolls Pritchard in 1773', *Philosophical Magazine and Annals of Philosophy*, vol. 11 (1832), p.183; T. Tredgold, *A Practical Essay on the strength of Cast Iron* (1824), pp.9-10; T. Telford, *Autobiography* (ed. J. Rickman, 1838), p. 29; *Chamber's Edinburgh Journal* (1832), vol.13, p.21.
2. For Wilkinson, see B. Trinder *The Industrial Revolution in Shropshire* (3rd ed., 2000), pp.73-4, 83-4.
3. J. Priestley Junr. – J. Wilkinson, 3 Oct. 1790, Warrington Public Library, Priestley Correspondence, 13.
4. A. Nimmo and T. Telford, 'Bridge', *Edinburgh Encyclopedia* (1830), vol. 6, p.539.
5. J. Ionides, *Thomas Farnolls Pritchard* (1999). We are also grateful to James Lawson for conversations about Pritchard over many years.
6. Lichfield Joint Record Office, will of Ann Farnolls, 12 Sepember 1745, prob. 14 April 1748; inventory, 13 May 1723 and admin., 17 October 1723 of Thomas Farnolls.
7. 13 Geo. III (1773), c.113; *Berrow's Worcester Journal* (12 August, 11 November, 16 December 1773; 3 February, 30 June, 28 July, 18, 25 August, 15 September, 17 November 1774; 16 February, 14 September 1775); J. White, 'On Cementitious Architecture', p.183; W. Camden, *Britannia* (ed. R. Gough, 1789),

vol. 2, pp.357-8; J.Ionides, *Thomas Farnolls Pritchard.*, pp.257-62.

8. J. White, 'On Cementitious Architecture', p.183; J. Ionides, *Thomas Farnolls Pritchard*, pp.120-3, 171; S.R.R. 1987/47/1, Abraham Darby's Cash Book 1769-81, ff. 25, 37.

9. *Shrewsbury Chronicle* (26 February 1774, 4 February, 26 August, 9 September 1775); *Berrow's Worcester Journal* (24 February 1774).

10. S.R.R. 6001/3689, Minute Book of the Proprietors of the Iron Bridge 1773-1799, 15 September, 17 October, 21 October 1775; S.R.R. 1987/47/1, f. 36.

11. Ironbridge Gorge Museum, Estimate for the erection of a Cast-Iron Bridge.

12. For details of shareholders see S.R.R. 6001/3689, and S.R.R. 6001/3690, Bridge Assignments and Transfers. Biographical details are drawn from the *Shrewsbury Chronicle* 1772-1810, from sundry documents in the Forester Collection, S.R.R. 1224, and from probate records of the Diocese of Hereford in the Herefordshire Record Office.

13. S.R.R. 6001/3689, 17 October 1775; S.R.R. 6001/3691, endpapers.

14. J. White, 'On Cementitious Architecture', p.183.

15. 'Estimate for the Erection of a Cast Iron Bridge', copy in Ironbridge Gorge Museum.

16. S.R.R. 6001/3689, 'Paid to Thos. Addenbrooke', account at the back of the minute book.

17. S.R.R. 6001/3691, endpapers.

18. *Journal of the House of Commons*, 1774-76, p.514; *Shrewsbury Chronicle* (17 February 1776).

19. *Journal of the House of Commons*, 1774-76, p.558.

20. *Journal of the House of Commons*, 1774-76, pp. 580, 598, 635, 640, 667, 679; *Journal of the House of Lords*, 1774-76, pp. 583, 587, 589, 593.

21. S.R.R. 6001/3689, 17 October 1775, 15 May, 24 July 1776; *Shrewsbury Chronicle* (18 May, 1 June, 13 July 1776).

22. S.R.R. 6001/3689, 1 October, 18 October 1776.

23. S.R.R. 6001/3689, 18 October 1776, 31 March, 14 July, 20 October 1777, 'Paid to Thos. Addenbrooke', account at the back of the minute book; S.R.R. 6001/3690, Bridge Assignments and Transfers; *Shrewsbury Chronicle* (26 October 1776).

24. S.R.R. 6001/3689, 14 July 1777.

25. S.R.R. 3689/6001; Ironbridge Gorge Museum, Cash Book of Abraham Darby III, 1769-81, ff. 44, 55.

26. See below, p.36.

27. National Museum of Scotland, Register No. T.1928.3. We are grateful to John Crompton, Curator of Engineering and Industry at the National Museum of Scotland, for much assistance in tracing the origins of the model.

28. J. Fisher, *An American Quaker in the British Isles* (ed. K. Morgan, 1991), p.266.

29. S.R.R. 1514/2/820. We are grateful to James Lawson for this reference.

30. National Museum of Scotland, Prof. A. H. Jameson – Science Museum, Edinburgh, 11 March 1927; Edgar Smith – Rowatt, 13 February 1927; F. & J. Wright, estimate for packing case for bridge, 30 March 1927. See also C. Hibbert, *George III: personal history* (1998), pp.193-94.

31. *Illustrated London News* (1 July 1843).

32. *Shrewsbury Chronicle* (27 December 1777).

33. J.Ionides, *Thomas Farnolls Pritchard*, p.171. See also fig.10, p.12.

34. S. Smith, *A View from the Iron Bridge* (1979), p.8. The portrait is held by the Ironbridge Gorge Museum.

III: Realisation

1. R.Labouchere, ed., *Abiah Darby of Coalbrookdale* (1988), pp. 97, 108, 154.

2. A. Raistrick, *Dynasty of Ironfounders*, (1953), pp.88-9; A. Raistrick, *Quakers in Science and Industry* (1950), pp.146-51; H.M.Rathbone, *Letters of Richard Reynolds* (1852), pp.31-2, 126.

3. B. Trinder, *The Industrial Revolution in Shropshire* (2000), pp. 106-08; *The Letter Book of Richard Crawshay 1788-1797*, ed. C. Evans and G.G.L. Hays (1990), p.70.

4. Birmingham Reference Library, Boulton & Watt Collection, Box 2 'R'; W. Reynolds – W. Rathbone, 30 12mo. 1777, quoted in A. Raistrick, *Dynasty of Ironfounders* (1953), p.94.

5. S.R.R. 749/29-32; E. Thomas, *Coalbrookdale and the Darbys* (1999), pp.79-80.

6. S.R.R. 3690, Iron Bridge Assignments and Transfers.

7. R. Labouchere, *Abiah Darby of Coalbrookdale*, pp.182-3.

8. S.R.R. 1987/47/1, Abraham Darby's Cash Book 1769-81, f. 17.

9. S.R.R. 1987/47/1, ff. 10-11, 20, 50; I.G.M., 1993:3374, Abraham Darby III's Ledger, f. 53.

10. S.R.R. 1987/47/1, ff.10, 25-26, 30; I.G.M. 1979.1076, Catalogue of Farming stock ... &c ... belonging to the late Mr Abraham Darby of the Hay Farm, Madeley, sale, 7/8/11/12 May 1789; *Shrewsbury Chronicle* (27 December 1777). Samuel Darby, iron merchant was elected a member of the Society of Arts on 16 October 1776, and Abraham Darby, ironmaster, on 19 February 1777. We are grateful to Susan Bennett, formerly archivist to the Royal Society of Arts, for this information.

11. S.R.R. 1987/47/1, f. 20; R. Labouchere, *Abiah Darby of Coalbrookdale*, p. 174.

12. R. Labouchere, *Abiah Darby of Coalbrookdale*, pp.183-4, 198, 204-5, 209; E. Thomas, *Coalbrookdale and the Darbys*, pp.95-6.

13. E. Thomas, *Coalbrookdale and the Darbys*, pp.69, 79-80.

14. S. Smith, *A View from the Iron Bridge* (1979), pp.20, 22-3; W. Camden, *Britannia* (ed. R. Gough, 1789),

vol. 2, pp.357-8.

15. I.G.M., 1993:3374, Abraham Darby III's Ledger.

16. S.R.R. 1987/47/1, Abraham Darby's Cash Book 1769-81; S.R.R. 1987/47/2, Abraham Darby's Cash Book 1784-89.

17. A. Young, *Tours in England and Wales* (ed. 1932), pp. 145-53; J.M. Fisher, *An American Quaker in the British Isles* (ed. K. Morgan, 1991), pp.264-7; *The Journal of John Wesley* (ed. N. Curnock, 1938), vol. 6, pp.225-6.

18. N. Scarfe, ed., *Innocent Espionage* (1985), pp. 93-6; M.W. Thompson, ed., *The Journeys of Sir Richard Colt Hoare* (1983), pp.167-8; R. Warner, *A Tour through the Northern Counties of England* (1802), vol. 2, pp.182, 185-7. See also B. Trinder, *The Most Extraordinary District in the World* (1988), *passim*.

19. *Edinburgh Encyclopedia*, vol. 6, p.539.

20. S. Smith, *A View from the Iron Bridge*, p.17.

21. *Ironbridge Quarterly* 1997 (3), p.15.

22. We are grateful to Shelley White of the Ironbridge Gorge Museum Archaeology Unit for her observations prior to the publication of a monograph.

23. 16 Geo. III, c.17, 1776.

24. S.R.R. 6001/3689, Minute Book of the Proprietors of the Iron Bridge 1773-1799, 15 May 1776; S.R.R. 1987/47/1, ff. 57, 61, 63, 65.

25. S.R.R. 240/6, Minute Book of the Proprietors of the Tontine Hotel, 17 January 1785.

26. S.R.R. 6001/3689, 10 July 1781, 19 July 1782, 15 July 1785.

27. S.R.R. 6001/3689, 25 April 1776, 2 May 1777, 28 April 1778, 30 April 1779; S.R.R. 1987/47/1, ff.32, 42, 52, 61, 62; I.G.M., 1993:3374, ff. 22-25.

28. S.R.R. 6001/3697, 4 June 1800.

29. I.G.M., 1993:3374, ff. 22-25; A. Blackwall, *Historic Bridges of Shropshire* (1985), p.108.

30. *The Iron Bridge cast at Coalbrookdale*, published 1782 by James Phillips, with 'an elevation of the bridge' (including text on its construction).

31. H. Hodson, 'The Iron Bridge: its manufacture and construction', *Industrial Archaeology Review* vol. 15 (1992), p.41.

32. J.M. Fisher, *An American Quaker in the British Isles*, p.265; R.Hayman, W. Horton and S. White, *Archaeology and Conservation in Ironbridge* (1999), 26-8, 36-7.

33. *The Hatchett Diary* (ed. A. Raistrick, 1967), pp.57-60; R. Warner, *A Tour through the Northern Counties of England* (1802), vol. 2, pp.185-7.

34. This suggestion was first made by the late W.K.V. Gale at a conference at the Shropshire Adult College, Attingham Park, in 1968, but that scrupulous scholar always emphasised that he was hazarding an opinion for which there was no evidence in original sources.

35. R. Hayman, W. Horton and S. White, *Archaeology and Conservation in Ironbridge*, pp.61-5.

36. *Ironbridge Quarterly*, 2001.4, p.1. See below p.50.

37. *The Journal of John Wesley* (ed. N. Curnock, 1938), vol. 6, pp.225-6.

38. *Shrewsbury Chronicle* (10 July 1779).

39. I.G.M., 1993:3374, f. 22-5; S.R.R. 1987/47/1, ff. 52-6.

40. H. Hodson, 'The Iron Bridge: its manufacture and construction', p.41; D.J. Parry, 'The Construction and Importance of the Iron Bridge', Liverpool School of Architecture, BA Dissertation, 1971; J. Smith, *A Conjectural Account of the erection of the Iron Bridge* (1979), North East London Polytechnic.

41. I.G.M., 1993:3374, f. 23; S.R.R. 1987/47/1, f. 55.

42. We are grateful to Shelley White for her observations on this matter.

43. I.G.M., 1993:3374, f. 23; S.R.R. 1987/47/1, f. 54.

44. I.G.M., 1993:3374, f. 23; S.R.R. 1987/47/1, f. 57.

45. I.G.M., 1993:3374, f. 23; S.R.R. 1987/47/1, ff. 55, 57-8, 61.

46. A. Blackwall, *Historic Bridges of Shropshire*, p.107.

47. I.G.M., 1993:3374, f. 23; Information from the late Charles Hadfield, and from a descendant of Edson.

48. I.G.M., 1993:3374, ff. 22-5; S. Smiles, *Industrial Biography: Ironworkers and Toolmakers* (1863), pp. v, 90-2; J. Randall, *History of Madeley* (1880), pp. 336-9; N. Scarfe, ed., *Innocent Espionage* p. 96; S.R.R. 1987/47/2, Abraham Darby's Cash Book, 1784-89, ff. 11, 15; S.R.R. transcript of Madeley burial register.

49. T. Telford, *The Life of Thomas Telford* (ed. J. Rickman, 1838), p.29; J. White, 'On Cementitious Architecture, as applied to the construction of bridges, with a prefatory note on the first introduction of iron as the constituent material for bridges of a large span by Thomas Farnolls Pritchard in 1773', *Philosophical Magazine and Annals of Philosophy*, vol. 11 (1832), p. 183; T. Tredgold, *A Practical Essay on the strength of Cast Iron* (1824), pp.9-10; B. Trinder, *The Industrial Revolution in Shropshire* (2000), p.102. An 18th-century portrait of 'G. Dixon, Engineer, Coalbrookdale, Ironbridge' is in private hands in Sydney, Australia (correspondence in I.G.M. Library), but no evidence has been found to link anyone of that name with the Iron Bridge.

50. *Shrewsbury Chronicle* (20 January 1781).

51. I.G.M., 1993:3374, ff. 22-5; S.R.R. 1987/47/1, f. 66.

52. See below p.38.

53. Quoted in B. Trinder, *The Most Extraordinary District in the World*, p.37.

54. *The Torrington Diaries* (ed. C.B. Andrews, 1934), vol. 1, pp.283-4.

55. N. Scarfe, ed., *Innocent Espionage* (1985), p.95.

56. S.R.R. 6001/3690, Bridge Assignments and Transfers.

57. E. Thomas, *Coalbrookdale and the Darbys*, pp.79-81.
58. I.G.M. 1979.1076.
59. S.R.R. 6001/3689, 24 Oct. 1783, 8 Dec. 1786, 4 Dec. 1795, 6 Dec. 1793; S.R.R. 6001/3697, 9 Dec. 1814, 1 Jan. 1829.
60. J. Edmunds, *A View of the Iron Bridge*; S. Smith, *A View from the Iron Bridge*, p.20.

IV: The Completed Bridge

1. See above pp.5, 23.
2. An Act for building a bridge across the River Severn from Preen's Eddy in the parish of Broseley to Sheep Wash in the parish of Sutton Maddock, 17 Geo. III c. 12 (1777).
3. S.R.R.6001/331, f. 19.
4 . S.R.R. 6001/3689, 5 Feb. 1779, 12 April, 7 December 1781, 1 November 1782, 17 June 1783, 3 June 1791; S.R.R. 6001/3697, 3 December 1819.
5. S.R.R. 6001/3697, 20 February 1827, 6 June 1828, 7 December 1832; S.R.R. 1649, Commonplace Book of Thomas Beard; J. Randall, *Broseley and its Surroundings* (1879), p.328.
6. S.R.R. 6001/3689, 19 July 1782. The Wharfage is depicted on Jean Rocque's *Carte Topographique de la Comté de Shropshire* of 1752.
7. S.R.R. 1681/196, Entering Book of Orders, Proceedings &c of the Trustees of the Turnpike Road leading from the Buck's Head &c, 19 July 1805, 30 August 1805, 18 April 1806, 6 June 1806, 13 July 1810.
8. S.R.R. 6001/3697, 9 June 1809.
9. 18 Geo. III, c. 88 (1778); *Shrewsbury Chronicle* (18 Oct. 1777, 13 June 1778); Abraham Darby III Cash Book 1770-80, f. 39.
10. *Shrewsbury Chronicle* (18 Sep. 1779).
11. S.R.R. 6001/3689, 7 March, 16 June 1783.
12. S.R.R. 1681/196, 9 January 1776, 16 January 1778, 2 November 1781, 11 April 1785, 5 December 1788, 2 December 1791
13. 57 Geo. III c.12; *Salopian Journal* (23 August 1816,1 January 1817,1 April 1818).
14. B. Trinder, *The Most Extraordinary District in the World* (1988), pp.22-4; S. Smith, *A View from the Iron Bridge* (1979) pp.12-17; Abraham Darby III Ledger 1769-81, f. 34. The Williams paintings are held by Shrewsbury Borough Museums. No copies of the engravings are known to survive.
15. S. Smith, *A View from the Iron Bridge*, p.18; Abraham Darby III Ledger 1769-81, f. 64.
16. Smith, *A View from the Iron Bridge*, p.20.
17. *Shrewsbury Chronicle* (10 June 1780); I.G.M., Abraham Darby III Ledger 1769-81, ff. 62, 66; S. Smith, *A View from the Iron Bridge*, pp.26-31.
18. S.R.R. 1987/47/2, ff. 11, 15-16, 26-27; copy of handbill in Ironbridge Gorge Museum Library.
19. S. Smith, *A View from the Iron Bridge*, pp.18-19; Minutes of the Society of Arts, 24 October, 28 November 1787; 6 February 1788; Minutes of the Committee of Mechanics, 15 November 1787, 20 February 1788. We are grateful to Susan Bennett for these references.
21. S.Smith, *op.cit.*, pp. 33-58; B. Trinder, *The Most Extraordinary District in the World* (1988), pp.1-13.
22. B. Trinder, ed., *A Description of Coalbrookdale in 1801* (1970), p.6.
23. S.R.R. 245/6, Minute Book of the Proprietors of the Tontine Hotel, *passim*.
24. S.R.R. 6001/3689, 16 July, 3 September 1784; S.R.R. 245/6, 22 October 1784.
25. S.R.R. 245/6, 20 April 1791.
26. S.R.R. 245/6, 29 April, 14 May 1784, 17 January 1785.
27. Hereford Record Office, probate of Michael Hodgkiss, 12 October 1796; J. Alfrey & K. Clark, *The Landscape of Industry* (1993), pp.136-9.
28. *Shrewsbury Chronicle* (7, 28 June 1805).
29. C. Hulbert, *The History & Description of the Country of Salop*, (1837), pp.343-8.
30. *Shrewsbury Chronicle* (23 March 1786, 14 May 1802).
31. *Eddowes's Salopian Journal* (10 June 1807); *Shrewsbury Chronicle* (19 June 1807, 13 June 1808).
32. *Shrewsbury Chronicle* (13 October 1781; S.R.R. 6001/3689, 16 October 1781, 7 March 1783.
33. *Shrewsbury Chronicle* (17 September 1785, 25 September 1786).
34. *Shrewsbury Chronicle* (9 September 1786, 13 September 1788).
35. *Shrewsbury Chronicle* (30 July 1798; *Eddowes's Salopian Journal* (18 July, 22 August 1798).
36. *Shrewsbury Chronicle* (19 May 1815, 14 July 1815, 14 February 1817, 25 April 1817).
37. *Shrewsbury Chronicle* (15 April 1817).
38. S.R.R. Watton Collection, vol. 7, p. 214; *Eddowes's Salopian Journal* (10 March 1841).
39. Pigot & Co, *National Commercial Directory: Cheshire, Derbyshire, Nottinghamshire, Shropshire* (1829). Manchester: Pigot, p.147.
40. S. Bagshaw, *A History, Gazetteer & Directory of Shropshire* (1851), p.578.
41. *Eddowes's Salopian Journal* (7 March 1838); *Wellington Journal* (1 November 1867); S.R.R. 6001/3698, 7 June 1839; J. Randall, *History of Madeley* (1880), p. 339; S. Smiles, *Industrial Biography: Ironworkers and Toolmakers* (1863), p.92, quoting William Gregory Norris.
42. S. Sidney, *Rides on Railways* (1851, ed. B. Trinder, 1973), p.139.
43. Quoted in *Ironbridge Quarterly* 1983.2. We are grateful to Shirley Strachan for this reference.
44. *Eddowes's Salopian Journal* (23 October 1878).

45. *Murray's Handbook for Shropshire* (1870), p.27.
46. *Ironbridge Quarterly* 1984.2.
47. *Borough of Wenlock Express* (22 July 1876, 26 May, 21 July 1877).
48. J. Randall, *History of Madeley* (1880), p.339.
49. J.J. Hissey, *A Leisurely Tour in England* (1913, pp.227/31. We are grateful to John Furlong for this reference.
50. *Railway Magazine*, vol. 61 (1927), pp.277-8.
51. *Shrewsbury Chronicle* (17 July 1925).
52. Quoted in J.A.R. Pimlott, *The Englishman's Holiday* (1947), pp.257-8.

V: Decay and Reconstruction

1. J.W. Fletcher, *A Dreadful Phenomenon described and Improved* (1773).
2. S.R.R. 6001/3689, 18 July 1783, 3 Dec. 1784.
3. S.R.R. 6001/3689, 19 Oct., 11 Dec. 1787, 6 June 1788; for Dundonald see B. Trinder, *The Industrial Revolution in Shropshire* (2000), pp.92-6.
4. S.R.R. 6001/3689, 3 June 1791, 7 Dec. 1792.
5. See below pp.76-7.
6. B. Trinder, *The Most Extraordinary District in the World* (1988), pp.66-7, quoting Letters from Simon Goodrich to General Sir Samuel Bentham, Goodrich Collection, Science Museum, London.
7. S.R.R. 6001/3697, 6 June, 5 Dec. 1800, 6 Mar. 1801; B. Trinder, *The Industrial Revolution in Shropshire*, p.91.
8. S.R.R. 6001/3697, 29 April, 6 May 1801. Sir R.C. Hoare, *The Journeys of Sir Richard Colt Hoare* (ed. M.W. Thompson, 1983), pp.167-8. See below pp.52-4.
9. S.R.R. 6001/3687, 4 Sep. 27 Nov. 1801; S. Smith, *A View from the Iron Bridge* (1979), p.49.
10. S.R.R. 6001/3697, 21 Feb., 6 July 1803. Memorial in St Chad's Church, Shrewsbury.
11. S.R.R. 6001/3697, 19 Aug. 1803, 6 Jan., 20 July 1804; I.G.M., Coalbrookdale MS 2, f. 271; S. Smith, *A View from the Iron Bridge*, p.58.
12. S.R.R. 6001/3697, 5 June 1807.
13. C. Hutton, *The History of Iron Bridges* (1812), p. 146.
14. S.R.R. 6001/3697, 4 Dec. 1818, 8 Dec. 1820, 6 June 1823; J. W. Hall, 'Joshua Field's Diary of a tour in 1821', *Transactions of the Newcomen Society*, vol. 6 (1925-6), pp.30-2.
15. S. Smith, *A View from the Iron Bridge*, p. 27; S.R.R. 6001/3698, 17 July 1835, 6 Dec. 1839, 8 Dec. 1843.
16. S.R.R. 6001/3698, 5 Dec. 1845; S. Smiles, *Industrial Biography: Ironworkers and Toolmakers* (1863), p.92, quoting William Gregory Norris.
17. *Wellington Journal* (30 August 1902; 25 July 1903); *Ironbridge Quarterly*, 2001.4, p.1, quoting evidence of W.H.Moore of Hastings, in *Wellington Journal* (15, 22 November 1958).
18. A. Blackwall, *Historic Bridges of Shropshire* (1985), p.19.
19. S.R.R. 760/1-47.
20. A. Blackwall, *Historic Bridges of Shropshire*, pp.81-2.
21. Report by Mott, Hay & Anderson, Civil Engineers, to the Trustees of the Iron Bridge, 19 March 1923, copy in I.G.M.
22. *Shrewsbury Chronicle* (15 May, 22 June, 3 Aug. 1934).
23. A. Raistrick, *Dynasty of Ironfounders* (1953), pp.193, 200.
24. A. Blackwall, *Historic Bridges of Shropshire*, pp.19, 101-12.
25. M. de Soissons, 119 (1991), pp.81-2; N. Cossons, 'Ironbridge – the First Ten Years', *Industrial Archaeology Review*, vol. 3 (1979), pp.179-86.
26. A. Blackwall, *Historic Bridges of Shropshire*, p.106.
27. M. de Soissons, Telford, p.119.
28. M. de Soissons, Telford, p.161.

VI: The Next Generations

1. J.G. James, 'Some Steps in the Evolution of Early Arched Bridge Designs', *Transactions of the Newcomen Society*, vol. 59 (1987-8); J.G. James, 'Iron Arched Bridge Designs in Pre-Revolutionary France', *History of Technology*, vol. 4 (1979); J.G. James, 'Russian Iron Bridges to 1850', *Transactions of the Newcomen Society*, vol. 54 (1982-3).
2. We are grateful to correspondents who have sent information about iron bridges to us personally, or to the Ironbridge Gorge Museum or the Science Museum, and in particular to Stuart Smith and John Powell who have passed on much valuable information.
3. J.G. James, 'Russian Iron Bridges to 1830', pp.347-54. Whether the Tsarskoe Selo bridges were of cast iron or wrought iron is queried in R.J.M. Sutherland, *Structural Iron 1750-1850* (1997), p.xxxiii.
4. B. Marrey, *Les Ponts Modernes* (1990), pp.107-9.
5. *Ironbridge Quarterly* (April 1972).
6. *Shrewsbury Chronicle* (23 Feb. 1791). Exhaustive enquiries by scholars in the Netherlands have failed to locate this bridge.
7. Quoted in Rev. John Burdon, *A Letter to the Wearmouth Bridge Commissioners* (1859). Copy in Sunderland Public Library.

8. B. Trinder, ed., *A Description of Coalbrookdale in 1801* (ed. 1979), p.12; I.G.M., Peskin Diaries; for the 19th-century wooden replacement see E. Thomas, *Coalbrookdale and the Darbys* (1999), p.172.

9. H. Torrens and B. Trinder, 'The Iron Bridge at Trentham', *Industrial Archaeology Review*, vol. 6 (1981-2), pp 44-55. The documents relating to the bridge are in Staffordshire Record Office, D593/F.3.2.68-69; D593/H/13/59; D593/N/2/1/1/6. See also *Shrewsbury Chronicle* (23 May 1794), *Eddowes's Salopian Journal* (21 May 1794).

10. D. Hague and S. Hughes, 'Pont-y-Cafnau: the first iron railway bridge and aqueduct', *AIA Bulletin*, vol. 9 (1982), pp.3-4; S. Hughes, *The Brecon Forest Tramroads* (1990), pp.328-9; S. Hughes, 'Aspects of the use of water power during the Industrial Revolution', *Melin*, No.4 (1988), pp.23-7; C. Hadfield, *Thomas Telford's Temptation* (1993), pp.79-81; S. Rowson and J. Wright, *The Glamorganshire and Aberdare Canals* (2001), p.65.

11. B. Trinder, *The Industrial Archaeology of Shropshire* (1996), pp.177-8; C.Hadfield, *The Canals of the East Midlands* (1966), p. 68; C. Hadfield, *The Canals of the West Midlands* (1966), pp.160-2; C. Hadfield, *Thomas Telford's Temptation*, pp.80-6; T. Ruddock, *Arch Bridge and their Builders 1735-1835* (1979), pp.149-50; C.Lewis, 'Josiah Clowes (1735-1794)', *Transactions of the Newcomen Society*, vol. 50 (1978-9), pp.157-9; S. Hughes, 'Aspects of the use of water power', pp.23-37.

12. *Derby Mercury* (17 February 1795); F. Nixon, *The Industrial Archaeology of Derbyshire* (1969), pp.107, 149; *Waterways World* (February 1980); R.B. Schofield, *Benjamin Outram* (2000), pp.65-9, 74-5.

13. C. Hutton, *History of Iron Bridges* (1812), p. 146; T. Ruddock, *Arch Bridge and their Builders*, pp.138-9. See below pp.68, 80.

14. W.White, *Directory of the Borough of Sheffield* (1833), p.62; Institution of Civil Engineers, J.G. James Collection; *The Cutting Edge* (journal of the Sheffield Trades Historical Society), No.4 (1988), No. 8 (1992).

15. E. DeLony, 'Tom Paine's Bridge', *American Heritage of Invention and Technology*, vol. 15 (2000), p.38.

16. J.G. James, 'Tom Paine's Iron Bridge Work 1785-1803', *Transactions of the Newcomen Society*, vol. 59 (1987-8), pp.193-5.

17. Thomas Paine to Sir George Staunton, 25 May 1780, *penes* Royal Society of Arts, copy in Sunderland Public Library.

18. J.G. James, 'Tom Paine's Iron Bridge Work', pp.207-10; E. DeLony, 'Tom Paine's Bridge', p. 43; A. Rees, *Cyclopaedia* (1819), vol. V, sub BRIDGE.

19. The drawing is inscribed 'Given to Isaac Rodds in 1823 by Samuel Clarke, Esq., this design was made and executed by Thomas Paine at The Holmes works'.

20. For Paine see also E. Kemp, 'Thomas Paine and his "Pontifical Matters"', *Transactions of the Newcomen Society*, vol. 49 (1977); W.H.G.Armytage, 'Thomas Paine and the Walkers', *Pennsylvania History*, vol. 18 (1951); T. Ruddock, *Arch Bridge and their Builders*, pp.135-7.

21. J. Summerson, *John Nash* (1935), pp.43-5, 53-4; *Shrewsbury Chronicle* (30 Oct. 1795); *Eddowes's Salopian Journal* (3 Oct. 1798); I.G.M., Coalbrookdale MS 2, f.89; C. Hutton, *History of Iron Bridges* (1812), pp.146-66; *Repository of Arts and Manufactures*, vol. 6 (1797), p. 361; T. Ruddock, *Arch Bridge and their Builders*, pp.140-1; J.G. James, 'Some Steps …', p.150.

22. Worcestershire Record Office, 250.1, BA 5512, Specifications for taking down and reconstructing Stanford Bridge; *Victoria History of Worcestershire*, vol. 4 (1971), p.341.

23. 30 Geo. III c.90; Sunderland Museum, Account Book of the Commissioners of Wearmouth Bridge 1792-1836; A. Rees, *Cyclopaedia* (1819), vol. 5, 'BRIDGE'. See also S. Miller, 'The Iron Bridge at Sunderland: a Revision', *Industrial Archaeology Review*, vol. 11 (1976), pp.70-2; J.G. James, 'The Cast-Iron Bridges of Thomas Wilson', pp.55-7; J.G. James, *The Cast Iron Bridge at Sunderland* (1986), *passim*; C. Hutton, *History of Iron Bridges*, pp.146-66; Revd. J. Burdon, A Letter to the Wearmouth Bridge Commissioners (1859), copy in Sunderland Public Library; T. Ruddock, *Arch Bridge and their Builders*, pp.137-9.

24. *Newcastle Courant* (13 Aug. 1796).

25. Revd. J. Burdon, A Letter to the Wearmouth Bridge Commissioners (1859), copy in Sunderland Public Library.

26. A. Raistrick, ed., *The Hatchett Diary* (1967), p.78.

27. A. Rees, *Cyclopaedia* (1819), vol. 5, 'BRIDGE'.

28. J. Summerson, *op.cit.*, pp.44-5; J.G. James, 'Some steps …', p.157.

29. *Newcastle Chronicle* (13 August, 10 September 1796).

30. E.T. Svedenstierna, *Svedenstierna's Tour of Great Britain 1802-03* (ed. M.W. Flinn, 1973), pp.117-18.

31. R. Warner, *A tour through the Northern Counties of England* (1802), vol. 1, p.308.

32. J.L. Ferns, 'The Walker Company of Rotherham', *Industrial Archaeology*, vol. 12 (1977), pp.213-15; D. Bayliss, *A Guide to the Industrial History of South Yorkshire* (1995), pp.20-1; A.H. John, ed., *The Walker Family* (1951); R. Warner, *A tour through the Northern Counties*, p.197; J. Gloag and D. Bridgwater, *A History of Cast Iron in Architecture* (1948), pp.73-6.

33. J.G. James, 'The Cast-Iron Bridges of Thomas Wilson', pp.58-60; L. Simond, *Journey of a Tour* (1815), pp. 63-4; J. Hakewill, *A Picturesque Tour of Jamaica* (1825), plate 'View of the Spanish Town bridge'.

34. J.G. James, 'The Cast-Iron Bridges of Thomas Wilson', p.60.

35. R. Warner, *A tour through the Northern Counties*, vol. 1, p.197; C. Hutton, *History of Iron Bridges*, p. 146; R. Southey, *Letters from England* (1951), pp.43-4; J.G. James, 'The Cast-Iron Bridges of Thomas Wilson', pp.60-3; J. Schopenhauer, *Reise nach England* (1982), p.236. We are grateful to Peter de Clercq for the last reference.

36. C. Hutton, *History of Iron Bridges*, p.146; J. Graves, *History of Cleveland* (1808), pp.64-8; *Newcastle Courant* (18 January 1806); J.G. James, 'The Cast-Iron Bridges of Thomas Wilson', pp.63-4.

37. J. Gloag and D. Bridgwater, *A History of Cast Iron in Architecture*, pp. 92, 98; J. G. James, 'The Cast-Iron Bridges of Thomas Wilson', pp.64-9; J.G.James, 'Some steps …', pp.158-61; N.W. Wright, *Lincolnshire Towns and Industry 1700-1914*, p.50; C.T.G. Boucher, *John Rennie 1761-1821*, p.122; C. Hutton, *The History of Iron Bridges*, pp.152-3; P.Thompson, *The History and Antiquities of Boston* (1856), p.38; T. Ruddock, *Arch Bridges and their Builders*, pp.138-9.

38. J.G. James, 'Some steps …', p. 158; J.G. James, 'The Cast-Iron Bridges of Thomas Wilson', pp.69-70; J. L. Ferns, 'The Walker Company of Rotherham', p.215; F.W.Bull, *A History of Newport Pagnell* (1900), pp.169-70.

39. *Derby Mercury* (18 February 1795); C. Hadfield and G. Biddle, *The Canals of North-West England* (1970), vol.2, pp.307-8; R.B. Schofield, *Benjamin Outram*, pp.131-6.

40. C. Hadfield and G. Biddle, *The Canals of North-West England*, vol.2, pp.324-6, 329; D. Chadderton, 'Outram's Iron Aqueduct at Stalybridge' (1977), pp.43-6; R.B. Schofield, *Benjamin Outram*, pp.97-100.

41. N. Cossons, *The BP Book of Industrial Archaeology* (1993), pp.264-7.

42. C. Hadfield and A.W. Skempton, *William Jessop: Engineer* (1979), pp.141-53; C. Hadfield, *Thomas Telford's Temptation*, pp. 87-114; A. Rees, *Cyclopaedia* (1819), vol. 6, 'CANAL'.

43. William Reynolds died in 1803. The Mr Reynolds who negotiated with the canal company was probably his half-brother Joseph.

44. A.H. Faulkner, *The Grand Junction Canal* (1993), pp.38-44; A.H. Faulkner, 'The Wolverton Aqueduct', *Transport History*, vol. 2 (1969), pp.155-60; J.G. James, 'The Evolution of Iron Bridge Trusses to 1850', *Transactions of the Newcomen Society*, vol. 52 (1980-1), p.68.

45. C. Hadfield, *The Canals of the West Midlands* (1966), pp.200-01, 223, 326-7.

46. C. Hadfield and J. Norris, *Waterways to Stratford* (1962), pp.88-9, 101-3, 121; A. Sealey, *Bridges and Aqueducts* (1976), p.48; Nicholson, *Guide to the Waterways, 3, Birmingham and the Heart of England* (1997), p.134.

47. J.R. Hume, *The Industrial Archaeology of Scotland, vol. 1: The Central Lowlands and Borders* (1976), pp.33-4, 259; G.D. Hay and G.P. Snell, *Monuments of Industry* (1986), pp.192-3.

48. T. Telford, *The Life of Thomas Telford*, pp.78-80; C. Hadfield, *The Canals of the West Midlands*, pp. 210-14.

49. N. Crowe, *The English Heritage Book of Canals* (1994), p.60; H. Compton, *The Oxford Canal* (1976), pp.92-100; F. Brook, *The Industrial Archaeology of the British Isles: The West Midlands* (1977), p.197; D.W. Hadley, 'The Role of Iron in Reconstructing the Oxford Canal', *Journal of the Railway and Canal Historical Society*, vol. 15 (1976), pp.9-15; J.S. Allen, *A History of Horseley, Tipton* (2000), p.25; A.W. Skempton *et al.*, *A Biographical Dictionary of Civil Engineers* (2002), pp.532-3.

50. See below pp.83-4.

51. J.H. Andrew, 'The Canal at Smethwick', *Industrial Archaeology Review*, vol. 17 (1995), pp.179, 182-3, 186; Institute of Civil Engineers, Historic Engineering Works Database.

52. N. Crowe, *English Heritage Book of Canals* (1994), p.60; J.G. James, 'The Evolution of Iron Bridge Trusses …', p.70; A.W. Skempton *et al.*, *A Biographical Dictionary of Civil Engineers*, pp. 398 400.

53. S. Hughes, *The Archaeology of the Montgomeryshire Canal* (1989), pp.25-31; W.J. Crompton, *A Guide to the Industrial Archaeology of the West Midland Iron District* (1991), p.29; F. Brook, *The Industrial Archaeology of the British Isles: the West Midlands*, p.197.

54. D. Hague and S. Hughes, 'Pont-y-Cafnau', p.3; W.L. Davies, *The Bridges of Merthyr* (1993), pp.85, 230, 233.

55. D. Hague and S. Hughes, 'Pont-y-Cafnau', p.3; W.L. Davies, *The Bridges of Merthyr*, pp.8, 239-42.

56. D. Hague and S. Hughes, 'Pont-y-Cafnau', pp.3-4; W.L. Davies, *The Bridges of Merthyr*, pp.150-5, 361-5, 404; S. Rowson and I.Wright, *The Glamorganshire and Aberdare Canals* (2001), p.45.

57. D. Hague and S. Hughes, 'Pont-y-Cafnau', p.3.; W.L. Davies, *The Bridges of Merthyr*, pp.134, 338-9, 403; S. Rowson and I. Wright, *The Glamorganshire and Aberdare Canals*, pp.84, 263-4.

58. M.V. Symonds, *Coal Mining in the Llanelli Area* (1979), vol.1, pp.95-100, 130-9, 202; S. Hughes, *The Brecon Forest Tramroads* (1990), p.328.

59. W.L. Davies, *The Bridges of Merthyr*, pp.107-9, 278.

60. W.L. Davies, *The Bridges of Merthyr*, pp.118, 296, 407.

61. W.L. Davies, *The Bridges of Merthyr*, pp.67, 119-20, 145-6, 175, 184, 353; S. Rowson and I. Wright, *The Glamorganshire and Aberdare Canals*, p.45.

62. S. Rowson and I. Wright, *The Glamorganshire and Aberdare Canals*, pp.45, 230, 239.

63. S. Hughes, *The Brecon Forest Tramroads*, p.329; D.M. Rees, *The Industrial Archaeology of South Wales* (1975), p.253.

64. We are grateful to Dr. Peter Wakelin of Cadw for information on this and other bridges in South Wales.

65. S. Hughes, *The Brecon Forest Tramroads*, p.328.

66. D.M.Rees, *The Industrial Archaeology of South Wales*, p.235.

67. D. Hague and S. Hughes, 'Pont-y-Cafnau', p.4; W.L. Davies, *The Bridges of Merthyr*, pp.18, 59.

68. A. Raistrick, *Dynasty of Ironfounders* (1953), pp.208-19.

69. *Shrewsbury Chronicle* (13 February 1795).

70. *Eddowes's Salopian Journal* (18 February 1795).

71. See above pp.47-9.

72. See above p.28.

73. We are grateful to James Lawson for information on the career of William Hayward.

74. For a detailed account of the bridge see B. Trinder, 'Coalport Bridge: A Study in Historical Interpretation', *Industrial Archaeology Review*, vol. 3 (1979), pp.153-7. See also A.H. Blackwall, *Historic Bridges of Shropshire* (1985), pp.19-22.

75. *Shrewsbury Chronicle* (17 April, 10 July 1795); A.H. Blackwall, *Historic Bridges of Shropshire*, pp.50-5; C. Hutton, *The History of Iron Bridges*, pp.147-9; J.G. James, 'Some Steps …', p.159.

76. *Shrewsbury Chronicle* (13 February, 10 July 1795); M.C. Hill, 'Iron and Steel Bridges in Shropshire 1788-1901', *Transactions of the Shropshire Archaeological Society*, vol. 56 (1956-7), p.113.

77. *Shrewsbury Chronicle* (19 July 1795, 5 October 1798); C. Hutton, *The History of Iron Bridges*, p.149.

78. See above p.65.

79. A.H. Blackwall, *Historic Bridges of Shropshire*, p.50.

80. I.G.M., CBD MS 2, Coalbrookdale Settling Journal, 1797-1808.

81. See below p.90.

82. I.G.M., CBD MS 2, f. 343; T. Ruddock, *Arch Bridges and their Builders*, pp.160-2; C. Hadfield and A.W. Skempton, *William Jessop: Engineer*, pp.231-4.

83. I.G.M., CBD MS 2, f.459.

84. *Eddowes's Salopian Journal* (5, 12 June 1816).

85. S.H. Spiker, *Travels through England, Wales & Scotland in the year 1816* (1820), pp.70-4; B. Trinder, *The Most Extraordinary District in the World* (1988), p.89.

86. *Shrewsbury Chronicle* (24 October 1817); *Gentleman's Magazine*, vol. 87 (1817), p.464.

87. A.H.Blackwall, *Historic Bridges of Shropshire*, p.43.

88. R.J.Sherlock, 'Industrial Archaeology in Administrative Staffordshire', *North Staffordshire Journal of Field Studies*, vol. 2 (1962), pp.81-2; R.J. Sherlock, *The Industrial Archaeology of Staffordshire* (1976), pp.114, 149-51; T. Ruddock, *Arch Bridges and their Builders 1735-1835*, p.169.

89. J.B. Lawson, 'Thomas Telford in Shrewsbury', A.Penfold, ed., *Thomas Telford: Engineer* (1980), pp.1-22.

90. See above pp.61-2, 70-1, 78.

91. J. Killer, *Die Werke der Baumeister Grubenmann* (4th ed., 1998), pp. 25-28; H.S.Smith, *The World's Great Bridges* (1954), p.61.

92. T. Telford, *The Life of Thomas Telford* (ed. J.Rickman, 1838), p.31.

93. A.H. Blackwall, *Historic Bridges of Shropshire*, p.51; B. Trinder, *The Industrial Archaeology of Shropshire* (1996), pp.194-5.

94. A.W. Skempton, 'Telford and the design for a new London Bridge', A. Penfold, ed., *Thomas Telford: Engineer*, pp.62-83; T. Ruddock, *Arch Bridges and their Builders*, pp.159-61; C. Hutton, *The History of Iron Bridges*, pp.157-9.

95. J. Banks, *A Treatise on Mills* (1795), subscribers' list; J. Banks, *On the Power of Machines* (1803), pp.89-91; T. Telford, *The Life of Thomas Telford*, p.682; J.F. Reigart, *The Life of Robert Fulton* (1856), pp.93-6.

96. C. Hutton, *The History of Iron Bridges*; T. Tredgold, *A Practical Essay on the Strength of Cast Iron* (1824); E. Hodgkinson, 'Theoretical and experimental researches to ascertain the strength and best forms of iron beams', *Memoirs of the Literary and Philosophical Society of Manchester*, 2nd Series, vol. 5 (1831), pp.407-544; W. Fairbairn, *On the Application of Cast and Wrought Iron to Building Purposes* (1854), pp.2, 31. The key articles analysing the development of structural theory in relation to iron are contained in R.J.M. Sutherland, ed., *Structural Iron, 1750-1850* (1997).

97. B. Trinder, *The Industrial Archaeology of Shropshire*, pp. 57-60.

98. A.H. Blackwall, *Historic Bridges of Shropshire*, pp.26-7, 48-9; *Eddowes's Salopian Journal* (21 August 1811).

99. A.H. Blackwall, *Historic Bridges of Shropshire*, pp.37, 48-50; *Eddowes's Salopian Journal* (15 April, 20 May 1812; 10 June, 22 July 1818).

100. *Eddowes's Salopian Journal* (7 August 1816).

101. A.H. Blackwall, *Historic Bridges of Shropshire*, p.43; T. Telford, *The Life of Thomas Telford*, plate 27; J. Gloag and D. Bridgwater, *A History of Cast Iron in Architecture*, pp.96-7.

102. T. Telford, *The Life of Thomas Telford*, pp.399, 458, plate 51; G. Nelson, *Highland Bridges* (1990), pp.149-52; *Building News*, vol. 62 (8 April 1892), p.592; T. Ruddock, *Arch Bridges and their Builders*, p.162; *Shrewsbury Chronicle* (5 June 1812).

103. T. Telford, *The Life of Thomas Telford*, pp.566-8 and plate 77.

104. T. Telford, *The Life of Thomas Telford*, pp.400, plate 47; G. Nelson, *Highland Bridges*, pp.87-9; J.R. Hume, 'Cast-Iron and Bridge-building in Scotland', *Industrial Archaeology Review*, vol. 2(1978), p. 296; J.R. Hume, 'Telford's Highland Bridges', A. Penfold, ed., *Thomas Telford Engineer* (1980), p.177.

105. Library of the Institution of Civil Engineers, J.G. James Collection.

106. T. Telford, *The Life of Thomas Telford*, pp.255-8, plate 81.

107. C.E. Welch, 'The Iron Bridge at Plymouth', *Report & Transactions of the Devonshire Association*, vol.98 (1966), pp.370-83. We are grateful to Keith Perkins for information on the Laira bridge.

108. T. Telford, *The Life of Thomas Telford*, p.85, plate 26; J.S. Allen, *A History of Horseley, Tipton*, p.25.

109. B. Trinder, *The Industrial Archaeology of Shropshire*, pp.57-60; J. Morris, *The Shropshire Union Canal* (1991), p.27; *Shrewsbury Chronicle* (30 November 1840) for Hazledine's obituary. None of the Hazledine company papers survive.

110. *Shrewsbury Chronicle* (16 April 1802; 22 April, 13 May 1803); British Parliamentary Papers, Report of

Commissioners appointed to enquire into the application of Iron to Railway Structures (1849), pp.287, 387.

111. J. Gloag and D. Bridgwater, *A History of Cast Iron in Architecture*, p.97; E. de Maré, *Bridges of Britain*, p.78; C.T.G. Boucher, *John Rennie 1761-1821*, p.133; *Gloucester Journal* (13 December 1813; 2 January 1815).

112. C.T. Boucher, *John Rennie 1761-1821*, pp.15, 49, 110-11, 122, 127, 129, 131, 134; C.T.G. Boucher, 'John Rennie 1761-1821', *Transactions of the Newcomen Society* vol. 34 (1961-2), pp.1-15; J.R. Hume, 'Cast Iron and Bridge-Building in Scotland', *Industrial Archaeology Review* vol. 2 (1978), p.290; P. Riden, *The Butterley Company 1790-1830* (1973), p.47; T. Ruddock, *Arch Bridges and their Builders 1735-1835* (1979), pp.166-7; J. Gloag and D. Bridgwater, *A History of Cast Iron in Architecture*, p.99; N.W. Wright, *Lincolnshire Towns and Industry 1700-1914*, pp.48-9; S. Croad, *London's Bridges* (1983), pp.13-14; J. Pudney, *Crossing London's River* (1972), pp.13-14.

113. J.L. Ferns, 'The Walker Company of Rotherham', *Industrial Archaeology*, vol. 12 (1977), p.215.

114. P. Riden, *The Butterley Company 1790-1830*, pp.6-36.

115. Library of the Institution of Civil Engineers, J.G.James Collection.

116. P. Riden, *The Butterley Company 1790-1830*, pp.47-49; J.G. James, 'Some Steps …', p.167; S. Croad, *London's Bridges* (1983), pp.38-40; J. Pudney, *Crossing London's River* (1972), pp.71-5; C. Hadfield and A.W. Skempton, *William Jessop: Engineer*, p.46.

117. J.G. James, 'Some Steps …', pp.171, 184-5; Library of the Institution of Civil Engineers, J.G. James Collection; *Building News* No.71 (1896), p.186.

118. J.I. Langford, *A Towpath Guide to the Staffordshire & Worcestershire Canal* (1974), pp.49-50, 168, 213-14, 219, plates 31, 36, 64, 65; Bridges 11 (SO 827744), 12 (SO 827756), 41 (SO 862908), 42 (SO 860913), 49 (SO 859949), 95 (SJ 936199).

119. SO 927867.

120. C. Hadfield and J. Norris, *Waterways to Stratford* (1962), pp. 88-9, plate 23; Stratford Canal examples includes bridges 32 and 33 by locks 7 and 8 of the Lapworth flight, at SP 176714 and SP 182712, on the northern section of the canal, three bridges at Kingswood Junction (SP 187708) and bridge 38 at SP 186708 on the southern section. There are more examples between Kingswood and Stratford.

121. Chirk Bank, Monks Bridge, No. 21 (SJ 292371); Trevor Basin, Scotch Hall Bridge, No. 29 (SJ 272423), and Rhos-y-Coed Bridge, No.32 (SJ 2704220); A.H.Blackwall, *Historic Bridges of Shropshire*, pp.58-9.

122. H. Torrens, *The Evolution of a Family Firm* (1978), pp.11-14.

123. C.T.G. Boucher, 'John Rennie 1761-1821', *Transactions of the Newcomen Society* vol. 34 (1961-62), p.15; J.R. Hume, 'Cast Iron and Bridge-Building in Scotland', *Industrial Archaeology Review* vol. 2 (1978), p.296; T. Telford, *The Life of Thomas Telford*, p.155; J.G. James, 'Some Steps …', p.170; J.S.Allen, *A History of Horseley*, p.25; E.Williamson and N.Pevsner, *The Buildings of England: London Docklands* (1998), p.214.

124. Mor Brook (SO 733885); Borle Brook (SO 753817); Abingdon (SU 496997); Tewkesbury (SO 892330). C.G. Maggs and G.Beale, *The Camerton Branch* (1985), pp.4, 25, 85-7.

125. C. Hadfield and A.W. Skempton, *William Jessop: Engineer*, p.166; p.15; J.R. Hume, 'Cast Iron and Bridge-Building in Scotland', *Industrial Archaeology Review* vol. 2 (1978), p.296; G. Nelson, *Highland Bridges*, pp.22-4.

126. Bridge No. 207 (TQ 163783); J.S. Allen, *A History of Horseley, Tipton* (n.d., 2000), p.25.

127. J.S. Allen, *A History of Horseley*, pp.25, 35; N. Crowe, *English Heritage Book of Canals*, pp.52-4; S. Broadbridge, *The Birmingham Canal Navigations 1768-1846* (1974), p.93.

128. H. Compton, *The Oxford Canal* (1976), pp.92-100; D.W. Hadley, 'The Role of Iron in Reconstructing the Oxford Canal', *Journal of the Railway and Canal Historical Society*, vol. 15, pp.9-15, 25, 35.

129. R. Southey, *Letters from England* (1951), p.44.

130. See above p.8.

131. J.G. James, 'Russian Iron Bridges to 1850', pp.86, 98; J.G. James, 'Some steps …', p.56.

132. *Shrewsbury Chronicle* (8 February 1826).

133. Richard Dearman to W.J.Chiswell, 5 12 mo. 1795, copy in I.G.M. Library.

134. *The Times* (18 May 1996); Northumberland Record Office, Buddle Collection, BUD/24/34, noted in Library of the Institution of Civil Engineers, J.G. James Collection.

135. Cadw Listing Record No. 17292. We are grateful to Dr Peter Wakelin for drawing this bridge to our attention.

136. Library of the Institution of Civil Engineers, HEW database; Acounts of Charles Heywood (clerk of works on the estate), 1804-33, Staffordshire Record office D615/E(F), 34; J.M.Robinson, *Shugborough* (1989), pp.79-80.

137. J.S. Allen, *A History of Horseley*, p.25; B. Trinder, ed., *The Blackwell Encyclopedia of Industrial Archaeology* (1992), p.414; J.R.Hume, 'Cast Iron and Bridge-Building in Scotland', p.296.

138. Institution of Civil Engineers, HEW database; Cathedral Close (SX 922925); Bourne bridges (TF 097200); Spa Bridge, Scarborough (TA 044882); North Street, Exeter (SX 917927).

139. *The Iris* or *Norfolk Weekly Advertiser* (10 December 1803).

140. D. Alderton and J. Booker, *The Batsford Guide to the Industrial Archaeology of East Anglia* (1980), pp.41,104-5, 130-1, 137, 150. We are also grateful to Norma Watt of Norfolk Museums Service for information on bridges in Norwich.

141. J.G. James, 'Some Steps …', pp.166, 169-70; R.N.C. Thornes, *West Yorkshire: A Noble Scene of Industry* (1981), p.33; W.J. Thompson, *A Brief Guide to the Industrial Heritage of West Yorkshire*

(1989), p.39. We are also grateful to Dr Ivor Brown for information on West Yorkshire bridges.

142. B. Marrey, *Les Ponts Modernes*, pp.109-13; J.G. James, 'Some Steps ...', pp.162-5.

143. J.G. James, 'Russian Iron Bridges to 1850', pp.347-71.

144. J. Rozpedowski, 'Iron bridges in the Lower Silesia region', ICCROM, *Ironworks and Iron Monuments* (1985), pp.409-13; E.T. Svedenstierna, *Sevedenstierna's Tour*, p.182 quoting notes in J.G.L. Blumhof, ed., *Erich T. Svedenstierna's Reise durch einen Theil von England und Schottland in den Jahren 1802 und 1803* (1811); *Schlesische Provinzialblatter* (October 1796), p.368; the bridge is illustrated in *Abbildung der Eisernen Waren welche auf den Konigl. Preuss. Eisenwerken zu Malapane, Gleiwitz und Greuzburg in Schlesien gegossen werden* (Leipzig).

145. J. Rozpedowski, 'Iron bridges in the Lower Silesa region', pp.413-17; J.G. James, 'Some Steps ...', pp.166-8; B.Trinder, *The Blackwell Encyclopedia of Industrial Archaeology* (1992), p.337.

VII: Beyond the Arch

1. B. Trinder, ed., *A Description of Coalbrookdale in 1801*, p.6; R. Warner, *A tour through the Northern Counties of England*, vol. 1, p.197.

2. C.T.G. Boucher, *John Rennie 1761-1821*, p.127; T. Telford, *The Life of Thomas Telford*, pp.566-8.

3. L.T.C. Rolt, *Thomas Telford*, pp.118-19; for Brown see T. Day, 'Samuel Brown: his influence on the design of suspension bridges', *History of Technology*, vol. 8 (1983), pp.61-90, reproduced in R.J.M. Sutherland, *Structural Iron, 1750-1850* (1997); G.D. Hay and G.P. Stell, *Monuments of Industry*, pp.186-7.

4. R.A. Paxton, 'Menai Bridge (1818-1826) and its influence on Suspension Bridge Development', *Transactions of the Newcomen Society*, vol. 49 (1977-8), pp.87-110; R.A. Paxton, 'Menai Bridge, 1818-26: evolution of design', A. Penfold, ed., *Thomas Telford: Engineer* (1980), pp.84-116.

5. D. Walters, *British Railway Bridges* (1966), pp.19-21.

6. R.J.M. Sutherland, 'The introduction of structural wrought iron', *Transactions of the Newcomen Society*, vol. 36 (1963-4), pp.271-9; L.T.C. Rolt, *Red for Danger* (ed. 1966), pp.94-5.

7. D. Walters, *British Railway Bridges*, pp.30-1.

8. E. Clark, *The Britannia and Conway Tubular Bridges* (1850); G.S. Dempsey, *Tubular and other Iron Bridges* (1850); W. Fairbairn, *An Account of the Construction of the Britannia and Conway Tubular Bridges* (1849); D. Walters, *British Railway Bridges*, pp.32-4.

9. A. Buchanan, *Brunel* (2002), pp.80-1; D. Walters, *British Railway Bridges*, pp.36-7, 43-6.

10. L.G. Booth, 'Timber Works', Sir A. Pugsley, ed., *The Works of Isambard Kingdom Brunel* (1976), pp.107-35.

11. See above p.63.

12. B. Trinder, 'Recent Research on Early Shropshire Railways', paper presented to the Second International Early Railways Conference: Manchester: September 2001; B. Trinder, *The Industrial Revolution in Shropshire* (2000), p.46. We are grateful to Richard Hayman for comments on the Cranages.

13. N. Cossons, 'Ironbridge – the First Ten Years', *Industrial Archaeology Review*, vol. 3 (1979), p.186.

Appendix: The Iron Bridge in America

1. Zaccheus Collins Papers, Folder 1810-1811, Historical Society of Pennsylvania, Philadelphia.

2. Richard Sanders Allen, authority on American covered wooden bridges, provided me with this information on 26 May 1997.

3. Zerah Colburn, 'American Iron Bridges', *Proceedings from the Institution of Civil Engineers* 22 (1863). This informative article goes into extensive detailed descriptions and evaluations of most of the important iron bridges built in America. Colburn points out the similarities between Polonceau's Pont du Carrousel and Delafield's Dunlaps Creek Bridge.

4. Eric DeLony, 'Surviving Cast and Wrought Iron Bridges in America', *IA: The Journal of the Society for Industrial Archeology*, Volume 19, Number 2, 1993. See also DeLony, 'The Golden Age of the Iron Bridge', *American Heritage of Invention & Technology*, Volume 10, Number 2, Fall 1994.

5. F.E. Griggs and A.J. DeLuzio, 'Stephen H. Long and Squire Whipple: The First American Structural Engineers', *Journal of Structural Engineering*, American Society of Civil Engineers, Vol. 121, No. 9, September 1995, pp.1352-61.

6. The other great collection of decorative cast-iron arches grace the grounds of Catherine the Great's royal palace, Tsarskoe Selo (Pushkin), in St Petersburg.

7. Llewellyn N. Edwards, 'The Evolution of Early American Bridges', *Transactions of the Newcomen Society*, Volume XIII, 1932-33, pp.161-2.

8. *Ibid.*

9. C. Shaler Smith, 'The Evolution of the Practice of American Bridge Building', *Transactions, American Society of Civil Engineers*, Paper 993, 1905, p.4.

10. Smith, pp.10-11.

11. An interesting debate illustrating the differences between American and British iron bridge construction is *American Versus English Methods of Bridge Designing*, reprinted from 'Japan Mail'. This was a series of letters which were published at intervals during 1885 and 1886, following the non-favourable review of John Alexander Low Waddell's *A System of Iron Railroad Bridges for Japan* by an anonymous Englishman. J.A.L. Waddell was one of America's most prominent consulting bridge engineers at the turn of the 19th and 20th centuries who taught civil engineering at the Imperial College in Tokyo.

Bibliography

1. Original Sources relating to the Iron Bridge

The minute and assignment books of the Proprietors of the Iron Bridge are in Shropshire Records & Research (S.R.R. 6001/3689-98) as are the Cash Books of Abraham Darby III covering the years 1769-81 (S.R.R. 1987/47/1) and 1784-9 (S.R.R., 1987/47/2), and the minute book of the proprietors of the *Tontine Hotel* (S.R.R. 245/6). The Ironbridge Gorge Museum holds Abraham Darby III's ledger, the accompanying volume to the Cash Books (I.G.M., 1993.3374), the 1775 estimate for building the bridge, and the Settling Journal of the Coalbrookdale Ironworks 1798-1808 (Coalbrookdale MS2), which includes material relating to early repairs. The Museum holds the originals or copies of most of the known prints, photographs and paintings of the bridge that have any historical significance.

2. Secondary works relating to the Iron Bridge

Alfrey, J. and Clark, K., *Landscape of Industry: patterns of change in the Ironbridge Gorge* (1993). London: Routledge

Blackwall, A.H., *Historic Bridges of Shropshire* (1985). Shrewsbury: Shropshire Books

Byng, J., *The Diary of John Byng, Viscount Torrington*, ed. C.B. Andrews (1934). London: Eyre & Spottiswoode

Camden, W., *Britannia, or a Chorographical Description of England, Scotland and Ireland* (ed. R. Gough, 1789). London; T. Payne

Chaplin, R., 'New Light on Thomas Farnolls Pritchard', *Shropshire Newsletter* No. 34 (1968)

Clark, K., *The Ironbridge Gorge* (1993). London: Batsford/English Heritage

Clark, P. and Corfield, P., *Industry and Urbanisation in Eighteenth Century England* (1994). Leicester: Centre for Urban History, University of Leicester

Cossons, N., *The BP Book of Industrial Archaeology* (3rd ed., 1993), Newton Abbot: David & Charles

Cossons, N. and Sowden, H., *Ironbridge: Landscape of Industry* (1977). London: Cassell

Cossons, N., 'Ironbridge - the First Ten Years', *Industrial Archaeology Review*, vol. 3 (1979)

Department of the Environment, Directorate of Ancient Monuments and Historic Buildings, *The Iron Bridge: Photographs taken during Repairs and Repainting, 1980* (1980). London: Department of the Environment, Directorate of Ancient Monuments and Historic Buildings

de Haan, D., 'Abraham Darby's Iron Bridge of 1779: Construction and Restoration' (unpublished working paper, 1999). Telford: Ironbridge Gorge Museum

de Soissons, M., *Telford: the making of Shropshire's New Town* (1991). Shrewsbury: Swan Hill

Dibdin, C., *Observations on a Tour through almost the whole of England and a considerable part of Scotland in a series of Letters* (1801-02). London: G. Goulding

Fisher, J.M., *An American Quaker in the British Isles: The Travel Journals of Jabez Maud Fisher, 1775-79*, ed. K. Morgan (1991). Oxford: Oxford University Press

Haddon, C.A., *The Iron Bridge, Coalbrookdale, Report on the Condition of the Bridge and proposed remedial works* (1966). Consultant's report to Sandford, Fawcett, Wilton & Bell, for Salop County Council

Hall, J.W., 'Joshua Field's Diary of a tour in 1821 through the Midlands', *Transactions of the Newcomen Society*, vol. 6 (1925-6)

Harris, J. 'Pritchard Redividus', *Journal of the Society of Architectural Historians*, vol. 11 (1968).

Hatchett, C., *The Hatchett Diary* ed. Raistrick, A. (1967). Truro: Bradford Barton

Hayman, R. and Horton, W., *Ironbridge: History and Guide* (1999). Stroud: Tempus

Hayman, R., Horton, W. and White, S., *Archaeology and Conservation in Ironbridge* (2000). London: Council for British Archaeology

Henderson, W.O., *Industrial Britain under the Regency: The Diaries of Escher, Bodmer, May and de Gallois 1814-18* (1968). London: Cass

Hibbert, C., *King George III: a personal history* (1998). London: Viking

Hissey, J.J., *A Leisurely Tour in England* (1913). London: Macmillan

Hoare, Sir R.C., *The Journeys of Sir Richard Colt Hoare through Wales and England 1793-1810*, ed. M.W. Thompson (1983). Gloucester: Sutton

Hodson, H., 'The Iron Bridge: its manufacture and construction', *Industrial Archaeology Review*, vol. 15 (1992), 36-44

Ionides, J., *Thomas Farnolls Pritchard of Shrewsbury: Architect and Inventor of Cast Iron Bridges* (1999). Ludlow: Dog Rose Press

Klingender, F.D., *Art and the Industrial Revolution* (ed. Sir Arthur Elton, 1968). London: Evelyn, Adam & Mackay

Labouchere, R., *Abiah Darby 1716-1793 of Coalbrookdale: Wife of Abraham Darby II* (1988). York: Sessions

Maguire, R. and Matthews, P., 'The Iron Bridge at Coalbrookdale', *Architectural Association Journal*, vol. 74 (1958)

Morriss, R.K., ed., *The Shropshire Severn* (1996). Shrewsbury: Shropshire Books

Morton, G.R. and Moseley, A.F., 'An Examination of Fractures in the First Iron Bridge at Coalbrookdale', *West Midland Studies*, vol. 2 (1972)

Mott, Hay and Anderson, *Iron Bridge, Shropshire: report to the Trustees of the Bridge* (1923). London: Mott, Hay & Anderson

Murray, J., *Murray's Handbook for Shropshire* (1870). London: John Murray

Muter, W. G., *The Buildings of an Industrial Community: Ironbridge and Coalbrookdale* (1979). Chichester: Phillimore

Parry, D.J., 'The Construction and Importance of the Iron Bridge', University of Liverpool School of Architecture, BA Dissertation (1971)

Perkins, T.R., 'Railways in the Severn Valley', *Railway Magazine*, vol. 61 (1927)

Plumptre, J., *James Plumptre's Britain: the Journals of a Tourist in the 1790s*, ed. I. Ousby (1992). London: Hutchinson

Powell, J. and Vanns, M.A., *The Archives Photographs Series: South Telford: Ironbridge Gorge, Madeley and Dawley* (1995). Stroud: Chalford

Raistrick, A., *Quakers in Science and Industry* (1950). London: Bannisdale

Raistrick, A., *Dynasty of Ironfounders: the Darbys and Coalbrookdale* (2nd edition 1989). York: Sessions

Randall, J., *The Severn Valley* (1862). London: Virtue

Randall, J., *Broseley and its Surroundings* (1879). Madeley: Randall

Randall, J., *The History of Madeley* (1880). Madeley: *Wrekin Echo*. Reprint, ed. Trinder, B. Shrewsbury: Shropshire Books, 1975

Randall, J., *The Wilkinsons* (n.d.). Madeley: *The Salopian*

Rix, M.M., 'Industrial Archeology', *The Amateur Historian*, vol.2 (1955)

Rix, M.M., 'A Proposal to Establish National Parks of Industrial Archaeology', *Journal of Industrial Archaeology*, vol. 1 (1964)

Rolt, L.T.C., *Landscape with Canals* (1977). London: Allen Lane

Sandford, Fawcett, Wilton & Bell, *Report on the Iron Bridge at Coalbrookdale* (1969). Consultant's report for Salop County Council. London: Sandford, Fawcett, Wilton & Bell

Scarfe, N., ed., *Innocent Espionage: the La Rochefoucauld Brothers' Tour of England in 1785* (1985). Woodbridge: Boydell

Sidney, S., *Rides on Railways* (1851, ed. B. Trinder, 1973). Chichester: Phillimore

Smiles, S., *Industrial Biography: Ironworkers and Toolmakers* (1863). London: John Murray

Smith, D.J., *The Severn Valley Railway* (1967). Bracknell: Town & Country Press

Smith, J., *A Conjectural Account of the erection of the Iron Bridge* (1979). London: North East London Polytechnic

Smith, S.B., *A View from the Iron Bridge* (1979). London: Thames & Hudson

Spiker, S.H., *Travels through England, Wales and Scotland in the year 1816*, 2 vols. (1820). London: Lacking

Sutherland, R.J.M., ed., *Structural Iron 1750-1850* (1997). Aldershot: Ashgate

Svedenstierna, E., *Svedenstierna's Tour in Great Britain 1802-03: the Travel Diary of an Industrial Spy*, ed. Flinn, M.W. (1973). Newton Abbot: David & Charles

Telford, T., *The Life of Thomas Telford* (ed. Rickman, J., 1838). London: Hansard

Telford, T. and Nimmo, A., 'Bridge', *Edinburgh Encyclopaedia* (1830), vol. 4, Edinburgh: Blackwood

Thomas, E., *Coalbrookdale and the Darbys* (1999). York: Sessions

Trinder, B., *A Description of Coalbrookdale in 1801* (1970). Telford: Ironbridge Gorge Museum Trust

Trinder, B., 'The First Iron Bridges', *Industrial Archaeology Review*, vol. 3 (1979). Reprinted in Sutherland, R.J.M., *Structural Iron* (1997)

Trinder, B., 'Coalport Bridge: a Study in Historical Interpretation', *Industrial Archaeology Review*, vol. 3 (1979)

Trinder, B., *The Most Extraordinary District in the World: Ironbridge and Coalbrookdale*, 2nd edition (1988). Chichester: Phillimore

Trinder, B., *The Darbys of Coalbrookdale* (2nd edition, 1992). Chichester: Phillimore

Trinder, B., 'The Shropshire Coalfield', Clark, P. and Corfield, P., *Industry and Urbanisation in Eighteenth Century England* (1994). Leicester; Centre for Urban History, University of Leicester

Trinder, B., *The Industrial Archaeology of Shropshire* (1996). Phillimore: Chichester

Trinder, B., 'The (Severn) Navigation', Morriss, R.K., ed., *The Shropshire Severn* (1996). Shrewsbury: Shropshire Books

Trinder, B., *The Industrial Revolution in Shropshire*, 2nd edition (2000). Chichester: Phillimore

Trinder, B. and Cox, N., eds., *Miners & Mariners of the Severn Gorge: the probate inventories of Benthall, Broseley, Little Wenlock and Madeley* (2000). Chichester: Phillimore

Victoria History of Shropshire, Volume 1 (1908). Oxford: Oxford University Press

Victoria History of Shropshire, Volume 10: Wenlock, Upper Corve Dale and the Stretton Hills (1999). Oxford: Oxford University Press

Victoria History of Shropshire, Volume 11: Telford (1985). Oxford: Oxford University Press

Warner, R., *A Tour through the Northern Counties of England* (1802). Bath: Gruttwell.

Watson, M. and Musson, C., *Shropshire from the Air: Man and the Landscape* (1993). Shrewsbury: Shropshire Books

Wesley, J., *Journals of the Rev. John Wesley,* ed. Curnock, N. (1938). London: Epworth

Weyman, H.T., *The Members of Parliament for Shropshire* (1895). Shrewsbury: Shropshire Archaeological Society

White, J., 'On Cementitious Architecture, as applicable to the construction of Bridges, with a prefatory note of the first introduction of iron as the constituent material for arches of a large span by Thomas Farnolls Pritchard', *Philosophical Magazine & Annals of Philosophy*, vol. 11 (1832)

Young, A., *Tours in England and Wales* (1932). London: L.S.E. Reprints

3. Works relating to other bridges or to the history of bridges in general

Alderton, D. and Booker, J., *The Batsford Guide to the Industrial Archaeology of East Anglia* (1980). London: Batsford

Allen, J.S., 'The History of the Horseley Company to 1865', *Transactions of the Newcomen Society* vol. 58 (1986-7)

Allen, J.S., *A History of Horseley, Tipton, Two centuries of Engineering Progress* (2000). Ashbourne: Landmark

Andrew, J.H., 'The Canal at Smethwick - under, over and finally through the high ground', *Industrial Archaeology Review* vol. 17 (1995)

Armytage, W.H.G., 'Thomas Paine and the Walkers', *Pennsylvania History* vol. 18 (1951)

Ashmore, O., *The Industrial Archaeology of Lancashire* (1969). Newton Abbot: David & Charles

Ashmore, O., *Historic Industries of Marple and Mellor* (1977). Stockport: Metropolitan Borough of Stockport

Banks, J., *A Treatise on Mills* (1795). London: Richardson

Banks, J. *On the Power of Machines* (1803). Kendal: Pennington

Bayliss, D., *A Guide to the Industrial History of South Yorkshire* (1995). Telford: Association for Industrial Archaeology

Berridge, P.S.A., *The Girder Bridge* (1969). London: Robert Maxwell

Blumhof, J.G.L., ed., *Erich Th. Svedenstierna's Reise durch einen Theil von England und Schottland in den Jahren 1802 und 1803* (1811). Marburg and Cassel: J. C. Krieger

Bone, M. and Stanier, P., *A Guide to the Industrial Archaeology of Devon* (1998). Telford: Association for Industrial Archaeology

Booth, L.G., 'Timber Works', Pugsley, Λ., *The Works of Isambard Kingdom Brunel: an engineering appreciation* (1976). London: Institution of Civil Engineers

Booth, L.G., Sutherland, R.J.M. and Billington, N.S.,'Thomas Tredgold (1788-1829): Some Aspects of his work', *Transactions of the Newcomen Society*, vol. 51 (1979-80)

Boucher, C.T.G., 'John Rennie, 1761-1821', *Transactions of the Newcomen Society*, vol. 34 (1961-2)

Boucher, C.T.G., *John Rennie 1761-1821* (1963). Manchester: Manchester University Press

Brear, B., 'The New Ferro-Concrete Bridge at Ironbridge, Coalbrookdale', *Ferro-Concrete*, vol. 1 (1909)

Bressey, C.H., *British Bridges* (1933). London: Public Works, Roads & Transport Congress

Broadbridge, S., *The Birmingham Canal Navigations 1768-1846* (1974). Newton Abbot: David & Charles

Brook, F., *The Industrial Archaeology of the British Isles: the West Midlands* (1977). London: Batsford

Buchanan, R. A., *Brunel: the Life and Times of Isambard Kingdom Brunel* (2002). London: Hambledon & London

Buchanan, R.A., and Cossons, N.,*The Industrial Archaeology of the Bristol Region* (1969). Newton Abbot: David & Charles

Bull, F.W., *A History of Newport Pagnell* (1900). Kettering: W.E. & J.Goss

Butcher, A., 'Development in Early Iron Bridges', *AIA Bulletin* vol. 9 (1982)

Chadderton, D., 'Outram's Iron Aqueduct at Stalybridge', *Saddleworth Historical Society Bulletin*, vol. 7 (1977).

Clark, E., *The Britannia and Conway Tubular Bridges* (1850). London: Day.

Clew, K., *The Somerset Coal Canal and Railway* (1970). Newton Abbot: David & Charles.

Cohen, P., 'The Origins of the Pontcysyllte Aqueduct', *Transactions of the Newcomen Society*, vol. 51 (1979-80)

Compton, H., *The Oxford Canal* (1976). Newton Abbot: David & Charles

Crawshay, R., *The Letter Book of Richard Crawshay 1788-1797* (ed. Evans, C. and Hays, G.G.L., 1990). Cardiff: South Wales Record Society

Croad, S., *London's Bridges* (1983). London: RCHME

Crompton, W. J., *A Guide to the Industrial Archaeology of the West Midland Iron District* (1991). Telford: Association for Industrial Archaeology

Crowe, N., *English Heritage Book of Canals* (1994). London: Batsford/English Heritage

Day, T., 'Samuel Brown: his influence on the design of suspension bridges', *History of Technology*, vol. 8 (1983)

Davies, W.L., *The Bridges of Merthyr* (1992). Cardiff: Glamorgan Record Office

DeLony, E., *Landmark American Bridges* (1992). New York: American Society of Civil Engineers

DeLony, E., 'Tom Paine's Bridge', *American Heritage of Invention and Technology*, vol. 15 (2000)

de Maré, E., *Bridges of Britain* (revised edition, 1974). London: Batsford

Dempsey, G.S., *Tubular and other Iron Girder Bridges, particularly describing the Britannia and Conway Tubular Bridges* (1864). London: Virtue. Reprint, Bath: Kingsmead, 1970

Dickinson, H.W., *Robert Fulton: engineer and artist; his life and works* (1912). London: John Lane, The Bodley Head

Dickinson, H.W., 'An Eighteenth Century Engineer's Sketchbook', *Transactions of the Newcomen Society*, vol. 2 (1921-2)

Dickinson, H.W. and Lee, A., 'The Rastricks: Civil Engineers', *Transactions of the Newcomen Society*, vol. 4 (1923-4)

Fairbairn, W., *An Account of the Construction of the Britannia and Conway Tubular Bridges* (1849). London: John Weale

Fairbairn, W., *On the Application of Cast and Wrought Iron to building purposes* (1854). London: John Weale

Fairbairn, W., *Iron: its history, properties and processes of manufacture* (1861). London: A.& C. Black

Fairbairn, W., *The Life of Sir William Fairbairn, partly written by himself and completed by William Pole* (1877). London: Longman. Reprint, ed. Musson, A.E., 1978, Newton Abbot: David & Charles

Falconer, K., *Guide to England's Industrial Heritage* (1980). London: Batsford

Faulkner, A.H., 'The Wolverton Aqueduct', *Transport History*, vol. 2 (1969)

Faulkner, A.H., *The Grand Junction Canal* (1993). Rickmansworth: W.H.Walker

Ferns, J.L., 'The Walker Company of Rotherham', *Industrial Archaeology* vol. 12 (1977)

Fulton, R., *A Treatise on the Improvement of Canal Navigation &c.* (1796). London: I. & J. Taylor

Gardner, J.S., *English Ironworks of the XVIIth and XVIIIth Centuries* (1911). London: Batsford

George, B., 'The Iron Bridge, North Street and St David's Hill, Exeter', *Devon Historian* No. 60 (2000)

Gibb, Sir A., *The Story of Telford* (1935). London: Maclehose

Gies, J., *Bridges and Men* (1964). London: Cresset

Gloag, J. and Bridgwater, D., *A History of Cast Iron in Architecture* (1948). London: Allen & Unwin

Graves, J., *The History of Cleveland* (1808). Carlisle: Jollie

Hadfield, C., *The Canals of the East Midlands* (1966). Newton Abbot: David & Charles

Hadfield, C., *The Canals of the West Midlands* (1966). Newton Abbot: David & Charles

Hadfield, C., 'Telford, Jessop and Pontcysyllte', *Journal of the Railway & Canal Historical Society*, vol. 15 (1969)

Hadfield, C., *Thomas Telford's Temptation* (1993). Cleobury Mortimer: Baldwin

Hadfield, C. and Biddle, G., *The Canals of North-West England* (1970). Newton Abbot: David & Charles

Hadfield, C. and Norris, J., *Waterways to Stratford* (1962). Dawlish: David & Charles

Hadfield, C. and Skempton, A.W., *William Jessop: Engineer* (1979). Newton Abbot: David & Charles

Hadley, D.W., 'The Role of Iron in Reconstructing the Oxford Canal', *Journal of the Railway and Canal Historical Society*, vol. 24 (1976)

Hague, D. and Hughes, S., 'Pont-y-Cafnau: the first iron railway bridge and aqueduct', *AIA Bulletin*, vol. 9 (1982)

Hakewill, J., *A Picturesque Tour of the Island of Jamaica* (1825). London: Hurst & Robinson

Hammond, R., *The Forth Bridge and its Builders* (1964). London: Eyre & Spottiswoode

Hatcher, J., *The Industrial Architecture of Yorkshire* (1985). Chichester: Phillimore

Hay, G.D. and Stell, G.P., *Monuments of Industry: an illustrated historical record* (1986). Edinburgh: Royal Commission on the Ancient and Historical Monuments of Scotland

Hayden, M., *The Book of Bridges* (1976). London: Marshall Cavendish

Hill, M.C., 'Iron and Steel Bridges in Shropshire 1788-1901', *Transactions of the Shropshire Archaeological Society*, vol. 56 (1956-7)

Hodgkinson, E., 'Theoretical and experimental researches to ascertain the strength and best forms of iron beams', *Memoirs of the Literary and Philosophical Society of Manchester*, 2nd Series, vol. 5 (1831)

Hughes, S., 'Aspects of the use of Water-Power during the Industrial Revolution', *Melin: Journal of the Welsh Mills Group*, No. 4 (1988)

Hughes, S., *The Archaeology of the Montgomeryshire Canal* (4th ed., 1989). Aberystwyth: The Royal Commission on Ancient and Historical Monuments in Wales

Hughes, S., *The Archaeology of an Early Railway System: the Brecon Forest Tramroads* (1990). Aberystwyth: The Royal Commission on Ancient and Historical Monuments in Wales

Hume, J.R., *The Industrial Archaeology of Scotland, vol. 1, The Lowlands and Borders* (1976). London: Batsford

Hume, J.R., *The Industrial Archaeology of Scotland, vol. 2, The Highlands and Islands* (1977). London: Batsford

Hume, J.R., 'Cast Iron and Bridge-Building in Scotland', *Industrial Archaeology Review*, vol. 2 (1978)

Hume, J.R., 'Telford's Highland bridges', Penfold, A., *Thomas Telford: Engineer* (1980). London: Thomas Telford

Hutton, C., *Tracts on Mathematical and Philosophical Subjects* (three volumes, 1812). London: Rivington

Ironbridge Gorge Archaeology Unit, *Cyfarthfa Ironworks, Merthyr Tydvil: An Archaeological Investigation* (1995). Telford: Ironbridge Gorge Museum

James, J.G., 'The Cast-Iron Bridges of Thomas Wilson', *Transactions of the Newcomen Society*, vol. 50 (1978-9)

James, J.G., 'Iron Arched Bridge Designs in Pre-Revolutionary France', *History of Technology*, vol. 4 (1979)

James, J.G., 'The Evolution of Wooden Bridge Trusses to 1850', *Journal of the Institute of Wood Science*, vol. 9 (1982)

James, J.G., 'Russian Iron Bridges to 1850', *Transactions of the Newcomen Society*, vol. 54 (1982-3), 79-104. Reprinted in Sutherland, R.J.M., *Structural Iron* (1997)

James, J.G., 'The Evolution of Iron Bridge Trusses to 1850', *Transactions of the Newcomen Society*, vol. 52 (1980-1). Reprinted in Sutherland, R.J.M., *Structural Iron* (1997)

James, J.G., *The Cast Iron Bridge at Sunderland* (1986). Newcastle on Tyne: Newcastle on Tyne Polytechnic Occasional Papers, History of Science and Technology No. 5

James, J.G., 'Some steps in the Evolution of Early Iron Arched Bridge Designs', *Transactions of the Newcomen Society*, vol. 59 (1987-8)

James, J.G., 'Tom Paine's Iron Bridge work 1785-1803', *Transactions of the Newcomen Society*, vol. 59 (1987-8)

John, A.H., ed., *The Walker Family* (1951). London: Diploma

Kemp, E.L., 'Thomas Paine and his "Pontifical Matters"', *Transactions of the Newcomen Society*, vol. 49 (1977)

Kemp, E.L., 'Samuel Brown: Britain's pioneer suspension bridge builder', *History of Technology*, vol. 2 (1977). Reprinted in Sutherland, R.J.M., *Structural Iron* (1997)

Killer, J., *Die Werke der Baumeister Grubenmann* (4th ed., 1998). Dietikon: Baufachverlag

Langford, J.I., *A Towpath Guide to the Staffordshire & Worcestershire Canal* (1974). Cambridge: Goose

Lawson, J.B., 'Thomas Telford in Shrewsbury: the metamorphosis of an architect into a civil engineer', in Penfold, A., ed., *Thomas Telford: Engineer* (1980). London: Thomas Telford

Lewis, C., 'Josiah Clowes (1735-1794)', *Transactions of the Newcomen Society*, vol. 50 (1978-9)

Lewis, M.J.T., 'Cast-iron Aqueducts', *Journal of the Railway & Canal Historical Society*, vol. 22 (1976)

Lewis, S., *Topographical Dictionary of England* (1835). London: S. Lewis

Lindstrum, D. *et al.*, *Timber: Iron: Clay* (1975). Stafford: West Midlands Arts

Maggs, C.G. and Beale, G., *The Camerton Branch* (1985). Upper Bucklebury: Wild Swan

Marrey, B., *Les Ponts modernes: 18e - 19e siècles* (1990). Paris: Picard

Martin, T., *The Circle of the Mechanical Arts* (1815). London: Rees

Middlemiss, J.T., *Some Account of Sunderland Bridge* (1907). Sunderland: Sunderland Antiquarian Society

Miller, R., 'Sunderland Bridge', *Industrial Archaeology Review*, vol. 1 (1976)

Minchinton, W., *A Guide to Industrial Archaeology Sites in Britain* (1984). London: Granada

Mock, E.B., *The Architecture of Bridges* (1949). New York: Museum of Modern Art

Morris, J., *The Shropshire Union Canal: a towpath guide* (1991). Shrewsbury: Management Update

Mutton, N., *An Engineer at Work in the West Midlands: J.U. Rastrick* (1969). Wolverhampton: West Midland Studies, Special Publication No. 1

Nash, T., *Collections for the History of Worcestershire* (2nd ed., 1799). London: T. Payne

Nelson, G., *Highland Bridges* (1990). Aberdeen: Aberdeen University Press

Newby, A.E., *The History of Engineering in Ipswich* (1950). Ipswich: Cowell

Newfield, W., *An Oration delivered at the Opening of the Iron Bridge at Wearmouth* (1796). Stockton: Christopher & Jennett

Nixon, F., *The Industrial Archaeology of Derbyshire* (1969). Newton Abbot: David & Charles

Northcliffe, D., *A preliminary report on the Kirklees Iron Bridge of 1769 and its builder* (1979). York: Yorkshire Archaeological Society

Paine, T., *Rights of Man* (ed. H. Collins, 1969). Harmondsworth: Pelican

Paxton, R.A., 'Menai Bridge (1818-1826) and its influence on Suspension Bridge Development', *Transactions of the Newcomen Society*, vol. 49 (1977-8)

Paxton, R.A., 'Menai Bridge, 1818-26: evolution of design', Penfold, A., *Thomas Telford: Engineer* (1980). London: Thomas Telford

Pendred, H.W., *Iron Bridges of Moderate Span: their construction and erection* (1894). London: Crosby Lockwood

Penfold, A., *Thomas Telford: Engineer* (1980). London: Thomas Telford

Pevsner, N. and Hubbard, E., *The Buildings of England: Cheshire* (1971). Harmondsworth: Penguin.

Plowden, D., *Bridges: the Spans of North America*, 1974). New York: Viking

Provis, W.A., *An historical and descriptive account of the suspension bridge constructed over the Menai Strait in North Wales* (1828). London: The Author

Pudney, J., *Crossing London's River* (1972). London: Dent

Pudney, J., *London's Docks* (1975). London: Thames & Hudson

Pugsley, A., *The Works of Isambard Kingdom Brunel: an engineering appreciation* (1976). London: Institution of Civil Engineers

Rees, A., *The Cyclopaedia or Universal Dictionary of Arts, Sciences and Literature* (39 vols., 1802-20). London: Longman

Rees, A., *Rees's Manufacturing Industry (1819-20): a selection from The Cyclopaedia or Universal Dictionary of Arts, Sciences and Literature by Abraham Rees* (ed. Cossons, N., 1972). Newton Abbot: David & Charles

Rees, D.M., *Mines, Mills and Furnaces: an introduction to Industrial Archaeology in Wales* (1969). London: HMSO

Rees, D. M., *The Industrial Archaeology of South Wales* (1975). Newton Abbot: David & Charles

Reigart, J.F., *The Life of Robert Fulton* (1856). Philadelphia: Henderson

Riden, P., *The Butterley Company 1790-1830* (1973). Chesterfield: privately published

Rix, M.M., 'The Second Iron Bridge', *Journal of Industrial Archaeology*, vol. 3 (1966)

Robins, F.W., *The Story of the Bridge* (n.d., c.1946). Birmingham: Cornish

Robinson, J.M., *Shugborough* (1989). London: The National Trust

Rolt, L.T.C., *Isambard Kingdom Brunel: a biography* (1957). London: Longman

Rolt, L.T.C., *Thomas Telford* (1958). London: Longman

Rolt, L.T.C., *Red for Danger* (1955). London: Bodley Head

Rosenberg, N. and Vicenti, W.G., *The Britannia Bridge: The Generation and Diffusion of Technological Knowledge* (1978). Boston, Mass

Rowson, S. and Wright, I., *The Glamorganshire and Aberdare Canals* (2001). Lydney: Black Dwarf

Rozpedowski, J., 'Iron Bridges in the Lower Silesia Region', ICCROM, *Ironworks and Iron Monuments: Study, Conservation and Adaptive Use* (1985). Rome: ICCROM

Ruddock, T., 'William Edwards's bridge at Pontypridd', *Industrial Archaeology*, vol. 11 (1974)

Ruddock, T., *Arch Bridges and their Builders 1735-1835* (1979). Cambridge: Cambridge University Press

Ruddock, T., ed., *Masonry Bridges, Viaducts and Aqueducts* (2000). Aldershot: Ashgate

Schofield, R.B., 'The Construction of the Huddersfield Narrow Canal', *Transactions of the Newcomen Society*, vol. 53 (1981-2)

Schofield, R.B., *Benjamin Outram 1764-1805: an Engineering Biography* (2000). Cardiff: Merton Priory Press

Schopenhauer, J., *Reise in den Jahren 1803, 1804 und 1805* ed. Konrad Paul (1982). Berlin: Rütten und Loening

Sealey, A., *Bridges and Aqueducts* (1976). London: Hugh Evelyn

Sherlock, R.J., 'Industrial Archaeology in Administrative Staffordshire', *North Staffordshire Journal of Field Studies*, vol. 2 (1962)

Sherlock, R.J., *The Industrial Archaeology of Staffordshire* (1976). Newton Abbot: David & Charles

Simond, L., *Journey of a Tour and Residence in Great Britain during the years 1810 and 1811 by a French traveller* (1815). Edinburgh: George Ramsay

Skempton, A.W., 'Engineering in the Port of London Authority, 1789-1808', *Transactions of the Newcomen Society*, vol. 50 (1978-9). Reprinted in Skempton A.W., *Civil Engineers and Engineering in Britain, 1600-1830* (1996)

Skempton, A.W., 'Telford and the design for a new London Bridge', Penfold, A., *Thomas Telford: Engineer* (1980). London: Thomas Telford

Skempton, A.W., 'Engineering in the Port of London Authority, 1808-1834', *Transactions of the Newcomen Society*, vol. 53 (1981-2). Reprinted in Skempton, A.W., *Civil Engineers and Engineering in Britain, 1600-1830* (1996)

Skempton, A.W., *Civil Engineers and Engineering in Britain, 1600-1830* (1996). Aldershot: Variorum.

Skempton, A.W. et al., *A Biographical Dictionary of Civil Engineers in Great Britain and Ireland, vol. I, 1500-1830* (2002). London: Thomas Telford

Smiles, S., *Industrial Biography: Iron Workers and Tool Makers* (1878). London: John Murray.

Smith, D., 'James Walker: Civil Engineer: 1781-1862', *Transactions of the Newcomen Society*, vol. 69 (1997)

Smith, H.S., *The World's Great Bridges* (1954). London: Scientific Book Club

Southey, R., *Letters from England*, ed. J. Simmons (1951). London: Cresset

Sutherland, R.J.M., 'The age of cast iron, 1780-1850: who sized the beams?', Thorne, R., ed., *The Iron Revolution: Architects, Engineers and Structural Innovation, 1780-1880*. Essays to accompany an exhibition at the RIBA Heinz Gallery (1990). Reprinted in Sutherland, R.J.M., *Structural Iron* (1997)

Sutherland, R.J.M., ed., *Structural Iron, 1750-1850* (1997). Aldershot: Ashgate

Summerson, J., *John Nash: Architect to King George IV* (1935). London: Allen & Unwin

Sweetman, J., *The Artist and the Bridge* (2000). Aldershot: Ashgate

Symons, M.V., *Coal-Mining in the Llanelli Area, vol. I, 16th Century to 1829* (1979). Llanelli: Llanelli Borough Council.

Telford, T. and Nimmo, A., 'Bridge', *Edinburgh Encyclopaedia* (1830). Edinburgh: Blackwood, vol. 4

Telford, T., *The Life of Thomas Telford* ed. Rickman, J. (1838). London: J. & L. G. Hansard

Thompson, P., *The History and Antiquities of Boston* (1856). Boston: John Noble

Thompson, W.J., ed., *A Brief Guide to the Industrial Heritage of West Yorkshire* (1989). Telford: Association for Industrial Archaeology

Thorne, R., ed., *Structural Iron and Steel 1850-1900* (2000). Aldershot: Ashgate

Torrens, H., *The Evolution of a Family Firm: Stothert & Pitt of Bath* (1978). Bath: Stothert & Pitt

Torrens, H. and Trinder, B., 'The Iron Bridge at Trentham', *Industrial Archaeology Review*, vol. 6 (1981-2)

Townley, P.A., 'Boston's Iron Bridge', *Lincolnshire Life*, vol. 6 (1966) [October]

Tredgold, T., *A Practical Essay on the Strength of Cast Iron* (2nd ed.,1824). London: J.Taylor

Trinder, B., 'The Use of Iron as a Building Material', in Lindstrum, D. *et al., Timber: Iron: Clay* (1975). Stafford: West Midlands Arts

Trinder, B., 'The Holyhead Road: an engineering project in its social context', in Penfold, A., *Thomas Telford: Engineer* (1980). London: Thomas Telford

Trinder, B., *The Making of the Industrial Landscape* (1982). London: Dent. Third edition, 1997. London: Orion

Trinder, B., ed., *The Blackwell Encyclopedia of Industrial Archaeology* (1992). Oxford: Blackwell

Waite, G.A., *The Conservation of Historic Bridges* (2001). Chester: Gifford & Partners

Walters, D., *British Railway Bridges* (1966). London: Ian Allan

Ward, A.W., *The Bridges of Shrewsbury* (1935). Shrewsbury: Wilding

Welch, C.E., 'The Iron Bridge at Plymouth', *Report & Transactions of the Devonshire Association*, vol.98 (1966)

White, S., *The Iron Bridge: Survey, Record and Analysis* (2002). Telford: Ironbridge Gorge Museum Archaeology Unit

White, W., *A Directory of the Borough of Sheffield* (1833). Sheffield: White

Williamson, E. and Pevsner, N., *The Buildings of England: London Docklands: An Architectural Guide* (1998). London: Penguin

Wilson, E.A., *The Llangollen Canal: an historical background* (1975). Chichester: Phillimore

Wright, N.R., *Lincolnshire Towns and Industry 1700-1914* (1982). Lincoln: Society for Lincolnshire History and Archaeology

Indices

Bridges are listed in the Index of Bridges and Aqueducts under the names by which they are most commonly known, with cross-references to other names, and, where appropriate, to the towns where they are situated. Companies responsible for the construction of bridges are listed under the heading 'Ironworks' in the Index of Places and Subject index, as are canal companies, museums, railway companies and rivers. Other companies are listed under the index of names.

Index of Bridges and Aqueducts
(including structures projected but not built)

The index includes projected bridges that were never built. References to counties in England and Wales are to historic counties. All are located in the United Kingdom unless otherwise indicated (by the names of the countries concerned current in 2002).

Index of Names

Index of Places and Subjects